Construction Since 1900
Materials

David Yeomans

BT Batsford Ltd. London

First published 1997

All rights reserved. No part of this
publication may be reproduced in any form
or by any means without permission from
the Publisher.

A CIP catalogue record for this book is
available from the British Library.
ISBN 0 7134 6684 7

Printed in Great Britain by
Butler and Tanner, Frome, Somerset

for the publishers
B.T. Batsford Ltd
583 Fulham Road
London SW6 5BY

Contents

List of Acronyms

List of Tables

List of Figures

Introduction

I'll tell you a tale that's true,

Just by way of convincing you,

How very little, since things were made,

Things have altered in the building trade.

Rudyard Kipling, *A Truthful Song*

The purpose of the book

No matter how much personal experience might lead us to concur with Kipling's view of building, all technologies change, even building technology, and at an ever-increasing pace. For well-established technologies such as building or artillery there may be centuries during which there is little development. Then, as new ideas are introduced, as some scientific understanding is applied to them, or possibly as ideas are transferred from other fields, so the pace of change gradually increases. Artillery became a science first with the invention of gunpowder, and then with the application of mechanics in the art of directing the guns. In recent years we have seen the introduction of electronics to the art of war. Somehow, building, for all its fundamental importance to human comfort, seems to have been rather late in enjoying the fruits of scientific understanding. While books on the science of gunnery appeared in the seventeenth century, early works on architecture and building did little more than convey conventional wisdom with little application of science until Fitzmaurice's Principles of Modern Building published in 1938. There had been studies of some aspects of building, such as Lord Rumford's work on the warming of buildings and the design of

fireplaces in 1796. During the nineteenth century, a growing number of books on the properties of materials and the mechanics of structures were published, but these seem slow beginnings and hardly resulted in major changes in construction methods. Understanding may have improved, but there was little change in the basic fabric of buildings until late in the nineteenth century. Compared with this slow development, changes in this century have been dramatic and this study is an attempt to look at the way in which technology has affected the practice of design and the form of building during this period of rapid change.

Originally the idea for this book was to produce something that would be of use to those concerned with the rehabilitation of an important part of our building stock: those buildings constructed since the turn of the century that are now being refurbished. Much of the material gathered for this purpose remains but it quickly became apparent that this could not be its only concern. A history which is simply a guide for rehabilitation might take either of two extreme forms: it could either be a slim account of major developments, perhaps with sets of tables and references where appropriate, or it could be a compendious tome, a comprehensive catalogue of the wide variety of materials and components used at different times. Practical considerations ruled out the latter but as material was gathered it became clear that there were a number of historical issues that remained unresolved and would have to remain so. This suggested that the former would be inadequate because these historical issues are not unrelated to some of the practical questions which may be asked by those confronted with understanding a building. It also became apparent that a work on this subject could be valuable to students, either in the study of the history, or in the understanding, of construction, and this second intention has helped the final shape of the book which, while less than encyclopaedic, is more than a brief summary.

The history of construction has become a significant subject for study in recent years, leading to the founding of the journal *Construction History* in 1985. Moreover, a history of architecture of this century can hardly be separated from a history of the construction methods that made so much of it possible. It might also be argued that, for students who want to tackle the history of a subject in greater depth, the study of more recent history has some advantages over the study of earlier periods. The issues of the time are closer to our own and therefore perhaps more accessible to students. In some ways it is a better period for those who want to engage in historical research themselves because the source material may be more readily accessible.

When studying construction methods, it is salutary to recognize that things do change — that the forms and methods of construction used today have not always been as they are — and to understand why and how the changes took place. Construction methods are still changing and it is important for students to realize what change has meant to the overall fabric of the building, to the nature of the construction process and to the industry. Attempts to improve the fabric of buildings and the efficiency of the construction process, or to accommodate new materials produced by the supply industry, may result in change, but in many instances the industry, including the design professions, has been strangely resistant. Change is often attended with some risk of failure and there have been instances where all has not been as simple as might have been supposed.

As well as charting some of the changes that have taken place, a number of historical questions have had to be addressed; before embarking on the history of various aspects of construction it is useful to consider some issues of historiography which this study has thrown up. History, which by its nature must be partial, is always a view of the past from a particular vantage point; here the viewpoint is technological change within building, although other views are possible. Marian Bowley (1960 & 1966) produced two histories of building in Britain (both sadly out of print) which examined the industry from the point of view of an economic historian. But as her books dealt with innovation in the industry they needed to consider technological issues in some detail and one of her observations on the changes in technology is a useful beginning. Writing about the inter-war period, she pointed out that there was no way of telling exactly what proportion of frame buildings were of steel and what proportion were of reinforced concrete. We do know that a simple majority were steel, even though concrete was cheaper, raising questions about the way in which design decisions were made, for which Bowley offers only tentative answers. There are several points which may be made from this simple observation. The relative popularity of particular building products is often impossible to determine because the statistics are not always available. The success or otherwise of even a single product can only be determined from the records of the company which produced it, always assuming that the company has survived to this day — many have not. Even so the factors which contributed to that success may not be the same in all cases, that is, for all products of that particular type.

Even today we do not have a clear idea of how design decisions may be made. It is only since the design methods movement of the 1960s, a period which saw the founding of the Design Research Society and such journals as *Design Studies* or the *Journal of Architectural and Planning Research*, that there has been any forum for the discussion of such issues, and research on the process of design still leaves many questions unanswered. If we do not know how decisions are made today still less can we tell how they were made in the past, since we have no measure of the factors which were affecting those decisions nor of their relative importance to the designer. As De Solla Price (1965) has pointed out, the history of a science may be written in the papers which are published in that field but the job of a designer is to produce designs, not to write about the process nor to describe those designs. When designers do describe their work, they do not necessarily discuss the factors affecting their decisions. This means that even if we know what was available to a building designer, both in terms of the building materials and products and the level of knowledge on which he or she could draw, there is nothing to tell us about the extent to which those resources were used. Concerns like this do not mean that a history cannot be written, simply that we have to be aware of the limitations that are present in the data that is available and the level of interpretation that is possible. One other limitation that cannot be ignored is that of geography. Today, building technology operates on an international scale with the manufacture and wide distribution of products as varied as sheet metal roofing and waterproof membranes and with the development of specialist component manufacturers, like those producing bespoke curtain walling. However, for the most part, this is a relatively recent phenomenon, though an example of an earlier international trade in building components was the shipping of roofing tiles which were both imported into Britain and exported at various times. The weight and shipping cost of materials has resulted as much in regional as in national differences in building; the industry has always tended to be somewhat parochial. This is, therefore, a study of British developments.

The form which the book has taken

There are also practical limitations to what may be covered and as material came to hand it became clear that some choices had to be made about the overall content as well as the form. A chronological history was not possible if some coherent structure was to be preserved. Therefore, the book has taken the form of a series of essays based on different types of construction rather than following a strict chronological sequence. It also became clear that limitations on size alone would prevent a complete coverage of the material in a single volume and the choice was made to restrict attention in the first instance to the major elements of structure and the major construction materials. This has meant that the servicing of buildings has had to be left to a later volume, as has cladding and the development of other manufactured building products in recent years. However, it will be apparent that this decision has involved an element of choice, one might say some historical judgement, for example, manufactured floor systems have been included as these have been an important part of construction since the turn of the century, even though more recent aspects of the industrialized building have not been considered.

The structure adopted has also meant that the timescale of the different elements is not the same. The important developments in steel and concrete construction took place largely in the first half of the century while major developments in timber engineering have been more recent. Also, if this book

was not to become largely a history of concrete design, developments in architectural form which may be regarded as a collaboration between modern movement architects and some of the more inventive structural engineers have had to be omitted, as have the more recent developments of pre-stressed concrete and shell design. These too will have to be left to a later work.

Almost inevitably the text deals more extensively with developments in the first half of the century, the period in which the basic methods of construction which we use today were established. The reader will therefore find a much briefer treatment of more recent developments for which information may be more readily available and whose techniques have changed less. The availability of data raises questions of how this may have affected the form of the book and how the approach adopted towards its selection has affected the picture that emerges. A number of historical questions cannot be answered in the present state of knowledge and the choice has been quite simply between presenting an incomplete picture and no picture at all. If there are readers who are stimulated by what appear to be interesting historical questions that would repay further work, then so much the better.

As others may need to explore further it may be useful to review briefly the sources that are available in this area because they vary considerably in the quality of the information that they provide and in their relative availability.

The sources used

The history of any technology may be traced partly in the artefacts that remain but buildings present a special case. Apart from a few exceptional types, we cannot keep them in museums; as for commercial buildings, more than any other human product, it is the unusual rather than the commonplace that survive. Standing structures are not readily accessible for inspection, so that it may often be difficult to know how they were built: it was not realized that the Jenny's Home Insurance Building was the first true steel-frame structure in Chicago until it was demolished in the 1930s. Significant buildings have been demolished before they could be examined, so destroying valuable evidence forever. Paradoxically, therefore, the buildings themselves are of limited use and we have to turn to other sources no matter how imperfect.

Building is a very public activity, and since the nineteenth century there have been journals concerned with its various aspects, discussing buildings as works of architecture as well as reporting on technological developments. It is thus possible to gain a picture of the history of building from these sources. The journals of the professional institutions fulfil a variety of roles, from social diaries to the repositories of learned papers. There are commercial journals like the *Architect's Journal* (a group that now includes the free journals which survive on advertising revenue). 'Trade journals', like *Roofing Contractor*, are directed at particular sectors of the industry, and house journals are produced by individual companies. In the last category are those which have been produced by contractors as advertising material, like *Kahncrete Engineering* or *FerroConcrete*, and those circulated mainly internally by large firms, like *Arup Review*.

Commercial journals are a valuable resource: as the principal sources for descriptions of major construction projects they give some indication of the state of the art at the time. Of those journals dealing with the majority of building issues, the extremes have been represented by *The Builder*, which has been concerned with the commercial aspects of construction, reporting major contracts and the prices of materials, and the *Architectural Review* which has dealt with the aesthetic aspects of architecture. Throughout much of this century *Architect's Journal* (AJ) and the *Architect and Building News* (A&BN) provided a good account of the state of the art with both descriptions of buildings and technical articles.

As the organ of its institution, a professional journal has a number of functions other than the publication of learned papers, but the form which these take provides a good indication of the concerns of the profession at the time. Journals for the engineering institutions have been concerned as much with the methods of design as with the products of design, but also with the process of construction. The contents of the *Journal of the Royal Institute of British Architects* (RIBAJ) during the early part of this century show considerable concern for developments in building technology. Before the First World War the profession had to come to terms with the introduction of reinforced concrete and the changes in the London building regulations to allow the use of steel frames. Articles appeared which dealt with the report of RIBA's Concrete Structures Committee, and

which considered the design of structural steelwork to a level of detail which would today be regarded as the province of the structural engineer. During the inter-war years there was a regular series reviewing construction methods and materials which relied on contributions from the Building Research Station and other research organizations. Today it seems less concerned with technical issues, but if the nature and possibly the quantity of the technical information which the historian may want has changed, this in itself gives some indication of the way in which professional attitudes and concerns may have changed.

Trade associations often produce regular publications more promotional than technical. They may be intended to provide designers with the kind of general knowledge about the use of their products or methods of construction but they may sometimes include technical information. In the post-war years, for example, *Concrete Quarterly* served to promote concrete as a material, providing information on technical developments; other publications have been produced to provide designers with the kind of technical information which they need in design.

Technical publications

Principally, journals have reported on what has been built and, while they may from time to time discuss the methods used in the process of design or make recommendations, this is not their principal function. Instead, designers draw upon the textbooks first encountered during their education and training, upon advice notes or bulletins, often published by government organizations, and, less frequently, research reports or design guides from particular materials interests. Most important is the technical information supplied by manufacturing companies describing their products and the published regulations to which designs must conform. There is therefore something of a paper trail to follow although, like the journals, such information has to be used with caution. Moreover, there is also the disadvantage that much of this is ephemeral and while some material, like British Standards, may not be actually lost, it may be difficult to access, an irritation to the historian but a major problem for those concerned with rehabilitation.

Textbooks and manuals

The most permanent of the literature that designers have to hand includes the handbooks, or manuals, for the materials which they are using and which may well have formed part of their training. Apart from a wide range of textbooks dealing with structural analysis and design, there are four standard engineering handbooks now available in Britain covering what may be regarded as the basic structural materials: steel, concrete, timber and masonry. It is only to be regretted that these have only recently appeared and so reference works showing earlier methods of design are not available. The oldest is Reynolds's *Concrete Designer's Handbook* (1932) but Grey's Steel *Designer's Manual* did not appear until 1955. Handbooks for other materials are even more recent (Ozelton & Baird 1976 ; Curtin et al. 1982).

Handbooks for architects present a more difficult picture than those for engineers because of the greater restlessness of architectural design. The basic works on construction like Mitchell's *Building Construction* (1888), McKay (1938) or those by Jaggard (1913) (though the latter is possibly better known in subsequent editions written in collaboration with Drury) — all of which went into many editions — had all been produced for students rather than practicing professionals. Occasionally a method of construction may grow to sufficient significance to warrant a special book, for example Rostron's *Light Cladding of Buildings* (1964), published when curtain walling had become common. There is no modern equivalent, probably because curtain walling is now a series of standard products manufactured and assembled by specialist sub-contractors, although Brookes (1983) has dealt with other aspects of cladding.

Another source is the material produced by the few research organizations, although this has often proved as ephemeral as trade literature. Research organizations established by the different sectional interests within the building industry are funded partly by levies on sales of materials with the disadvantage that they are vulnerable to the vicissitudes of trade and the politics of their sponsoring bodies. Some have had well-established laboratories producing a variety of publications. Their scientists may publish in the scientific journals appropriate to their field but to have had the desired effect on the building industry they need to produce publications directed particularly at designers: information leaflets, reference works produced in book form and research reports whose circulation may be limited to members. Some of these are dealt with in more detail in Chapter 1.

This brings up the difficult question of the extent to which these various sources of information were used. Ensuring the dissemination of the results of scientific work to designers has been a constant problem for both research and trade organizations.

That scientific information is available is no guarantee that it will be used. It may not reach those whose designs it could affect, or it may be simply ignored. The attitude of steel designers to the findings of the Steel Structures Research Committee, discussed in Chapter 4, is a clear example but similar attitudes can be seen in other areas. It is not simply a question of the information being deliberately ignored, there is also the question of how widely known particular information may have been. Recent studies of how designers receive information shows that most is transmitted by 'warm body contact', that is, there are some within organizations who are more forward-looking or more up to date than others. They act to influence their seemingly less motivated colleagues. Possibly, their colleagues have not developed the skills to research the latest developments, a sad reflection on the education of professional designers.

Equally, while some firms have a reputation for being innovative in their designs there are more perhaps who work to the lowest common denominator. 'Quick and dirty' design is not to be despised; it is often the most cost-effective solution, satisfying the client more by the rapidity with which it can be produced than a more sophisticated design. It may also produce a more robust product, that is, one more capable of being adapted to changing requirements. Other designers have greater ambitions and have attracted clients who require more sophisticated design; it is often they who pioneer ideas which are later absorbed into more conventional practice. Of course, this high-calibre work is most often reported in the journals, so that a picture of go-ahead professionals may be projected which does not correspond with what is happening in general practice.

Codes and regulations

Scientific information is incorporated into a technology when it finds its way into the regulations or the standards, and so changes in these might seem to represent a secure source for the development of the technology. Once again a great deal of material has been produced, although the historian may be faced with the problem of the availability of these, if not of their survival. This kind of material should be purged from the designer's library as soon as it becomes out of date. At the same time it is important for those involved in the rehabilitation of existing buildings to be aware of the regulations in force at the time of construction. For example, with increasing structural knowledge the allowable stresses for structural steel have been raised and it is useful for the engineer to know this and thus to understand the methods of design which have been used at different times. The pattern of legislative control over building was far more complex in the past than it is today with the effect that standards were issued by a larger number of authorities. The changing state of the building regulations is discussed in Chapter 1 and while the actual regulations in force at different times may be available to the historian, there are questions about their interpretation and application which require some discussion. These were issues frequently discussed within professional organizations.

Although one might assume that regulations and standards represent an absolute definition of the state of the art at any one time, it is clear that this cannot be so. The rate at which scientific developments are officially recognized in this way is variable; for example, there have been a number of occasions in which designers anticipated the publication of standards and regulations. The London Building Acts were simply unable to keep pace with the developments in technology, an inevitable effect of the time taken to draft legislation, although there have been examples where there has been an apparent resistance to the official recognition of developments in technology. It is not for me to say whether this reflects appropriate caution or official inertia but an example is provided in the slow acceptance of flat-slab construction described in Chapter 5.

British building regulations have increasingly drawn on British Standards in recent years so that today these are the most important standards after the Building Regulations which so frequently refer to them.

Historically the manufacturing standards are important as indicators of the quality of materials used in existing buildings but there has been no published source of information on this. The British Standard catalogue does not indicate the dates of earlier editions, still less any amendments that may have been made, and the current standards themselves now rarely summarize the history of the standard as they once did. Naturally the British Standards Institution keeps an archive of early standards and a 'history book' which lists all the standards with dates of both early editions and amendments and an extract of some of those relating to building is provided in Appendix I.

Trade organizations have occasionally issued standards as a way of attempting to control materials and workmanship within their sector of the industry. As they are produced to inform suppliers and installers, they may have been of little relevance to the contemporary designer. If assured of a satisfactory performance by a product supplied and installed by a trade organization member (whether it be a structural fire protection or a flooring finish), the designer may be little concerned about the details of its specification. Nevertheless, such standards may be historically significant. They may also be of interest to the conservator, particularly where the standards of a product have changed or where different grades of a product were made for use in different situations. Regrettably, however, it may prove difficult to locate such 'trade standards'.

Trade literature

Designers today most commonly draw upon trade literature in the development of their designs; it represents the current state of the art, but here the historian faces a serious problem of survival of the material. As trade literature becomes out of date it is most often destroyed — and for fairly good reasons. There is no comprehensive archive of such material for the historian of technology and therefore no source of information for someone concerned with the historic artifact, or the architect, surveyor or engineer who may be concerned with its rehabilitation (see Yeomans, 1994). Of the various forms of trade literature produced, the most likely to survive are promotional books, either those of a technical nature or those illustrating buildings using the company's product. The British Gypsum 'White Book' or the Redland 'Tile

Book' are well-known recent examples, but there have been books and booklets for as long as there have been manufacturers. Perhaps the earliest was that produced to describe Coade Stone at the end of the eighteenth century (Coade, 1784). Early in this century there were firms who produced books describing their products and steel companies have included standard details and information on specifications in their bound handbooks, whose principal task is to list the properties of their products.

Again the effect of such publications is difficult to gauge. Steel tables are an obvious necessity, reproduced in engineers' diaries as much as in special handbooks because of the designer's constant recourse to them, but the same is not true of other materials where there may be direct competition with equivalent products. The pattern seems to be that firms would produce such guides when they were trying to break into a market and when their method of selling depended upon specification by the designer rather than their offering a supply-and-design service. If, like some of the early reinforced concrete companies, a manufacturer offered a design service, there was no need for a design manual to be supplied to the architect or structural engineer. While this means that the pattern of information available will reflect contractual arrangements and show similar variations in the past as it does today, it raises questions about the methods used to promote products. How important was, and is, the trade representative?

Compendia of trade information

The task of finding details of building products and materials is helped by the compendia of such products which have been regularly published. The best-known today is probably the *Architects' Standard Catalogue* while others have been published under a bewildering variety of names. They were never comprehensive and so can only provide a sample of the products available at any time, and the technical information in them is limited and seldom as comprehensive as the information provided in a manufacturer's leaflet. Nevertheless, they can give an indication of the types of products which were available at different times and so some idea of general trends of development. Regrettably their survival rate has also been poor and, paradoxically, the most difficult one to find is the largest and potentially the most useful — the *Architects' Standard Catalogue*. Perhaps its large size encouraged its

destruction and the British Library and the RIBA library have only two or three editions between them. The annual *Specification* which first appeared in 1898 is also a valuable source. Although it always contained some advertising material, it was principally concerned with the correct specification of materials and workmanship and so provides a guide to contemporary orthodox thinking. In this respect it is better than the catalogues because it gives more specific information on product use and the standards of workmanship required. Some early editions even included drawings of buildings but this practice was regrettably abandoned. Longer lasting was the practice of including articles by specialists on technical subjects.

Survival of information

The survival of all technical information, apart from that included in books from ordinary publishers and in journal articles, is a somewhat haphazard affair. It is unlikely to be kept by those to whom it is addressed. The designer requires immediate access to information, possibly for very short periods, and it is essential that the information be up to date. There is every incentive to acquire only information which will be of direct use and to weed the collection regularly. While records of completed jobs may be reduced to microfilm form for long-term storage, there is no incentive to keep out-of-date trade or technical information in a similar way. Equally, there is no guarantee that material will be kept by its producers. Some manufacturers and trade organizations do have archives of early technical material, and publications of professional institutions will be kept by their libraries, but in the commercial world the survival of any material is likely to be only as good as the survival of the organisations which produced it. Once an organisation ceases to exist so might much of the material that it has published. The survival in institution libraries of technical information other than that produced by the institution itself will again be rather haphazard.

Even where trade literature is available, its claims should be treated with a degree of circumspection. The function of the literature is to sell a product as well as to inform the designer of its performance characteristics. The former is served by emphasizing the ease and universality of its application, the latter serves the designer best by noting the limitations in its use.

It is clear that the conflict between these interests may lead to false claims being made (Yeomans, 1988a). There is also a learning period associated with new building products as their performance is assessed in use and this may lead to changes in the formulation of a material or the design of a product or even to restrictions placed upon its use over a period of time. Thus, information produced early in the life of a product may be significantly different from that produced at a later date: this may be important if the date of the literature source is different from that of the building in question.

Original drawings

Another important primary source are drawings and specifications produced by designers. The survival of drawings and specifications made for particular buildings makes these as problematic as any other source. Firms may have ceased to exist, and their drawings lost; even when the firms do survive there is no guarantee that they will have preserved their records. For example, a student researching a well-known and historically significant firm visited them as they were about to move offices; he discovered that drawings of interest to him were being discarded. The same is true of manufacturing companies, once important in their day but whose products ceased to be in demand and which eventually ceased to trade. It may be feasible to search for such material when tracing the history of an individual building or firm, or possibly where it is important to trace the development of a particular technique in detail, but his kind of material cannot form a major part of a general history. While there are some occasions in which such material has been used here, the scope of this book has generally made it impracticable to use material of this detailed kind.

Conventions within the text

Time

References to time need to be commented on. The terms pre-war and post-war are still commonly used and are significant because of the major changes which the 1939-45 war stimulated, but as the period covered by this book includes two world wars this could lead to some potential confusion. To avoid this I use the term post-war to mean post-Second World War, avoiding the term pre-war except where it is immediately obvious from the context which war is being referred to. Elsewhere the term inter-war period will be used to avoid ambiguity, and for the period before 1914, pre-First World War.

Names of journals and organizations

Both journals and organizations occasionally change their names and some policy has to be adopted towards these, especially when there is one journal which has recently changed its name to coincide with that of another which no longer exists. *The Builder* has recently changed its name to *Building*, the name of a journal which was published between 1926 and 1960 (and which will be referred to in subsequent chapters) but which was originally *The British Builder*. Here my policy has been to always use one name and that most commonly used which, with the exception of the two journals just referred to, is the most recent. Therefore, the name *Architect's Journal* is used even for the period before 1919 when this journal was first called *The Builder's and Architectural Record* until 1910 when it briefly became *The Architect's and Builder's Journal*.

The policy towards other organizations which have changed their names is different. Building Research Station (BRS) became the Building Research Establishment (BRE) and as it did so it absorbed the Forest Products Research Laboratory (FPRL) which confusingly became Prince's Risborough Laboratory (PRL). For this and other organizations the names referred to are those at the time and so contemporary with their publications.

Dimensions

Since the period of this history encompasses the change from imperial to metric units some clear policy has been necessary for the reporting of dimensions. The simplest seems to be to report all dimensions in the units current at the time. This means that the dimension given will be the same as in contemporary accounts. I have chosen not to fill the text with translations into metric units (or vice versa).

1 A century of change

The building industry's development in this century has taken place against a background of increased scientific understanding and changing regulations. Building, as is frequently observed, is a craft-based industry and this has given it a rather peculiar relationship to scientific knowledge. Craft training means that the neophytes learn from those who are already skilled in the trade — this is just as true of designers as it is of the tradesmen who build the things that they design. Just as the apprentice bricklayer learns the correct way to butter the end of a brick from those who have learned and practiced the skill before him, so the 'articled pupil', as he was called at the turn of the century, learned the correct form of eaves detail and all the other mysteries of design from his seniors in the 'trade'. This was the expectation of all ranks in the industry and, to a certain degree, such a pattern of learning is resistant to change. New methods of construction may be regarded with suspicion if only because the unknown brings with it risks. But the craft-based approach develops a habit of mind that is hard to break even when new methods of construction are introduced. Once a technique is adopted, even though it may be shown to rest on false assumptions, it may be hard to introduce change based on scientific understanding. The attention of the designer is focused on other issues and once a way to do something has been learnt it is with difficulty that those practicing it can be persuaded that it may be wrong or that there may be other and better ways.

Neither is it the habit of the industry to seek out the latest scientific findings. Buildings are not high-performance machines where scientific knowledge is needed to keep a competitive edge; the result is that science tends to be invoked only when necessity demands. Besides, there is considerable investment in existing methods, sometimes in plant but often more important investment in trained personnel and in management structures. There is even a disincentive within the industry to invest in training to accommodate new technologies because the labour force is highly mobile. For the scientifically minded, the application of scientific understanding in building can look like the gradual pushing forward of the frontiers of enlightenment against the armies of ignorance and superstition.

Does this seem too harsh? A personal anecdote might help illustrate the point. Only recently a teacher was heard telling a student that the way to prevent timber decay was to keep it well ventilated. True, that is one way, but the fact is that the way to prevent decay in timber is to remove the conditions for fungal growth, that is, moisture. Keeping the timber dry is the essence of good detailing but ventilation is only one way of doing that. Part of the problem is that timber, above all materials, is the one we know best, or rather, think that we do. It is the oldest building material still in use today, the one that every do-it-yourself enthusiast will have handled, and as such it is the material about which there may be the greatest number of myths in circulation.

Neither has the architectural profession shown a consuming interest in participating in scientific development, in spite of occasional polemics on the importance of science and the existence from the turn of the century of RIBA's Standing Science Committee. When the Building Research Station (BRS) wanted to begin work on the decay and preservation of building materials, it sent a circular to all members of RIBA pointing out that this work would be helped if they could obtain data from members. The result was only three or four replies.[1]

One can hardly avoid the impression that scientific understanding has been forced upon the industry through necessity. This may have been because of failures of various methods of construction, because the industry was seen to be failing adequately to serve social needs, or when changes within the industry demonstrated that existing craft practices were inadequate. Sometimes new methods of construction were introduced for which there was no craft experience so that scientific understanding, even if rather primitive, was essential. What then are the scientific needs of the industry? This can be answered in two ways: the needs of manufacturers in the development of their products and the needs of design. Of course, designers need to know both about the performance of materials and the assemblies which they construct from these materials.

During the nineteenth century, the industry changed from being almost entirely site-based, in which brick, stone, timber and some simple building products were assembled on site into the required forms, to one which used an increasing number of manufactured products. Nevertheless, the value of these was still low compared with the cost of site work. In this century the value of manufactured components in building has increased considerably, making the manufacturing sector a more important influence upon design and construction. With the restructuring of the manufacturing sector of the industry, craftsmen were faced with unfamiliar materials; both this and the need for some means to assess the alternative methods of construction which became available after the First World War required scientific understanding of building. Manufacturers could make use of science in understanding the factors involved both in the manufacturing and in the performance of their products but architects needed some collaborative organization to carry out research. Although the profession had its Science Standing Committee it did not have laboratories and these were required if there was to be any real progress in the understanding of buildings.

Fire resistance

Concern for fire protection led to the first significant attempts to introduce some scientific understanding into building design. This is hardly surprising since it was concern for fire that had driven earlier developments in building technology. Just as the burning-down of the Albion Mill at the end of the eighteenth century focused the attention of the nineteenth-century mill builders on the need for fireproof construction, so a series of disastrous fires at the end of the nineteenth century drew this problem once again to the attention of architects and stimulated the establishment of the British Fire Prevention Committee (BFPC). In 1897, *The Builder* had complained about the lack of attention given to the causes of fires, calling for them to be studied to see

what lessons might be drawn from them.[2] Shortly after this there was a major fire at Cripplegate and *The Builder*, at the same time as it reported this, was also able to announce the establishment of the BFPC which became the country's first scientific establishment concerned with building.[3] The Cripplegate fire had followed another particularly severe fire only three years before, partly attributable to the poor planning of the building, but an early report of the committee (Goad, 1899) noted ten major fires in London alone in the decade between 1889 and 1899. If fires of this kind were to be prevented, there was a need for improvement in both building design and methods of construction to prevent their spread. But this in turn depended upon a better understanding of the behaviour of building materials in fire. The task facing the committee was therefore to improve knowledge on several fronts.

The first issue to be tackled, before there could be any serious study of fire protection, was to define the terms being used. The word 'fireproof', commonly used by many companies advertising their methods of floor or wall construction, was hardly a scientific description of performance. In 1900, *The Builder* in a review of Freitag's book on fireproof building had complained about the 'pious belief' that structural iron and steel were fireproof and cited the new Record Office and Admiralty as public buildings which were built with unprotected steel structures.[4] A first step towards a clear specification of the fire resistance of either materials or methods of construction was to define and measure different grades of fire resistance. In 1903, the BFPC organized an International Fire Prevention Congress at which it was officially recognized that the term 'fireproof' was a poor description of construction and 'fire resisting' was substituted. The BFPC also proposed standards which were accepted by the Congress and which divided fire-resisting construction into three classes, depending upon whether they provided 'temporary resistance', 'partial resistance' or 'permanent resistance' (Table 1.1). A set of standard conditions was then issued (BFPC, 1904) defining the periods for which floors, ceilings, partitions and doors had to resist a fire of a given temperature to meet these standards for two different classes of building, though the classes of buildings themselves were undefined.

This was an important step forward, but if building methods and the performance of building components

Table 1.1 Grades of fire resistance				
Temporary	A	45	1500°F	
	B	60	1500	
Partial	A	90	1800	1cwt./sq. ft.
	B	120	1800	1.5 "
Full	A	150	1800	2 "
	B	240	1800	2.5 "

Source: The Fire Prevention Congress of July 1903

were to be described in this way then they had to be tested to determine their performance under standard conditions. To do this the committee established a testing station where it was able to carry out such tests and although this testing station led a somewhat peripatetic life it managed to carry out a large number of tests in its first few years. First opened in 1898, the station moved in 1901 and again in 1905. The committee was run on a largely voluntary basis and as a result was only able to acquire temporary sites in London. However, it was anxious that the testing station should be within a taxi ride from Charing Cross for the convenience of the specialists who were prepared to give their time voluntarily and on whose services the station relied. In spite of this somewhat shoestring operation the station had three brick-built testing chambers each measuring about 10 ft. x 22 ft. on plan. These were gas-fired and had recording pyrometers, while photographic records were also made of the tests. Some tests were undertaken as part of the committee's own research but the majority were for manufacturers of flooring, partitions, fireproof doors and in some cases safes.

Presumably the BFPC's own tests were carried out in the hope that elements of construction of known fire resistance could be incorporated into regulations. The New York Building Department had already (in 1896) carried out tests to determine the fire resistance of floors[5] but there was no similar official investigation of fire resistance in Britain. The tests which the BFPC applied to these elements of construction were more severe than those in the present British Standard test and, although their severity was recognized at the time, this was justified on the assumption that specimens for the test would be built to a higher standard than that of

normal construction. Commenting on this, Holt (1913) disputed that this was so for Britain, although, assuming lower standards of supervision there, he conceded that it might be true in the United States, but there is no indication of whether he had any evidence for this belief. Apart from his display of chauvinism, Holt's observation is an early example of whether standards used in one country are applicable elsewhere. In producing his useful summary of the state of the art, Holt would have been able to draw on the early publications of the committee.[6] Some of these dealt with general aspects of fire protection while the most numerous were the test reports called 'Red Books', giving full details of various forms of construction, and their performance in fire.

An influential series of tests carried out by the committee compared the performance of concretes made with different aggregates.[7] Slag, broken brick, granite, burnt ballast, coke breeze, clinker, and Thames ballast were all tested. The Thames ballast failed in the test which was probably no surprise to those at the time who had been reading the reports of fires that had been appearing in the AJ 'Fire Supplements'. It could also have been no surprise that it was the aggregates produced from some refractory process that performed best: burnt ballast, breeze, brick slag and clinker all passed the test. These tests were reported in one of the AJ's 'Fire Supplements', a series whose regular appearance during 1904 and 1905 is some indication of a general interest in fire resistance at the time. There was very little scientific information in these which were predominantly a series of reports of actual fires with the view to drawing some lessons from them. For example, by reporting the failure of steel and granite columns in fires, one issue showed that materials normally assumed to be fireproof were not so. The impression given is of a serious concern for the fire safety of modern buildings and in particular the fire resistance of the modern building materials that were becoming available. While there was considerable experience of the behaviour of masonry structures in fire, there was little knowledge of how steel or concrete structures might behave and, in the absence of any scientific data, designers could only rely on the information that could be obtained from actual incidents.

In 1905, a 'Fire Supplement' complained that the General Standard Fire Office Rules were only sent out on request by the Fire Officers' Committee and that many architects were ignorant of them. They therefore published the most important of these rules together with the definitions of fire-resisting materials from the London Building Act.[8] Unfortunately, in the absence of well-established methods of fire-testing, it was not possible for the rules at that time to refer to the BFPC's standards of protection and they failed to go beyond simple descriptions of acceptable methods of construction. The thickness of external walls required was to be 6 in. with party walls 13 in. thick, unless of concrete when they were to be 20 in. thick. Floors were to be a minimum of 5 in. thick and the cover to reinforcing steel was to be between 1 and 2 in, but otherwise at least twice the bar diameter. There was a height limit for buildings and a limit on the size of separate compartments to 60,000 cu. ft. There was also a requirement for scuppers in some buildings to carry off the water used in fire-fighting. The rules made no reference to the standards of fire resistance that the BFPC had proposed nor to the possibility of acceptable standards of test performance for new methods of construction, even though by this time nearly one hundred tests had been carried out. Science, it seems, was not yet to be trusted. These rules were also quite separate from those applied by the London County Council (LCC).

The BFPC's work largely came to an end with the death of its chairman E. O. Sachs in 1920; there was then no satisfactory establishment for fire-prevention research for some time. A Royal Commission was set up in 1921 which noted the risks associated with ducting in buildings but otherwise a hiatus in fire-prevention activities prevailed.[9] Fire was, of course, an international problem and in 1927 BRS reviewed the published accounts of fire-testing methods adopted by various authorities in different countries and noted four conditions that were necessary to ensure comparative test results: that the design of the furnace should be such as to ensure even heating; the temperature accurately controlled to give a standard rate of temperature rise; there should be a standard method of quenching or cooling the tested construction, and provision for applying loads (Stradling & Brady, 1927). A RIBA initiative in 1929 led to the first British Standard on fire testing, and while the Building Research Board through the BRS made a contribution to the work on this standard, the chairman's report in

1933 still noted the lack of fire-testing facilities.[10] The Fire Officers' Committee had a testing furnace in Manchester but there was nowhere to test manufacturers' products on a routine basis. It was not until the opening of the Fire Testing Station at Elstree in 1935 that fire testing of building components was put on a sounder footing.

A problem with any laboratory tests of building materials is in being able to relate the results of the tests to the performance of the materials in service. A standard test only provided a comparison of different materials and relating the test conditions to actual fires only became possible after the Second World War. As part of a survey of war-damaged buildings, an examination was made of the colour changes which occurred in building materials in fires (Parker et al., 1950) so providing an assessment of temperatures reached. This work also estimated the radiation from fires, which was related to their ability to cross streets.

All of the early work was concerned with fire resistance of building materials and such work has continued into recent years. Thus the Timber Research and Development Association (TRADA) began a series of tests of the fire resistance of timber-building components in the 1970s and, through the work of its fire laboratory, has a quality-assurance scheme for fire-resisting timber doors. But the focus of fire research has shifted away from simply testing the fire-resisting properties of building materials and is now as much concerned with the processes by which fires develop and with the mechanisms of fire and smoke spread. These processes affect the ability to escape a fire while the effects of smoke have become much more important with the increasing use for furnishings of flammable materials which give off toxic fumes and with the development of new building forms with large public spaces. If a particular event is to be associated with this last concern, it must surely be the disastrous fire at Summerland, Isle of Man in 1973. The need is such that fire engineering has now become a recognized professional specialization in building design.

Government research: the Building Research Station and the National Physical Laboratory

Much of this later work on fire has been government-sponsored through what is now the Building Research

Establishment (BRE) but government research in building was not prompted by the issue of fire. The need for industrial research was first officially recognized in 1915[11] and the Department of Scientific and Industrial Research (DSIR) was established in 1916. This led to the establishment of the Building Research Board (BRB) and the Building Research Station (BRS) which claims to be the first research organization specifically concerned with issues of building. Scientists were recruited to work for the Board and research laboratories were established at East Acton before moving to their present location at Garston at the end of 1925. The memorandum which had advised the formation of the BRB had stressed the lack of scientific knowledge in the industry and identified particular areas of concern: problems of durability and manufacture, the development of new materials, housing problems and fire prevention.

Even during the war it had been clear to the government that once hostilities were over it would have to tackle a housing shortage of a scale beyond the capacity of the traditional building industry: as a result, alternative methods of construction needed to be examined. After the war, the Standardisation and Construction Committee was established to examine alternative methods of construction but many of the methods proposed were quite bizarre. The approved methods even included one by Captain Adams which consisted of a building whose framework 'is composed of disused under-parts of motor cars, lorries, tram rails, etc.'.[12] If this was an example of the ideas coming before the committee the need for some scientific method of assessing the proposals can hardly be underestimated. While this was the kind of task that the BRS might address, there were more immediate practical problems which needed to be solved, particularly if research was to contribute to relieving the housing shortage of the time. It also quickly became apparent to those working at the Station that much fundamental work on the science of building materials was necessary before there could be any serious exploration of such problems. And while for much of its work the Station could draw upon established scientific methods, in other areas new techniques had to be developed before research could progress. This can be seen in the number of papers which members of the Station published in the *Journal of Scientific Instruments*.

The Station Director's first report in 1926 noted that the work of the Station fell into two major areas. Basic research considered the properties of building materials and the development of analytical techniques, research into the performance of building materials in service, manufacturing methods, and the performance of buildings from the user's point of view. The other major division, Intelligence and Special Investigations, was responsible for work at the request of outside organizations and for the investigation of building failures. Of course, there were inevitable overlaps between these two. Neither is this a complete list: two important pieces of work which the Station carried out in the inter-war years involved the design of building structures. The BRS was thus carrying out work of a varied nature much of which has already been reviewed by Lea (1971). Rather than use the official divisions of research it is more useful to consider the work of the BRS in relation to the process of manufacture and construction. BRS research was directly involved with the manufacture of building materials and products and related to this was research which concerned building materials' specification.

Materials and products manufacture

Cement and concrete are good examples of the need for fundamental research. Reinforced concrete was by then an established construction material, with the first regulations published in 1915; however, the poorly understood chemistry of cement and concrete meant that the quality of cements could not be improved. The problem at the time was controlling the free lime content of the material. At the same time, there was no rational basis for the selection of aggregates. This was the area in which Lea worked, publishing a number of papers on the properties of aggregates in the late 1920s and on their chemistry in the 1930s.

Manufacturing problems were tackled early; the first considered being the production of sand-lime bricks which was the subject of the Station's first report in 1921 (later revised). The Station also made contributions to the British Standards for these bricks in 1923 and 1934. This work (discussed in Chapter 2) is an excellent example of the need for research into the manufacture of a building product. The Station's facilities and organization enabled trade bodies who could not afford to establish their own research organizations to sponsor research. Various organizations, among others, the Cast Concrete Products Association (CCPA), the Greystone Lime Burners Association and the Natural Asphalt Mine Owners and Manufacturers Council, engaged in co-operative research with the Station. The results of co-operative work were generally the subject of confidential reports to the sponsors. This research presumably had a very direct affect on either their manufacturing methods or on the products which they produced; cast-concrete products are a good example. The details of this research are also discussed in Chapter 2 but when research on cast-concrete products first began in 1931, there were over a hundred firms in the CCPA and the first report was based on visits to over twenty of these.

The extent to which the BRS was able to undertake such collaborative work naturally depended upon the existence of trade organizations through which it could be funded and the willingness of those organizations to sponsor work in this way. Not all industries were convinced of the need for such research; for example, in 1935, Raymond Unwin, in his chairman's report, noted the failure of the heavy clay industry (i.e., the brickmakers) to carry out its own research even though it had an annual turnover of £14 million. As a result of the Station's own work, the need and demand for routine testing of building products and an awareness of the need for qualitative performance measures must have been increased. The Station received a large number of requests for such testing but did not have the staff or the capacity to undertake this clearly valuable work without severely disrupting its normal programme and in 1931 alternative ways of meeting this demand were discussed. One proposal was that a national testing house should be established but the alternative favoured by the BRB was to use existing testing houses and in the following year eight such organizations were approved and formed into a panel of co-operating laboratories.

Materials specification

Knowing *how* to produce something was one problem but this was sometimes related to the issue of *what* to produce. There was, for example, a poor understanding of the way in which the measurable properties of sand-lime bricks affected their performance in service so that the Station was as concerned with the required properties of this type of brick as they were with the

process of manufacture. Much the same was true of clay bricks but here there was also a concern for the problems of efflorescence. In 1924, there were more than 1600 firms manufacturing clay bricks. Flettons were known to have a high sulphate content and, with little knowledge of the effect this content might have in practice, there was a prejudice against specifying them. There was also a tendency to limit the level of water absorption in specifications, but the BRS showed that there was no link between this property and durability. Neither were bricks the only material where a more rational basis for specification was needed.

Work was done on the durability of roofing slates with the intention of producing a British Standard. The need to establish routine tests for weathering qualities was an example where existing properties of materials were known but where the testing method developed was related more to a fundamental understanding of the mechanism of decay than it was to being able to replicate the conditions of service. A collection of slates was divided into three categories of weathering qualities and subjected to tests to establish which could be used to discriminate between these grades. None of the physical tests were of value (and strength was not a suitable basis for specification purposes), but an acid test appeared to work, with decay linked to calcium carbonate and iron sulphides as impurities. Repeated wetting and drying was shown by others to have produced lamination and although work was started at the Station on similar lines, the test gave similar results to the acid test which was simpler to carry out. Although Lea reported some opposition to the tests proposed, this was overcome, and a specification for Welsh slates was produced in 1936. The specification was revised in 1944 to cover all types of slates.

The work on slates produced relatively rapid results, while the major work on weathering which the Station carried out in its early years was on natural building stones. Here the problems were much more difficult because so little was known about the mechanisms of decay and there was no science of weathering. Work was carried out on a number of fronts but it took ten years' work before the appearance of R. J. Schaffer's report, *The Weathering of Natural Building Stone* (1932). Until the performance of materials was understood, specification was to an extent based on traditional practice which might be unrelated to actual performance, a reliance on mythology rather than scientific understanding. Architects might not, for example, have been getting the best stone because old-fashioned specification practices required stone to be 'free from shells' while shelly stone may weather better.[13]

The investigation of asphalt mastic roofings started as early as 1926 because there was insufficient knowledge to distinguish between a good roofing which would last many years, and one which would rapidly show signs of deterioration. An increasing number of reported failures of asphalt roofing was also an indication of the need for a standard and in 1927 the difference between the materials in good and bad roofs was shown to be in their acid content. While asphalts in use were normally a mixture of natural rock asphalt and natural bitumen, lighter bitumen or oils was added as a flux but it was noted that the common practice of adulterating the material with petroleum bitumen was also associated with failures of this kind of roofing. Artificial asphalts were being manufactured by combining ground limestone with bitumen and in 1930 the Station investigated the properties of these.

Standards for site work

Of course, a material's performance was not simply a matter of specification. It was as much related to standards of workmanship and design, and asphalt was one such material. There were reports which attributed failure to poor handling of the material and poor workmanship.[14] Another cause of failure was movement of the supporting structure where in some cases cracking of the roof structure could be associated with cracking of the asphalt. Of course, a good asphalt roof should be sufficiently flexible to cope with this extent of movement and in 1931 the annual report noted that it was becoming common to include a layer of felt bitumen between the supporting concrete and the asphalt to facilitate movement, a practice recommended by the Station, as was the use of white chippings to reduce solar heat gain.

Traditional methods of construction needed attention because of developments which were occurring within the structure of the manufacturing side of the industry. The restructuring of the plaster industry (see Chapter 2) meant that builders were often working with unfamiliar materials as different products became available and problems were associated with both lime and gypsum plasters. An aspect of work on lime

specification, carried out for a British Standards Institute (BSI) committee, was to find a method of slaking because limes vary in their requirements. In 1928 it was reported that practical trials had been carried out and shown that the Emley plasticimeter gave a true index of the working plasticity of the material. At that time a specification for quicklime finishing coat was practically ready and they anticipated being in a position to complete a specification for mortar lime within a year.

Work on lime in general seems to have begun with devising methods of measurement. By 1930 there was a satisfactory test for workability and a good understanding of the setting mechanisms for lime-based plasters and by 1931 progress had been made in drawing up specifications for building limes by a BSI committee. The 1927 chairman's report discussed the problems of gypsum plaster. A large number of proprietary and patent plasters were available on the market as well as traditional products like 'Keene's cement', but these differed considerably in their constituents and properties. Because these plasters were poorly understood by their users, there were a large number of failures even in carefully supervised work. The report compared the per capita consumption of gypsum plasters in this country with that in the United States which was much higher, indicating a greater confidence in the material because of generally better products and commented:

This may be legitimately associated with the existence there of a complete series of official specifications for the various gypsum plasters and gypsum products in common use and with the growth of standardisation of quality… amongst the larger producing firms.[15]

Although the Board hoped to be able to draw up a specification for this type of plaster, it was clear that work would be slow because there was no co-operation from the manufacturers. This appears to have been short-sighted for, in 1929, the Board's report noted: 'The continuous sequence of cases in which failures of gypsum plasters have been reported to the Station, together with the evidence accumulating of the variability of the commercial product, clearly points to the need for more scientific control of the industry.'[16]

Calcium sulphate plasters were also used for gauging lime, the other common material used for this being Portland cement, but in 1933 it was noted that not all calcium sulphate plasters were suitable for this purpose. Because of their variability and the difficulty which the user faced in distinguishing the different types, Portland cement was probably the simpler material to use.

The importance of standards for site practices was demonstrated by the problems associated with magnesium oxychloride (magnesite) flooring, where poor standards of construction had led to failures. This method of flooring was based on nineteenth-century invention. A mixture of magnesium oxide and an aqueous solution of magnesium chloride produces a cementitious material to which fillers could be added to modify its properties. Fillers of sawdust, wood flour, broken cork, asbestos fabric and powder, quartz sand and a variety of others were used, the choice depending upon the required properties of the floor. Two-coat floors were used with different properties in each coat and the material could be reinforced for use over wooden flooring. The process was simple to carry out but there were many failures because of incorrect use, and the material began to develop a poor reputation because of poor contractors. The process led to steel corrosion, a factor often ignored in construction. The Station patented a substitute material using ferrous chloride instead of magnesium chloride to avoid the corrosion problem; the work by the Station, in association with the Magnesium Oxychloride Flooring Association, eventually led to the publication of a British Standard in 1938.[17]

An understanding of site operations is as important for productivity in construction as it is for obtaining adequate standards, although the former was of less concern to the Station in its early years and only became a part of the work of the Station in post-war years. Work on block-laying productivity, for example, demonstrated that composite walls were cheaper than those made entirely of bricks and this has certainly become the standard method of construction.[18] But the results of research into productivity did not necessarily have much effect on the industry. The BRS was sceptical about the likely advantages to be obtained from industrialized building following the Second World War when a housing shortage once again led to an interest in prefabricated construction. But while the results of research were not encouraging, showing that houses designed to be produced in the factory were no cheaper than traditional site construction, there was a significant shift towards factory methods.

Work by industry

Raymond Unwin's complaint in 1935 about the lack of research by the brickmakers was not entirely justifiable because the London Brick Company had opened a research department in 1928. Research of some kind is essential to the development of new products and manufacturing methods but beyond the simple ability to produce a workable product at a reasonable price the need for further research needs to be apparent to the manufacturer. Improvement of the manufacturing process, making it cheaper in order to compete with competitors or concern to improve the performance of the product, again with the intention of making it more competitive, might justify research, but both incentives depend upon the working of the market. There is no need to reduce costs if there is no direct competition, and this was true of most of the basic materials of construction in the early years of this century because of the costs of transport. Powell (1970) has pointed out that transport costs in the early part of the century protected local producers who may not have been competitive in either price or quality once wider competition became possible. Research to improve the performance of a product also assumes that buyers are in a position to compare the relative performance of competing products, whether they be similar products by different manufacturers or substitute products. Examples of the latter are concrete blocks as a replacement for bricks or artificial, as a substitute for natural, stone.

Concrete-block production is an example of the failure of the industry to carry out research. It had been possible to cast these on relatively simple equipment from an early date but as late as 1951, when the BRS published its report on block-making machinery, it noted the wide variety of practices that were in existence because of a lack of any real scientific investigation of the process.[19] Individual firms, lacking any guidance and with little or no communication between them had developed their own working practices which were often at odds with each other. This effect may have been a function of an industry which consists of large number of small firms with local markets. Where large firms compete with each other there may be both the incentive and the capability of carrying out research to develop new products or otherwise to gain an advantage over competitors, or simply to retain customer satisfaction. For example, plaster manufacturers employed chemists in the inter-war period. Caffereata employed a chemist following the First World War which led to their development of a keratin-based retarder in the 1920s and later, Aegrit retarder for finishing coats which was patented in the early 1930s. The Gotham Co. also employed a chemist in the late 1920s, principally to develop methods of testing because there had been complaints as a result of the variability of the materials being supplied. This also led to the development of Gothite, a backing coat gauged with sand which was intended to replace the traditional Portland cement/lime/sand mixtures which had given trouble with some paints. This new backing coat was intended to be a chemically neutral base to avoid reaction with this problem. The BRS had also done work on the reaction between paints and plaster.

Where firms saw the need for research, whether they saw fit to combine together to do this or whether they preferred to work alone, must have depended upon both the kinds of issue that they wished to tackle and upon some commercial judgement. In some cases it was in their interest to be independent while others saw the need for a general improvement in knowledge. The latter was more likely where a group of firms were in direct competition with producers of alternative products. Thus, the natural asphalt producers formed a group to combat the products of artificial asphalts while the research that the Cast Concrete Products Association sponsored would have improved their products *vis-à-vis* natural stone.

Trade associations

The function of trade associations needs to be considered quite separately because of the variety in the kind of organizations and in the way in which they operate. Put simply, the function of a trade association is to promote the interests of its members in a variety of ways not all of which may contribute to technical development. The interests of members may be served through activities as diverse as political lobbying, by the simple advertising of members' products, by offering information services to users or by the publication of technical literature, whether or not the last is based upon research. The major associations have done all these things but it is difficult to get a full picture of the effect of trade associations because of their variety and to some extent their fugitive nature: the history of these associations is difficult to research because they have

often left little or no trace. These associations are naturally subject to the vicissitudes of trade. They survive only as long as their products thrive in the marketplace but they may be brought to an untimely end simply because the captains of that particular industry no longer see the need for the association. This may happen under the pressure of falling profits, the fate that recently befell the Cement and Concrete Association, or because the association has fulfilled its function. Thus, the Sand Lime Brick Association was concerned with improving production methods; once the production problems had been solved, the association was wound up.

In 1937, an exhibition of building science demonstrated not only the work of the BRB but also had exhibits by a number of trade organizations.[20] The catalogue noted that at that time there were twenty such organizations but failed to say how this list was determined or how many of these were carrying out work which involved building. The exhibition gave those trade organizations which were carrying out their own research a chance to show what they were doing. The Research Association of British Rubber Manufacturers seems to have been the oldest of the associations, founded in 1920 and, although not principally concerned with building, was carrying out development work on jointing in pipes, methods of vibration insulation, thermal insulation, rubber paints and rubber floor and roofing materials. The British Non-Ferrous Metals Research Association was another organization not primarily concerned with building but it did research on the use of copper for domestic plumbing. The Research Association of British Paint, Colour and Varnish Manufacturers, like many manufacturers' research associations, was initially concerned with problems of manufacture but its Paint Research Station published a number of bulletins dealing with painting issues during the 1930s. These covered issues as diverse as the preservation of iron and steel by means of paint, priming joinery timbers and the decoration of new plaster and cement.

The trade association representing the cement manufacturers, the Cement Manufacturers Federation, set up the Cement and Concrete Association in 1935 absorbing the older British Portland Cement Research Association. The aim was to increase cement sales through technical excellence although they restricted their activities to the promotion of Portland cement.

Laboratories at Wexham Springs were set up in the years immediately after the war and since then this organization has carried out extensive work, developing an international reputation for structural concrete research. It has carried out pioneering work on model structures, for example. Nevertheless it restricted its activities to the interests of the Portland cement industry and is an example of the difficulties of commercially based organizations: in this instance fly ash and slag were regarded as part of the competition rather than subjects for parallel research. Neither did it take an active interest in the precast or ready-mixed concrete industries which developed their own associations.

The brick industry separated publicity from research: the former was carried out through the Brick Development Association while research was done through the Clay Products Technical Bureau, a rather short-lived organization publishing its bulletins in the late 1960s. The Timber Development Association (TDA) was established before the war and quickly made its presence felt through a house design competition.[21] The association established laboratories in the post-war years, first at Tylers Green and then at its present home in Hughenden Valley adding the word 'Research' to its name to emphasize that it was not simply a promotional organization (eventually to become TRADA). As timber has a wide range of uses, not all the work carried out by TRADA has been concerned with building, but it has made major contributions to the design of timber roof structures and timber-frame buildings (see Chapter 6) and provided test facilities for the fire resistance of timber construction. It has also been concerned with the establishment of quality assurance schemes in recent years.

These associations represented manufacturing rather than contracting interests. It was not until much more recently that contractors have been drawn into a research association with the formation of the present Construction Industry Research and Information Association (CIRIA). Not all major contractors belong to this and there are those, like John Laing, who have their own research organizations.

Quality control

A growing function of trade associations has been to establish standards of performance for its members. The obvious means by which it might do this is through the BSI, the working of which will be discussed below, but we have already seen how standards for sand-lime bricks and jointless flooring were issued through collaboration between the BSI, the BRS and the trade associations concerned. The former was an example of a manufacturing standard and these have the advantage that they offer the purchaser some guarantee of the properties of the materials being purchased.

A knowledge of the performance of particular components is essential to their correct specification in design but the designer may also rely upon certain minimal standards being guaranteed within a class of materials or products. Part of the service provided by architects in Britain has been the supervision of construction, thus providing some assurance to the client of workmanship standards. For traditional construction this was a relatively simple matter. Although a characteristic of building construction is that much of the work cannot be readily tested or inspected once in place, considerable reliance was placed upon the employment of trained craftsmen. It was a satisfactory system while building remained a bespoke product but could not work when it became a speculatively built product and the National House Building Council was needed to try to remedy this.

The introduction of new building technologies and of a market in buildings changed working relationships. New technologies often required specialist contractors or sub-contractors and with this came specialist knowledge and skills, knowledge which the architect might not share. Even if the architect did have the necessary knowledge, the degree of supervision required might change completely. This became apparent with the introduction of frame structures. Bylander was to make much of the supervision required for steel fabrication (see Chapter 4) and it was recognized that reinforced concrete required a greater degree of site supervision than other forms of construction (see Chapter 5). The solution was for the supervision of the structure to be taken into the hands of a structural engineer who had the necessary knowledge and who would, in most circumstances, have been responsible for the structural design.

Changes in smaller elements of construction have presented similar problems but not of a kind which could be solved in the same way. There is no fire engineer to oversee the application of fire-protective treatments to structural steel, for example, although this is exactly the kind of construction that presents problems of quality control. Control of the properties of materials and standards of workmanship may require knowledge which the architect does not have while their application may also require new skills and so a degree of specialist training. Control over the process is essential in such situations where it is often not easy to inspect work even though it is critical to an aspect of the building's performance.

Trade associations have responded to this by taking on a new role, that is, the issuing of trade standards or advisory documents to designers which have become more important as construction has depended more upon new, and therefore unfamiliar, materials. Individual firms may train and approve contractors in the use of their products, a role which reflects the methods adopted by reinforced concrete companies in the early years of the century (see Chapter 5). Some companies have approved contractors as well as issuing approved details to which the designer must conform. This training function has also been taken on by some trade associations, fire protection being an obvious example. In this way trade associations may assume part of the role of the architect or structural engineer in providing some assurance of workmanship standards. Site operations are one thing but, given its traditional structure, standards are also a problem for the building industry when operations are removed from the site to the factory where processes are not easily open to scrutiny. The issue here is not the standard of manufactured items like bricks or plasterboard, which may be controlled by ensuring compliance with fixed manufacturing standards, but for the supply of items previously 'assembled' on-site to the designer's specification. Ready-mixed concrete, an idea begun here in the inter-war years but which developed rapidly after the war, is an example of this kind of change in the supply pattern.

Twelvetrees (1925) reported the use of central mixing plants in the United States for the construction of roads for which these plants were clearly suited because large quantities of material were needed on what was essentially a moving site. In Britain there was some interest in this American development which was reported in the pages of *Concrete*. At first the Americans used ordinary tip-up trucks for delivery although, by 1930, mixer trucks were in use there. A year later there was a report of a ready-mix plant opening in London

with an illustration of a delivery to a road construction site. In 1938, there were a few plants in operation in different parts of the country with their use reported for major building work at the Olympia and Savoy sites in London. Development remained fairly limited until the post-war years when, by the early 1960s, it had become the common method of obtaining concrete. It was still possible, of course, for test cubes to be taken to ensure adequate strength but, given the lag between casting and the results of test cubes — and as the purchaser had no direct influence over the running of the mixing plant, and thus no direct way of ensuring a consistency in standards — some other assurance was desirable. This degree of control was provided by the British Ready Mixed Concrete Association who ran a scheme by which regular samples were taken from their members' mixing plants and tested. This scheme also allowed the application of statistical techniques to provided a link between quality control and production control.

In the 1970s TRADA established quality assurance schemes for trussed rafter roofs and fire-check doors although these address different problems. The purchaser of trussed rafters needs some assurance that the structures supplied have been manufactured from properly graded timbers and have been assembled correctly. The purchaser of a fire-check door needs to know what grade of door is being supplied — doors providing different degrees of fire protection may nevertheless look exactly the same. A more recent development has been the establishment of the Agrément Board with its own testing laboratories. The certificates issued by this organization not only provide some assurance of the manufactured product's quality, but also cover its proper installation, thus providing the designer with a guide for the supervision of site workmanship.

Building performance

We have been concerned up until now with developments in building materials and contracting methods, but research into the performance of buildings themselves has also been necessary to improve building design. Changes in technology have had a profound effect on the performance of buildings in a way that has needed a level of exploration beyond the capability of individual professionals and even of professional firms unless of sufficient size. New structural techniques, new types of building, developments in building services, stricter performance requirements and radically new methods of construction have all presented problems which have required collective effort of some kind. The first example of this was the interest taken by various professionals in reinforced concrete (see Chapter 5).

Building performance was one of the divisions of work carried out by the BRS which initially dealt with what we would today call 'environmental control'. Much of the early experimental work on aspects of building performance was carried out by the National Physical Laboratory (NPL) rather than by the BRS at Garston. This included work on lighting, acoustics and the thermal performance of building materials. The first task on lighting was to define the terminology of the subject while work at the NPL was carried out to devise methods for predicting levels of lighting so that the designer could assess its adequacy for particular tasks. This work involved both natural and artificial, i.e gas and electric, lighting. Work was also done on the efficiency of light-wells based on models. The subject of lighting produced its own learned society, the Illuminating Engineering Society, which at that time decided not to become a professional association as a matter of policy. This was, of course, to change. The establishment of standards of illumination in buildings was not to become a serious issue until the Second World War when factory lighting became important for the war effort.

Experimental work on room acoustics was carried out at the NPL and in 1932 the Station was called upon to advise on the acoustics of the League of Nations hall in Geneva. There was also an increasing awareness of the problems of noise, a subject which had been discussed by Hope Bagenal (1924), but it was not until 1933 that the BRB noted that the public were becoming increasingly noise-conscious. In the following year the BRB formed a sub-committee of the Architectural Acoustics Committee to consider sound transmission with special attention being paid to problems of impact noise. Life was simply becoming noisier. The increasing use of motor transport created a problem of street noise and the popularity of the gramophone and the radio created noises that could be transmitted between dwellings — flat construction particularly raised the issue of design to minimize the transmission of structure-bourne sound. In 1935 a noise abatement exhibition was held at the Science Museum and the Building Centre and in 1938 the AJ had a special issue on methods of construction, in both building planning and insulation, to prevent noise transmission.[22]

Establishing a scientific base to predict the thermal performance of buildings involved a number of parallel experiments: work was needed on both the thermal properties of building materials and of elements of construction, on methods for measuring conditions of human comfort and on the performance of heating appliances. This was an area where the interest of the BRB overlapped with those of other organizations. It had always been recognized that the comfort, and possibly the health of occupants, depended upon adequate ventilation and this had been a particular concern of the Board of Education during its early years, and a determinant of the planning recommendations for the design of school buildings. Ventilation had also been of concern in the planning of hospitals and in 1931 an *ad hoc* committee was formed in conjunction with the Medical Research Council 'to review the physical criteria, psychological considerations and nomenclature in research on heating and ventilation and to examine the possibility of adopting standard terminologies & methods of measurement'.[23] There was also an overlap here in the research interests of the BRS and the Industrial Health Research Board and therefore a need for common methods and terminologies to be adopted. Some impetus was given to work in this area in the 1930s by the introduction of new methods of heating, particularly radiant heating, which raised questions of human comfort — to tackle this an instrument to measure comfort conditions, the 'Eupatheoscope', was developed at the Station.

The Institute of Heating and Ventilating Engineers was also interested in work on the heating of rooms and worked with the Station on the design of a heating laboratory. This essentially comprised an enclosed space representing the heated room enclosed in a controlled environment. While the original suggestion for the establishment of such a laboratory had been made in 1930, design and construction took a rather long time and it did not come into use until 1936. There seems to have been little sense of urgency at this time but heating and ventilation were to become far more important in post-war years with radical changes in the design of dwellings.

With the common use of individual room heating, either by solid fuel or gas fires, dwellings in Britain had been generally well ventilated, more by accident than by design. However, the post-war years saw the growing use of central heating in private houses and the construction of local authority flats which not only had heating systems that failed to provide adequate ventilation as a by-product, but which also had impermeable concrete walls — and who would open the window when several floors above the ground? The result in both situations was the appearance of condensation and the development of mould growth. In response to a request from the DoE's Housing Directorate, the BRS set up a programme to identify the conditions for mould growth and to establish the factors in the design of buildings which produced such conditions. By this means they were able to show how to avoid the problem in new designs and suggest remedial action for existing buildings.

Buildings could no longer be considered as shells against the weather whose performance depended simply upon an understanding of the properties of individual constituent materials. New materials and forms of design were creating systems that behaved in ways that were not fully understood by designers and there needed to be a shift in the focus of research. This is amply illustrated by the differences between the three editions of *Principles of Modern Buildings* and commented on by Lea in his introduction to the third edition: 'What in 1938 was unfamiliar has now entered into the common stock of ideas' (Ministry of Technology, 1959). He also observed 'Research starts with the materials and components and progresses to the study of functional elements and then of the building as a whole.' While design research, if this last may be so called, may be considered the province of the professions it was not something in which professional bodies had shown a continuing interest. There had been some professional research, in addition to that by the BFPC before the First World War, but what there was had been on a rather *ad hoc* basis. RIBA, for example, had carried out some tests on the strength of brickwork in the 1890s, although this does not seem to have led to anything, and it had also developed an interest in lighting conductors for which a committee had established design rules. It was also RIBA who instigated the establishment of the Joint Committee on Reinforced Concrete in 1906, although work on reinforced concrete design was to become the province of the new Institution of Structural Engineers. This new

professional body naturally was interested in the development of design methods and codes of practice.

Though there was little actual building activity during the Second World War, members of the professions had a strong presence on the committees responsible for drawing up the Post War Building Studies series which had been set up by the Ministry of Health. However, these publications were not particularly influential. Much more important were the committees responsible for codes of practice, although here again it was the structural codes that were most influential (see below). It was more common for trade associations to carry out development work or research into the design of buildings, especially where this was likely to lead to an increased market share for the products of its members. In 1934 Council for Research on Housing Construction produced a report, *Slum Clearance and Rehousing*, on the design of flats, essentially promoting the use of steel frame construction by providing figures which purported to show the economies that could be achieved with steel.[24] The Council, under the chairmanship of Lord Dudley, was not an independent research organization, but was sponsored by the steel industry. This is perhaps not the best example of research by a trade association since it seemed to be based on little actual research. A better example is the TDA which did work on roof design in the years immediately following the Second World War but which had always had an interest in the promotion of timber for framing housing, eventually leading to the publication of its design guide in 1966.

Dissemination

What means has the building industry found for disseminating the results of research? If design as well as construction is as suggested a craft activity, then this is not a trivial question. Cole and Cooper (1988) have discussed the way in which the architectural profession has responded to developments in technology and increased scientific understanding of buildings, though perhaps it would be more accurate to say the way in which the profession has not responded. Cole and Cooper observe that architects have been reluctant to take on these aspects of design, although theirs is not the only profession to be slow to respond to new ideas. Structural engineers have from time to time also displayed some reluctance to change their practices, as will be shown in the following chapters. Research results will directly affect design when they are incorporated into standards, codes of practice or legislation and it may be argued that research's effect on building design has often depended upon the ability to turn research findings into design guides, rather than the willingness of professionals to respond.

BRS publications

The results of the Building Research Station's work were disseminated in three kinds of official publications: bulletins which were written in a non-scientific language and addressed to the building industry, special reports and technical papers which were much more scientific in their language and their intended audience. These were only a small proportion of the Station's output — its members also produced scientific papers for various specialist journals as well as articles of a practical nature in building and other professional journals. By 1936 when the annual report produced its last cumulative list of publications the total output amounted to some 400 publications of which only 25 per cent were in the form of bulletins, special reports or technical papers. The titles of the remainder testify to the pioneering work which the Station did in a number of fields, show the balance of concerns within the Station and also the shift in emphasis that occurred from time to time.

The Station also published *Building Science Abstracts* from 1928 which summarized current research publications in the field. Clearly it was necessary for the Station itself to keep abreast of research elsewhere but this would have had little effect on designers. Its value was to other research workers. Much the same might be said of the papers and special reports which the Station produced. Many of these were of potential value to the industry although at a strategic level rather than at the individual design level.

In 1930 the BRS began to include notes on building performance as a supplement to the *RIBAJ*. This reported the queries that had been addressed to the Station and the replies, most naturally concerned with the performance of building materials. The Station also contributed to regular articles in journals dealing with imediate technical issues and providing practical guidance, for example, the advice given on the handling of external renders which were becoming

more popular in the 1930s with the modern taste for white surfaces. The Station took a more direct approach after the war with the publication of BRS Digests in 1948 and Information Papers in 1979. It also adopted a policy of publishing Current Papers, sometimes reprints of journal articles which provided more information on research for those who were interested.

Design guides

Other important publications were concerned with particular building types, often the work of government departments, for example, the Department of Education and Science (DES) produced a constant flow of work on the design of schools. Other building types have also attracted attention: in 1956 the *Factory Building Research Commitee* was formed on the initiative of the Midland Regional Board for Industry and this resulted in a series of 'Factory building studies', published in 1960 and 1962. The initiative for work of this kind can be seen as a response to the particular needs of the time as seen in the appearance of *Better Factories* in 1963 (National Productivity Year). However, this was published by the Institute of Directors rather than being an initiative of the building industry or profession.

While professional bodies are naturally concerned with the development of the science of their trades they are not always in a position to ensure that research is carried out and their normal function is to disseminate through their journals knowledge generated by others. The *RIBAJ's* regular reports on the work of the BRS have attempted this. Whether such publications were the cause or the result of an interest in science within the architectural profession of the time — a characteristic of the modern movement in architecture — is hard to say. Research and the publication of results was certainly contributing to a climate of awareness in the industry, and the 1937 exhibition 'Science and Building' mounted by the DSIR had a wide range of exhibitors from both government laboratotries and the industrial organizations referred to above. By the 1950s the Station was only one of a number of laboratories carrying out regular research in building although, without commercial pressures, it was able to take a rather longer-term view than some of the other organizations.

In post-war years we have seen far more publications from such organizations directed towards informing the designer. Their format has varied from one organization to another and it would be difficult to say how effective each may have been in its field. The interests of steel, represented by the British Constructional Steelwork Association (BCSA) booklets in the 1960s and 1970s and more recently by Constrado Publications, take the form of design guides on specific topics. The Clay Products Technical Bureau took a similar line as have TRADA with their Wood Information Sheets. Concrete Publications, in contrast, began during the inter-war years to produce a series of rather more substantial books which dealt with a range of issues from the theoretical treatment of concrete structures and the mathematics of structural analysis to the practical design of particular types of structure and of works on site. Concrete has also been served since 1949 by the publication *Magazine of Concrete Research*.

Regulations

Ultimately scientific understanding must be reflected in the building regulations, either shaping those regulations to bring about changes in construction methods, as has recently happened with the requirement for improved thermal insulation standards, or because the regulations have needed to change to respond to new construction methods. Unfortunately the form of regulations in Britain until recently has had the effect of limiting developments in construction, a situation only too clear to many in the industry. Regulations were naturally the subject of interest to the professional bodies, whose journals occasionally carried critical articles, and they might also be of more than passing interest to the commercial journals, depending upon editorial attitudes. *Architect and Building News* (*A&BN*) appeared to wage a campaign against what it considered to be archaic plumbing regulations in the inter-war years.[25] A review of the response of regulations during that period to changing construction methods shows that the form in which they were framed, and in some cases administered, was ill-suited to a rapidly changing technology.

While the purpose of regulations is naturally to ensure sound building it is important to recognize how that is seen because regulations are inevitably a response to the perceived needs of the time. The first Parliamentary bill dealing with building in London was to control its rebuilding after the Fire of 1666 and was naturally particularly concerned with fire precautions.

During the nineteenth century public health became an important issue and so shaped regulations, while concerns for the structural strength and stability of buildings followed the development of frame structures in the first decades of this century. Today, while fire protection issues remain of considerable importance, it is concern for energy savings which are, for the first time, having an influence. Such shifts of emphasis can be seen in the approach taken towards structural safety. In today's climate of highly stressed materials it seems natural that design loads and working stresses should be specified. Although such specifications might have been attempted by the end of the nineteenth century, it was only the appearance of frame buidings that led to the incorporation of design loads in regulations and then only for those frame structures (see Appendix II).

The state of building regulations at the beginning of this century can only be called confusing; not only confusing when studied from this distance, but also to designers at the time: control was exercised in a variety of ways and different regulations applied in different parts of the country. General Acts of Parliament, principally the Public Health Acts and the Shops and Factory Acts imposed regulations. The Public Health Acts of 1875 and 1890 led to subordinate regulations by giving local authorities powers to impose local by-laws and regulations. However, by-laws needed to be confirmed by the Minister of Health while regulations did not. Model by-laws were issued by the Ministry of Health; local authorities generally based their own by-laws on these but were also given discretionary powers to grant waivers. Some cities were even governed by local Acts of Parliament, the most important being the London Building Act of 1894. There were also local Acts for Birmingham, Cardiff, Bristol, Leeds, Liverpool, Manchester, Sheffield, Bradford and Huddersfield and Glasgow.[26] One problem with such Acts was that they could only be modified by resorting to Parliament, a clumsy process, hardly enabling regulations to adapt quickly to changes in building technology.

This variety of means of control naturally led to some divergence in the regulations although Wood (1933), presenting a paper to the Institution of Structural Engineers, was of the opinion that there was not as much divergence as commonly alleged at the time, nor many unreasonable provisions within by-laws, although he did not think the system was without faults. At the time he was writing, the legislation in force was still the 1875 Public Health Act which, for buildings, regulated the construction of walls, roofs, foundations and chimneys. An amendment Act of 1890 covered the structure of staircases and hearths, the height of habitable rooms, the prevention of alterations which might contravene the provisions of the act, the heights of buildings and chimneys, and the structure of chimney shafts.

The model by-laws of 1905 which were published as a guide to local authorities were regularly updated by the ministry but local authorities did not always follow suit, with the result that individual by-laws might be out of step with the recommendations. However, it was not the law that was the problem but their interpretation by the local authority. This sometimes took the form of 'unwritten by-laws', that is, by-laws which only existed in the mind of the district surveyor who was applying them. Nevertheless, variations of the regulations sometimes created an unwillingness by contractors to quote for work outside their area. Buildings were also controlled by regulations other than the by-laws, so that while accommodation and safety standards were regulated in the Shops, Offices and Factory Acts, regulations made under the Cinematograph Act (1909) controlled the construction of cinemas. Government circulars were issued to regulate the construction of schools which lay outside the control of local authorities. It was then, as it is today, also possible for local authority surveyors to invoke other regulations to support demands for certain standards of construction. For example, the Petroleum Act might be used to control the construction of filling stations.[27]

The situation in and around London was, if anything, more complex than in the rest of the country. Within the LCC area, building was controlled by the 1894 London Building Act but there there were numerous amending Acts,[28] the most important being the so-called Steel Frame Act of 1909 and the 1930 Act. These various Acts were necessary because control was exercised through an Act of Parliament and the LCC had no powers to make changes themselves, although they might have powers to grant waivers. Regrettably, the 1930 Act only consolidated the earlier amendments rather than creating radically new legislation — regrettably because the Act, as with the model by-laws, made no provision for the possibility of new forms of construction. For example, although the

London underground railway used escalators and they could be installed in provincial towns, there was a time when they could not be incorporated into department stores in London because there was no reference to either escalators or moving staircases in the Act.

The system of employment of surveyors in London was also a potential source of difficulty. Surveyors were appointed by the LCC but were not paid by them. Instead, they acted as independent consultants and were paid a fee by the applicant although, in districts round the LCC area, surveyors were employees of the local authorities, as they were elsewhere. Under this system there was the obvious possibility of different interpretations of parts of the Act by different surveyors. Some details of this will be given in Chapter 4 but it is mentioned here as an example of the difficulties created by the structure of the regulations. The London Building Act of 1909 was important in that, although the model by-laws covered general building construction, they did not deal with frame buildings and other authorities chose to follow the lead set by London and use their regulations.[29]

The London Building Act of 1894 assumed that buildings would be of masonry and timber construction and there were rules covering the thickness of walls, the dimensions of wooden bressumers and floor joists, the protection of ironwork against fire and the provision of means of escape.[30] Protection against fire was an important part of these regulations but having been framed on the assumption of masonry construction, the fire regulations were quickly overtaken by other methods of building. This was changed when the London Building (Amendment) Act of 1905 gave a definition of fire-resisting materials and, while applying the requirements for means of escape to existing as well as new buildings, did allow for the use of new materials subject to the approval of the building control officer.[31] The weakness was that no criteria were laid down by which the new materials could be assessed in spite of the work of the BFPC. Fire protection was further modified by the LCC (General Powers) Act 1908 Pt III which defined the cubical extent of buildings and requirements for division walls. However, the major change which came in 1909 was the provision for the erection of steel-framed buildings in the so-called Steel Frame Act which regulated for steel frames and specified the fire protection required.[32] This Act made it economical to use steel frames in London and in

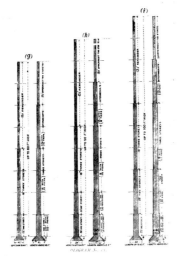

Fig. 1.1

other cities which adopted the same regulations. It also authorized regulations for concrete although these were not issued until 1915.

While local authority by-laws specified the thickness of walls (Fig. 1.1) it was unusual for them to specify the sizes of structural timbers. This was a matter of policy because in drawing up the model by-laws the Ministry of Health was reluctant to include regulations for floor sizes, arguing that local authorities might not have the necessary inspectors to enforce such regulations. Nevertheless, there were some authorities who did include such regulations in their by-laws. Liverpool was one such city, possibly because of the large number of warehouse buildings that it had (see Table 1.2).

In 1952 there was a change in the form of the model by-laws which for the first time relied upon 'deemed to satisfy' clauses. These were introduced to allow more freedom in the use of new construction methods. The functional requirements to be satisfied were stated and then examples of methods and materials that would satisfy the regulations were given. In order to do this, the 'deemed to satisfy' clauses drew extensively on British Standards and Codes of Practice (CP). The same pattern was used when the national Building Regulations were introduced in 1966. These replaced the old system of local by-laws and for the first time brought the whole of England and Wales under one set of regulations. However, the regulations were still complex and continued to govern aspects of construction which could not be shown materially to

affect the safety of buildings or their occupants' health. Present building regulations represent a radical change with the aim of controlling simply the health and safety of the occupants of buildings and the conservation of energy, moving away from a direct specification of forms

Table 1.2
Sizes of structual timbers in Liverpool

Floor joists at 15 in. centres.				Beams at 10ft centres.		
span	depth	width		span	depth	width
ft	ins	ins	ins	ft	ins	ins
3	4	3	3	10	10	6
5	4	3.5	3	12	11	7
7	4	4	3	14	12	8
9	4	5	2.5	16	13	9
11	4	6	2.5	18	14	10
13	4	7	2.5	20	15	11
14	4	7	3			
16	4	8	3			
18	4	9	3			
20	4	10	3			
22	4	11	3			

Warehouses

Joists			Beams		
span	depth	width	span	depth	width
ft	ins	ins	ft	ins	ins
3	4.5	3	10	12	11
4	6	2.5	12	13	12
5	7	2.5	14	14	13
6	7	3	16	15	14
7	7.5	3	18	15	18
8	8	3	20	15	24
10	9	3			
12	10	3			
14	11	3			
16	12	3			
18	9	6			
20	11	4.5			

of construction. The Approved Documents which support the present regulations are not intended to restrict the form of building and have the effect that changes may be made relatively easily.

These Approved Documents continue to draw upon the provisions of British Standards but, while the present arrangement may have improved the flexibility of the regulations, it is not clear that British Standards can be brought up to date sufficiently rapidly to deal effectively with developments in construction methods.

British Standards

The other area of influence in building science has been in the development of British Standards. The earliest of these which applied to building were BS 4, in 1903, and BS 12 the following year. Until the first of these defined standard sizes for rolled steel sections, manufacturers had all produced their own sizes: the publication of the standard was a step towards simplifying steel design. BS 12 established a standard of performance for cement produced in Britain and the number of revisions shows that manufacturing standards were continually being improved. The first of these two standards set a pattern for many others, i.e. the standardization of component sizes, and a number of building products were treated in this way. BS 12, however, involved some quantitative testing of the manufactured products and therefore some implicit relationship to its performance in service and it was in this area that scientific work was needed, both to develop appropriate tests and to ensure that they had some relevance to the performance of the product. It was in this area that the BRS was able to contribute to the work of the BSI, an example of this seen in the way in which the standard for sand-lime bricks was changed (see above) as a response to better scientific understanding.

Different kinds of standards were beginning to appear: some were simple manufacturing dimensions to ensure compatibility of different products; some, although still manufacturing standards, defined performance-related properties while others simply defined standards terms to be used in some areas of methods for testing the properties of materials. BS 648 (1938) *Weights of Building Materials* hardly fits into any of these categories, being more an information sheet than a standard, but it is a useful reference for presenting calculations to building control officers. Even

when British Standards are simply manufacturing standards there are differences in approach which depend upon the nature of the product being defined and to some extent the intentions of the drafting committee. This is not the place to examine the working of the committees but the effect has been that some standards provide a measure of quality assurance, i.e. of a standard of performance in service, while others do not. This is not always clear to those specifying who may not take care to read the standard and who may assume that its function is to assure adequate performance. Naturally this is not always possible. As we have seen, simple comparative tests of some property of the product may be all that is possible within the state of knowledge, particularly when laboratory tests are not be able to replicate service conditions or where there is no known relationship between performance and measurable characteristics.

The establishment of standards which provide a measure of quality assurance, reflecting the safety of building fabric and providing recommendations for methods of design, have increasingly been developed and relied upon by building regulations. The British Standards codes of practice for design date from 1942 when the Council for Codes of Practice for Buildings was set up within the Ministry of Works, eventually becoming part of the work of the British Standards Institution. The publication of these codes enabled first the by-laws and then the Building Regulations to refer to them rather than having structural design recommendations included within these documents, compliance with the relevant Code of Practice being 'deemed to satisfy' the legal requirements. Reference to such codes naturally ensured a degree of uniformity before the publication of Building Regulations. Those produced for the various aspects of structural design have become standard works of reference, although the same seems not to be true of others. CP 3, Chapter 5, *Loading*, was well known but few architects seemed to even know the general title of the code itself, *Code of Functional Requirements of Buildings*.

In recent years there has been a shift in the philosophy of structural design with a general move towards limit-state design rather than allowable-stress design. The first change of this kind came with the introduction of load-factor design in reinforced concrete, no doubt a popular move because it simplified the calculations. However, the more recent changes towards limit-state design have been less popular because they have had the opposite effect. Put simply, limit-state design depends upon identifying a number of possible states at which the structure may be said to become unserviceable, failure of the materials of the structure, unacceptable deflections, unacceptable levels of cracking in reinforced concrete, etc. The intention in design is to limit the working loads to a proportion of the load that will produce such an effect, thus providing a safety factor against failure. Following the appearance of the concrete code framed in this way, the speed with which it was possible to introduce the same design method for other materials has varied, with timber long resisting attempts to apply such an approach. But it has also to be said that engineers have been divided about the desirability of such codes and, as the change has been introduced with both old and new codes in use at the same time, many engineers have resisted adopting the new approach for as long as possible. Given the history of Steel Structures Research Committee (see Chapter 4) such resistance might well have been anticipated.

Notes

1   *RIBAJ*, 35, (1927—8), p. 311. The original request had appeared in an earlier issue of the journal.

2   *The Builder*, 72, (1897), p. 473.

3   *The Builder*, 73, (1897), p. 443. An account of the working of the testing station was given in the AJ 'Fire Supplement' of 15 February 1905, pp. 56—7.

4   *The Builder*, 78 (1900), pp. 413—16.

5   *The Builder*, 78 (1900), p. 415. These test were of two thicknesses of 7/8 in. board with either 'Salamander' or asbestos between them. At the same time tests were carried out on terracotta floors and on partitions.

6   British Fire Prevention Committee, Publications 1—89, (Vol 1—9), 1898—1905, Red Books 90—257, 1906—21.

7   These were reported in the AJ 'Fire Supplement', 22 Nov. 1905, p. 47.

8   AJ 'Fire Supplement', 25 Oct. 1905, pp. 35—8.

9   Royal Commission on Fire Brigades and Fire Prevention, Cmnd. 1945, HMSO: 1923.

10   Chairman's Report, 1933, p. 6. Raymond Unwin was the chairman at the time.

11   Scheme for the Organization and Development of Scientific and Industrial Research, Cmnd. 8005, HMSO: 1915.

12   *AJ, 50* (1919), p. 585. However, Adams later produced a design for houses using specially designed steel studs and floor joists. *AJ*, 51 (1920), p. 29.

13   Review of construction and materials — Weathering of Portland stone', *RIBAJ*, 41, (1933—4), p. 83.

14   For example, Chairman's reports, 1928, p. 106 and 1929, p. 102.

15   Chairman's report, 1927, p. 58.

16   Chairman's report, 1929, pp. 39—40.

17   BS 776: 1938, Magnesium Oxychloride (Magnesite) Flooring.

18   *A work study in block laying*, NBS Technical Papers, No. 1, HMSO: 1948.

19   *Concrete Block-making Machines*, BRB Special Report, No. 17, HMSO: 1951.

20   'Science and Building, Exhibition at the Building Centre' *RIBAJ*, 44 (1936—7), pp. 441—3.

21   Wood, 1 (1936), pp. 46—7.

22   AJ, 87 (1938) May 19, pp. 849 et seq.

23   Chairman's Report for 1931, p. 3.

24   A summary of the report was published in *Building*, 9 (1934), p. 262.

25   Their concern was the requirement for external drainage which was needed because of the risk of leaks (*A&BN*, 121, p. 295). It advocated US plumbing practice (*A&BN*, 122, p. 294 and 130, p. 213). The one-pipe plumbing system was reported used in the Cumberland Hotel, London, in 1933 (*A&BN*, 133, p. 79).

26   Birmingham Consolidation Act 1883 and Birmingham Corporation Act 1903; Cardiff Corporation Act 1894; Bristol Improvement Acts 1840 & 1847; Public Health Acts 1871 & 1896; Bristol Corporation Act 1907; Leeds Corporation and Consolidations Act 1905; Liverpool Building Act 1842, Liverpool Sanitary Act 1846 (amended 1854 & 1864), Liverpool Improvement Act 1882 and Liverpool Corporation Act 1889; Sheffield Corporation Act 1900; Glasgow Building Regulations Act 1900.

27   The Petroleum (Consolidation) Act 1928.

28   1898, 1905, 1908, 1909, 1915, 1920, 1921, 1923, 1926, 1927, 1928, 1930.

29   For a history of building regulations in London see Pitt and Knowles, 1972.

30   Under Pt xiv, Sec 164.

31   5 Edw. vii c209.

32   9 Edw, vii c130.

2 Traditional construction

The term 'traditional construction' is still used to describe some of the forms which we are building today, but building has moved so far from the brick wall and the slate roof that the use of the term seems little more than a habit of language. Unfortunately, it may also be a habit of mind. While craft training is an essential part of design learning, and of trade skills, it brings with it the assumption that things are done in a certain way because that is how they have always been done and have proved successful. Such an approach does not always facilitate changes in technology, because it discourages taking a fresh look at the established methods and because it assumes that 'improvements' may be adopted without the need for a radical consideration of their implications. Construction at the turn of the century was a mixture of genuine traditional forms and the beginnings of some new methods that have become familiar today. Most construction was still of load-bearing masonry and, although new methods were already being introduced, timber floors were still common in commercial construction. Transport costs made the supply of building materials and components a very local affair and this affected not simply the basic materials like bricks or stone, and lime for mortar and plaster, but also manufactured components such as patent fire-proof floors. Because the production of building materials depended upon local sources of raw materials the properties of the resulting products, particularly bricks and plastering materials, varied considerably in different parts of the country.

Of course, the local nature of building materials is most visible in vernacular buildings: more expensive, 'polite' construction has always been able to draw on imported supplies. There are also parts of the country which have never been able to supply all the materials for some of their building needs and so have had to import one or more from elsewhere. By and large, though, buildings displayed a distinctive regional pattern derived from the walling and roofing materials used which were drawn in one way or another from the soil of the region. England is a country with clay lowlands where brick predominates. In chalky areas, vernacular buildings were often built of flint and in other upland areas the local stone can usually be seen in the buildings. But this pattern is not restricted simply to rural buildings nor to the vernacular of the remote past. The industrial towns of the Pennines and much of Scotland are noticeably of local stone, used for both domestic and commercial building well into the inter-war period. In at least one area, Bolton, the stone was so plentiful, and its working so well established, that eaves gutters were made of stone rather than cast iron.

The general trend during the century has been one of change from this very local pattern of construction, reflecting the nature of local supplies, to one in which construction is much the same throughout the country, a process which began with canal and rail transport in the late eighteenth and the nineteenth centuries but which has accelerated in this century. It has not simply been that improved transport widened the choice available. That did happen in some instances as companies built up a national reputation for specialist products which they could supply by rail — terracotta from such works as Edwards at Ruabon or Burmantofts at Leeds for example. But transport also allowed cheaper materials from elsewhere to compete successfully against relatively expensive local materials so that the latter were no longer used. In some cases this has simply meant a cheaper supply of a similar material, one kind of brick substituted for another for example, while in other areas it has meant the substitution of alternative materials and products, sometimes quite different from the original. The obvious example is the now almost universal use of brick as a facing material for walls even in areas which had traditionally used stone. A related trend is the growth of large companies who have come to dominate the supply of particular building materials, partly through amalgamations and partly through the ability to compete successfully in either price or quality. While specially manufactured components must always be carried long distances, it is the bulk materials that this development has affected most, those materials that go to make the basic carcase of the building, the 'bricks and mortar' but also the roofing materials and the window glass.

In this chapter we shall consider this basic carcase, the external walls and the roof, composed of so-called 'traditional' materials, i.e. masonry walls with tile or slate roofs. It will also be convenient to deal with 'wet' surface treatments, i.e. plasters and renders, since they use much the same materials as the mortars that are used in the construction of the wall and are also bulky products subject to the trends discussed above. Before considering walls or roofs as elements of construction we need to examine the range of materials that can be used for each, especially for walls because materials differed considerably and the development of these materials during the century has brought about changes in the way in which walls have been constructed. Timber floors and roofs will be discussed in Chapter 6.

Stone

Where stone was the basic material of construction it sometimes remained so even for quite modest buildings. Many of the industrial towns and cities on both sides of the Pennines have large stocks of predominantly stone houses, many built in this century. The stones were generally the local limestones or sandstones but in places like the Lake District it is even possible to find buildings of this century constructed of the local slate. In chalk districts the use of flint persisted while near the coast of East Anglia beach pebble was used. These methods of construction have been discussed by Clifton-Taylor and Ireson (1983) but the persistence of such local vernacular traditions has had relatively little influence since the Second World War except to the extent that planning restrictions may be placed upon the materials to be used in order to conform with the appearance of traditional construction. This often means resorting to artificial stone (see below) because the original stone is now no longer available or has become prohibitively expensive. The use of stone for commercial buildings persisted even after the steel frame had been introduced; while the *Modern Building Review* claimed in 1910 that this was the 'age of steel' it noted that it was also the 'age

of stone', which it continued to be until well into the inter-war period, with steel-framed buildings clad in 'stone' walling. For such buildings the range of materials is naturally much greater. While there may have been a tendency to use the local stone where it was available in sufficiently large sizes, Portland stone and granite were the most popular stones for commercial and public buildings and a wide range of other stones was still available well into the inter-war period.

Before the First World War, *The Builder* listed a large number of types of stone in its review of current prices although some were more important than others. Gradually most of the stones listed became unavailable but they were still sufficiently important in the 1920s for BRS to carry out work on their properties, much of which culminated in R. J. Schaffer's (1932) classic work on the weathering of stones. The frequency of freezing and thawing in Britain makes it one of the harshest climates for building materials and part of the problem was to find a satisfactory index of durability to freeze—thaw cycles. The saturation coefficient was a useful but not sufficient index. Another problem which researchers needed to examine was the various forms of chemical attack. There was concern for attack on limestones by sulphates which caused the formation of a surface skin which is impervious to water. (The formation of surface skins on sandstones was attributed to a similar cause.) It was not known whether these skins were to be regarded as harmful or 'protective'. It was also observed that there are variations in the porosity of walls and there was concern for possible attack on stone by free lime which might be present in the mortar. A suggested remedy for this was to use pozzolanic materials in the mortars; although the BRS was to carry out research on these materials, there is little evidence that they became popular in Britain.

How much effect the results of the work on the durability of stone made to architects' use of the materials is difficult to say. One of the results of the BRS's work was to show that various proprietary surface treatments to preserve stone had all proved harmful. It was also clear that some old-fashioned specification practices by architects might not ensure the best results. While there is no geological distinction between Portland stone Whitbed and Basebed, the former is better for resisting acid attack from air pollution. The effect of requiring stone to be 'free from shells' has already been noted (in Chapter 1). In those areas where stone was readily available it may have persisted for such features as door and window jambs, as well as sills and lintels, even after the appearance of brick for the rest of the wall. That it was able to persist in this way depended not just upon the local availability of the material but also upon the use of stone-working machinery which had been developed in the nineteenth century and enabled the material to be worked into such components: builders were drawing on supplies which might be both quarried and worked in their own locality.

Artificial stone

Artificial stone was used as an alternative to natural stone masonry during the inter-war period, intended to give the appearance of natural stone at much lower cost. Grundy (1930) listed a number of different kinds of artificial stone including Ford's silicate of limestone, Thon's reconstructed limestone and Ransome's artificial stone. This last was said to be almost obsolete but indicates the unlikely formulae sometimes adopted. It was formed of sands and sodium silicate placed in a mould to which was added a solution of calcium chloride. But, the most important type of artificial stone was precast concrete; its importance during the early years of the century is suggested by the many editions of Childe's Manufacture and Uses of *Concrete Products and Cast Stone* which discussed the methods of manufacture used. First published in 1927, this work illustrated a number of complete artificial stone elevations in styles varying from tudor to baroque. The frontispiece was an all-concrete house by Sir Reginald Bloomfield. When the BRS began work on cast stone in 1931, in co-operation with the CCPA there were over 100 firms in this association. (A list of cast-stone products can be found in the Concrete Year Book.) The artificial material was itself cheaper than the quarried stone and artificial stone could also be cast into shapes much more easily than working the natural material. This was not simply for decoration or for the complex shapes of architraves or cornices but because stone, whether real or artificial, was shaped to fit round the steel structure as brickwork and masonry ceased to be load-bearing. As a facing material, precast concrete could not only be cast into complex shapes, it could also be given a variety of surface treatments, sometimes the surface material being different from the body of the piece.

Various methods of moulding were adopted and the quality of the product probably varied as a result. Childe shows the use of simple wooden moulds for making components, but 'cast stone' could also be made like cast iron, i.e. with the liquid run into sand moulds. This is a better process because it allows the repetitive use of timber patterns which are not damaged by wetting from the concrete. As water is drawn out of the concrete by the sand of the mould the resulting material is denser, and hence stronger and with better weathering properties than would be suggested by the initially high water content of the concrete necessary for the casting process.

A problem faced by the manufacturers of this type of product was surface crazing. It seems to have been generally assumed that this was associated with drying shrinkage of the products, the outer layers drying and shrinking earlier than the body of the material and unable to sustain the tensile stresses so developed. However, this did not seem to fit with the observation that cracking might take some time to develop and tests carried out by the BRS showed that the phenomenon was associated with carbonation of the concrete. Work was thus directed to examining the mechanism of cracking in more detail and devising methods of preventing it. By allowing partial hydration of the mix before casting, there was some reduction of both drying and carbonation shrinkages, while the mix's workability could be restored to a limited extent by reworking the material. The alternative, which was to add more water, had a deleterious effect. In addition to the work on cracking the Station carried out an investigation of the use of pigments in cast products and of Dolerites as aggregates. Problems had been found in association with the use of both which made the concrete unsound . Problems with the pigments centred on the manufacturers' addition of extenders, some of which were positively harmful and it was clearly desirable to have some standards to control these. Dolerites were shown to expand with oxidation. Clearly the substitution of natural stone with artificial products was not a simple affair.

Stone walling — natural and artificial

Stone in this century has been essentially a facing material used initially in conjunction with a brickwork backing to form a wall. Warland (1947, p. 270) distinguished two types of facing (Fig 2.1);

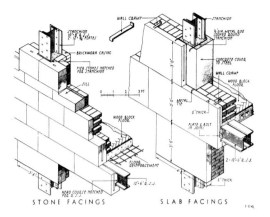

Fig. 2.1

'stone facings' in which the stone was cut into blocks and bonded into the brickwork, and 'slab facings' where relatively thin slabs were fixed back to the brickwork with cramps. In its first form, the stone was still part of the masonry wall and it continued to be used in this way when used with steel frames even though the wall was no longer load-bearing. In the second, it was already making the transition to a thin independent facing even though at that time Warland showed these stones to be 5 in. thick. Warland had already noted the change in the use of stone that had been brought about by the introduction of the steel frame: 'The introduction of steel into the construction of buildings has revolutionised orthodox methods, instead of being the art of building in stone, has become the means whereby the carcase of the building may be pleasingly covered with stone.' This had an effect on the craft so that:

Today it is necessary that the setter out should have a knowledge of steel construction, and should be in a position to interpret steel work drawings in order that he may fully appreciate the cutting and construction necessary where steelwork and stonework are in combination (Warland, 1929, p. 16).

But while this constructional change was occuring, much the same architectural forms continued to be used: At one time masonry was entirely constructional . . . large openings were spanned by stones of considerable size and where the span was too large for one stone, several stones were introduced, with radiating or secret-joggled joints. These joints are still used in modified form in conjunction with steelwork. A rolled steel joist is placed across the opening . . . and

the stones are notched and bolted to this joist, giving the appearance on the elevation of solid stones (Warland, 1947, p.271).

Stone needed to be fitted round the steelwork and attached to it: either the columns and beams were cased in concrete and the stone cramped to that, or it was cut to fit round these members. It could be fixed back to the steel with rag bolts, fitted to holes in the stone with lead, with cramp bolts into the top bed of the stone, or with anchor bolts or plates and bolts. These last two were let into mortices or slots in the sides of the stones. Heavy cornices often needed considerable supplementary steelwork for their support and Warland suggests how cast stone cornices might simplify the construction (Fig.2.2).

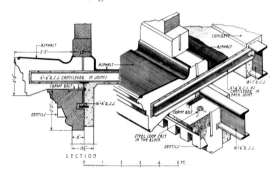

C A S T   S T O N E   C O R N I C E
Fig. 2.2

If stone, or artificial stone, is to be used in the form of thin slabs there is no reason why it should be fixed directly to a masonry wall. The thin stone might also be carried on an independent frame in front of a masonry wall, thus separating the construction of the wall from that of the facing. But before this could happen there

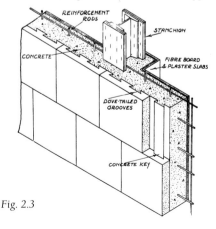

Fig. 2.3

had to be a change to an architecture of smooth surfaces. Cast stone made it possible for modern architects to use smooth 'stone' facings against cast concrete walls, possibly using them as permanent shuttering.(Fig 2.3) Curtis Green did this at the Dorchester Hotel as did Wells Coates at the Palace Gate flats. More recently, stone has been used as a light cladding in conjunction with frame buildings using techniques developed with earlier precast concrete claddings, this change in material depending upon a change in architectural fashions.

Brick

Brick was, of course, the principal material of construction in most of England but methods of manufacture and the structure of the industry were changing. In the late nineteenth century, *Rivington's Notes on Building Construction* noted that: 'operations in brickmaking are very numerous, though not intricate; they differ in several particulars in different localities, according to local custom, generally influenced by the nature of the clay (Twelvetrees, 1875—89, Vol. 3, p. 89.)

The details of many of these operations need not concern us here but what is important for the properties of the brick are the nature of the clays and the firing. Brick colour depends partly upon the composition of the clay and partly upon the conditions of firing. Suffolk whites, for example, which were used in London, had a high calcium-carbonate content which gave them their colour.

What was important to the brickmaker was the amount of shrinkage of the clay body. Because of shrinkage, pure clays are useless for brickmaking unless they are mixed with a non-plastic material. London clay has a high shrinkage and London stocks were made from a mixture of chalk, cinder dust and clay, the chalk combining with the clay while the cinder dust formed a fuel. Sand reduces the shrinkage and improves the shape of the bricks but an excessive silica content makes the bricks soft, so producing 'rubbers'. There is some evidence that designers were becoming more careful in their selection of bricks when Searle (1912) noted:

Formerly it was sufficient if bricks had a reasonably good shape & colour, but builders and engineers are now specifying vitrified and non-absorbent bricks, or those in which the absorption is within certain limits, and are much more exacting as regards shape and colour (p. 125).

The effect of this was to reduce the range of clays (or rather earths since the materials were not pure clays) which were suitable for making bricks.

Although machinery for making bricks came into use during the nineteenth century, hand-made bricks continued to be used because architects preferred their appearance. There were three ways of making bricks by machine, the simplest being the wire-cut brick: the clay extruded in a rectangular section and cut by wire into the correct length. The result is a brick which has no frog. This type of brick was popular with Victorian architects because of its smooth face, and it could be made with the same kind of plastic clay that was used for hand-made bricks. In the mid-nineteenth century machines for producing pressed bricks were perfected. Using a much drier clay, the process was suitable for much harder clay bodies than could be used for making wire-cut bricks, and was known as the stiff-plastic method. It had the advantage that the bricks did not need drying before being placed in the kiln and, together with the semi-dry process, accounted for the majority of the bricks being produced by the turn of the century. The semi-dry process also involves pressing the bricks into a mould although, as the name suggests, the clay body contains far less water

The production of bricks from plastic clay required the addition of water, thus the bricks needed drying before firing and the method of working was seasonal. As dry-pressing of bricks reduced the need for drying, so brickmaking became a continuous rather than a seasonal process with considerable economies in firing. This was not simply because the bricks needed less fuel but because the continuous nature of production enabled the Hoffmann kiln to be used. This is a circular arrangement of firing chambers used in sequence and continuously (Fig. 2.4); its use not only resulted in greater economies of fuel but it also produced bricks of much more even quality than either the use of clamps for firing or the 'Scotch (or Dutch) kiln' which were still being used. Previously, it had not been possible to obtain an even temperature throughout these so that the quality of bricks varied considerably. Moreover, because it was costly to transport bricks or any other heavy building material, local suppliers dominated the markets, and brickmaking and quarrying were carried

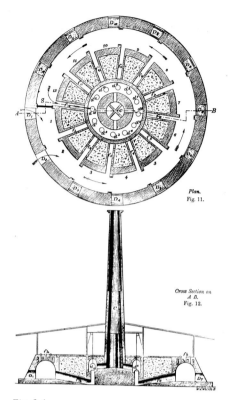

Plan.
Fig. 11.

Cross Section on
A B.
Fig. 12.

Fig. 2.4

out on a small scale. Now the conditions were available which favoured larger companies.

As the properties of clays vary throughout the country, it will be apparent from this discussion that different kinds of bricks were to predominate in different regions. Wire-cut bricks and those made by the stiff-plastic method predominated in the north of England while the much more plastic clays of the south-east favoured the 'full-plastic' method and handmade bricks. This kind of clay, that produced the London stock brick, does not lend itself to the kind of mechanization used for other kinds of brick. Using *Clay Brickmaking* in Great Britain as her source, Bowley (1960, p. 172) produced a table of the approximate distribution of brickworks in Great Britain which provides a picture of the industry's diversity in the mid-1930s and the way in which the clays affected the distribution of the different processes. In 1937 there were a total of 1462 brickworks. North of the line from the Severn to the Wash there were 877 of which 825 used the stiff-plastic or the wire-cut methods of

production. In the south and south-east, which included London, there were 365 works with 298 of these making handmade bricks or using the full-plastic method. But the number of brickyards in an area is not an indication of the total output and the all-important Fletton bricks came from just 31 works.

The wide variety of bricks that resulted from the different clays and the different methods of moulding and firing naturally produced a bewildering variety of names as well as a variety of properties. Cutters and rubbers were named for the way in which they were to be used. Grizzles, chuffs and shippers were all inferior bricks. Gault bricks indicate the clay used, which resulted in a light-coloured brick, and in some cases the process of manufacture was indicated in the names. With properties and their appearance depending upon properties of the clay available, there was a distinctive regional variation in the appearance of brick buildings. Only where transport was cheap could materials be supplied from a distance — Lincolnshire bricks, for example, could be shipped cheaply to London by sea. This inevitably meant that there was also a wide variation in brick prices, but eventually the manufacturers of Flettons were to use cheap railway rates to compete with local bricks and although they were not suitable as facing bricks they came to be the commonly used brick in backing work.

Fletton bricks

The Fletton brick came to dominate brick construction in the post-war years. The industry is based upon the lower Oxford clay, first worked for brickmaking in Fletton near Peterborough. This shaley clay can be ground to a powder and pressed into bricks without the addition of water and the high proportion of carbonaceous material in the clay provided sufficient 'fuel' that little additional fuel was required for firing. In addition, some bricks were made using the plastic process at Fletton to use the overlying layers of clay that were not suitable for the dry process. The introduction of the Fletton brick was significant: production costs were low and the economies in the brickmaking process, combined with the proximity of the Fletton brickfields to the Great Northern Railway, enabled the makers to ship bricks to London and sell them at prices that were competitive with local stock bricks, made using the plastic-clay process.

Mechanization introduced into the Fletton brick

fields was derived from earlier developments in the Lancashire brick fields. Consolidation of the many companies into the giant London Brick Company that we know today began about the turn of the century but the major consolidations were in the inter-war years. Hillier (1981) has claimed that this greatly increased the efficiency of production and so reduced the costs of the bricks (especially in the mid 1930s), improving their competitive position *vis-à-vis* other brick companies. However, Bowley's account of the development of the Fletton industry suggests that the issue is a little more complex than this. Because the price of locally-made bricks varied so much, depending upon local production costs, the London Brick Company (LBC) was able to adjust its prices accordingly. The company also depended upon the shipping rates which it could obtain from the railways. Hillier noted that when the railways raised their rates it reduced the geographical area over which these bricks were competitive; Bowley (1960) however has pointed out the advantageous rates that the LBC was able to negotiate which enabled it to compete with local bricks in Halifax and suggests that this may not be the only instance of a policy to undersell local producers.

All Fletton bricks had been 'commons' until 1923 when a facing brick was introduced. This was a rustic brick produced by machining a zig-zag pattern into the surface, devised by LBC and Forders so giving them an advantage over other Fletton producers — and an advantage over other facing bricks. In spite of its cheapness, a disadvantage with the Fletton brick was its high sulphate content which eventually caused some concern. Considered unsuitable in areas with high atmospheric pollution, the Fletton brick could not take cement-based renders until Sulphacrete was developed to overcome this difficulty.

Sand-lime bricks

Sand-lime bricks, also called calcium-silicate bricks, are essentially a mixture of lime and sand pressed together to form a brick shape and then cured in an autoclave. Alternative mixtures were also possible: while quartz sand was regarded as the best material for making these bricks, clinker from a municipal refuse destroyer, slag and crushed rock were also used. Blast-furnace slag was the cheapest of the substitutes for sand. Of the various limes available, calcium oxide was preferred to magnesium oxide.

Originating in Germany with the Michaelis process in the late nineteenth century and patented in 1868, sand-lime bricks were first produced in Britain in 1905 (Lea, 1971, p. 47); they were only used in a few areas where there was no suitable clay available for brickmaking. Production remained limited with only 8 works in operation in 1920, 15 in 1932 and 25 by 1939. The difficulty facing the brick manufacturers at that time, and so those specifying their use, was that there was little knowledge to relate the properties of these bricks to their durability and specifications varied considerably. It was recognized that the properties of the bricks were affected by the qualities of the constituent materials and their proportions, which was discussed by Searle (1915) in a general way. However, the effect of these variables and also the conditions of manufacture were not to be investigated in detail until the work of the BRS which began in the 1920s and continued for over a decade (see Weller, 1921; Bessey, 1934). After early work on sand-lime bricks for the development of the British Standard the BRS did further work in the late 1930s in co-operation with the Association of Sand-lime Brick Manufacturers. This association was not formed until 1936 and was principally concerned with improving manufacturing processes.

Sand-lime bricks had been the subject of the Station's first publication in 1921, although it was little more than a simple account of the process of manufacture. It recognized sand-lime bricks as a satisfactory form of construction but contained little information on their properties and, more particularly, the way in which the manufacturing process could affect these. The properties were clearly dependent upon the nature of the mix, both the proportions of sand and lime and the grading of the sand, and upon the autoclaving conditions, but it was not clear how. Thus, when the first British Standard on sand-lime bricks (BS 187) appeared in 1923 it was based on little more than received wisdom and much work remained to be done. Research then carried out at the BRS on both the manufacture and the durability of these bricks led to revisions of the BS in 1934 and in 1942. This research showed how strength is affected by the proportion of coarse to fine sand in the mixture and the clay content of the sand. Later measurements by the BRS also showed that there was wide divergence in the properties of the bricks actually being manufactured though the degree of variation reduced over the years, partly due to increased knowledge of the factors affecting brick strength but partly as a result of closures of works producing inferior products.

Sand-lime bricks were often used for their light colour but in London this presented architects with a difficulty that illustrates the restrictive nature of the way in which the regulations were framed. The requirement of the LCC by-laws was for bricks used in construction to be 'well-burnt' and since sand-lime bricks were not burnt at all in their manufacture they did not constitute a brick within the definition of the regulations. The effect of this was that any architect or builder wishing to use them had to obtain a waiver. A correspondent to the *RIBAJ* argued that, as the process of manufacture produced what was essentially a limestone block the sand-lime brick should be classed as such.[1] He appears to have been unsuccessful but sand-lime bricks were used for facings of the RIBA building. Judging by the report on this building (Hamilton *et al.*, 1964) they appear to have been susceptible to sulphate attack in the London atmosphere.

Perforated bricks

Another kind of brick whose use was restricted by regulations was the perforated brick which has achieved only limited popularity even although Twelvetrees (1875—89) was illustrating perforated bricks and noting their advantages in the 1870s. These are lighter than solid bricks, give better thermal insulation and, because they contain less clay, require less fuel in firing. In spite of these advantages there were only a small number of plants making perforated bricks in the immediate post-war period, partly perhaps because of the industry's conservatism but also the specifier's and those responsible for drafting regulations. Whitaker's of Leeds developed a perforated brick in the 1930s intended for the London market but its adoption had been inhibited by the regulation which required eight inches of solid incombustible materials for external walls and the experiment had been abandoned. However, in the 1950s, the firm revived the idea and were able to produce a perforated facing brick below the cost of equivalent solid bricks.

Hollow clay tiles were used for the backing of walling (Fig. 2.5) in the late 1930s but they did not become as popular here as on the continent even though it must have improved thermal performance. Warland

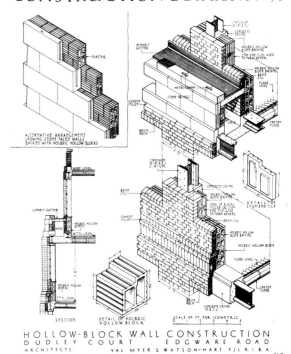

CONSTRUCTION DETAILS : Nº 38

HOLLOW-BLOCK WALL CONSTRUCTION
DUDLEY COURT   EDGWARE ROAD
ARCHITECTS: VAL MYER & WATSON-HART F/L R I B A

Fig. 2.5

(1937) showed hollow clay blocks used in a number of different ways in association with steel framing: as a backing to brickwork cladding (pp. 49—50), as a backing to stone facing slabs held to the hollow-block wall with cramps (p. 42) and used by themselves with an external cement stucco rendering (p. 51). How frequently any of these techniques were used in practice is difficult to say and Warland himself (p. 52) expressed surprise that this last method had not been more extensively used in association with light steel framing. It was one of the methods that had been officially recommended for the construction of school buildings although an aspect of these that should be noted was that they were exempt from local authority bylaws and could use techniques that might not have been otherwise approved.[2]

The BRS showed considerable interest in the development of this type of brick and by the time Bowley (1960) was discussing innovations in the building industry she was able to report a growing interest in it. However, the BRS had greater ambitions

Fig. 2.6

than just to change the form of the brick. The strength of a brick is far greater than actually required for domestic construction; it is the other properties of the material that are more important, in particular cost, and thermal and weathering properties. As perforations lightened the brick they could surely enable a much larger unit to be laid, so reducing the cost on-site and with sufficient voids the thermal performance could be considerable enhanced. Based on this logic the BRS experimented with extruded clay units, the intention in the post-war years being to produce a unit wide enough to comprise the full width of the wall and incorporate the cavity, that is to make a single unit with the same

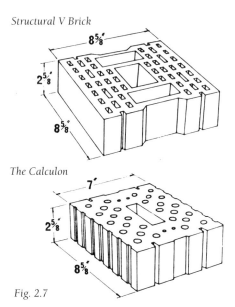

Structural V Brick

$8\frac{5}{8}$"

$2\frac{5}{8}$"

$8\frac{5}{8}$"

The Calculon

7"

$2\frac{5}{8}$"

$8\frac{5}{8}$"

Fig. 2.7

effect as a cavity wall. The result was the V brick developed by the BRS in collaboration with the Western Counties Brick Co. and the Sussex and Dorking Brick Co. (Fig. 2.6). This brick was 8⅝ in. wide and resembled two thin perforated bricks connected by thin webs so that it could be easily handled for laying. A special closer was needed for forming corners. In 1959 some bungalows built by Fred Pooley at Aylesbury[3] and in the 1960s a 13-storey block of flats in Southwark demonstrated the scope of these bricks. It was followed by the Calculon brick, a 7-in.-wide perforated brick suitable for the internal walls of tall blocks but these bricks failed to establish themselves as a regularly used type (Fig. 2.7).

Brick sizes

We are familiar with standard-sized bricks but simple observation of earlier construction shows that they have not always been the same size. Sutcliffe (1902), in a list of the properties of 14 different bricks, gives sizes varying from 8.6 x 4.1 x 2.4 in. (pressed Metalline made at Buckley near Chester) to 9.8 x 4.9 x 3.1 in. (red rubbers made at Bracknell, Berks.). In 1904 a standard brick size was decided between RIBA, the Brickmakers Association and representatives of the Institution of Civil Engineers.[4] The dimensions of this were: 8 stretchers = 72 in. — 8 headers = 35 in. — 8 bricks (frogs alternating) = 21.5 in.. However, in 1919 a conference at the RIBA led to changes when the Northern Federation of Building and Engineering Brick Trades, which covered Northumberland, Cumberland, Durham, Westmorland, Yorkshire and Lancashire, agreed with the government to make a standard-sized brick 2 ⅞ in. high making the height of 4 courses + 4 joints =13 in. and 8 bricks as above between 23 in. and 23.5 in., that is, northern bricks were to be larger. Then in 1924 the size of bricks for use in local authority housing was fixed by the Housing (Regulation of Size of Bricks) Act 1924.

Terracotta and faience

Terracotta was beloved of the Victorians because it enabled expressive architecture by means of decorative sculptural forms and also because it produced a surface which was unaffected by atmospheric pollution. Not only durable, it also retained its surface finish and its colour, washed as it was by every shower of rain. In public buildings, Waterhouse at the Natural History Museum had shown how it could be used as the basic material of construction, while at the Albert Hall, Scott and Townroe had successfully combined it with brickwork. By the end of the era it was well established and had become the means of embellishing apartment blocks, public houses and theatres. In this century it gradually ceased to be the material of public buildings and churches, perhaps because it had become so readily available and was being used for the embellishment of more modest buildings, even for cheap working-class houses, especially in those areas with easy access to the works. Thus, the terraces of Liverpool and some of the towns in North Wales were embellished with terracotta details used for lintels or eaves cornices: the product of Edwards works at Ruabon. Nevertheless, terracotta had a continuing life in commercial buildings well into the inter-war period. Of course, styles had changed by then but, even as architecture became much more restrained in its surface treatment, terracotta and faience remained valuable surfacing materials well known for their use in the new cinemas but also used in a variety of other buildings. It was not until the Second World War that it fell out of favour and virtually disappeared from use. Today only two firms are producing terracotta.

While, like bricks, terracotta is made of clay, the process is much more demanding in the type of clay used so that only a few brickmakers had suitable resources. The process appears deceptively simple but requires some skill and understanding of the material. Large terracotta units are formed as a hollow box by pressing the clay by hand into plaster-of-Paris moulds. The sides of the moulds are made separately to the required pattern and strapped together for the pressing process. As the clay dries, it shrinks. It shrinks even further during firing so that some allowance must be made for both shrinkages in the size of the pattern. Also, hollow pieces tend to warp so that stiffening ribs or even knock-out panels may have to be incorporated into large pieces to avoid this. While the hollow terracotta components were bespoke items, the same manufacturers made special bricks as standard items used for such features as string courses and window mullions, as well as clay tiles for walls, which were illustrated in their catalogues.

Like bricks, the colour of terracotta depends upon the clay used, but the addition of minerals to the clay body can alter this and the product can also be glazed.

The colour of glazed ware depends upon both the formulation of the glaze and upon the temperature and atmosphere within the kiln, all of which may make its reproduction in repair work very difficult. Glaze formulae were often closely guarded secrets so that matching an existing colour today is almost certain to be a difficult process of trial and error. Moreover, some colours are very sensitive to the temperature of firing which results in the differences of shade often seen in this kind of work. Ironically the accuracy with which kiln temperatures can be controlled today may be a disadvantage, because they can ensure a far greater uniformity of colour which may contrast with the variations in the original construction.

Concrete blocks and bricks

Although they are similar in their manufacture, raw materials and properties, it is probably wise to distinguish between simple concrete blocks and the many special forms which have been patented from time to time as new ways of building walls. For some reason the design of specially shaped concrete units as an alternative way of making walls seems to have attracted more inventions than any other aspect of construction. A number had already been invented when Kempton Dyson (1908) discussed the manufacture of concrete blocks in an early issue of *Concrete* and the housing needs after the First World War then served to encourage many other inventors. However, none of these has had much importance as a building method. The simple rectangular concrete block became important, whether solid or hollow, it could be used just as any other masonry unit.

The first hollow block-making machines in this country were patented as early as 1875 by both Holt of Leeds and Sellars of Birkenhead. Some machines made single blocks, others several blocks at a time; some made solid blocks and others hollow ones, and their performance had been improved by the development of a vibrating table incorporated into some machines to facilitate compaction. At the turn of the century a number of these were available on the market and Stuarts Granolithic Company and the Patent Victoria Stone Co. were by then making artificial stone blocks using block-making machines. By the 1920s the machines available ranged from simple hand-operated devices to electrically and hydraulically-powered

automatic and semi-automatic machines
(see Childe, 1927).

The basic concrete block was discussed extensively by Searle (1913). Their advantage was that the blocks could be made on site with relatively inexpensive equipment and alternative materials could be used for the aggregates. Block-making machines were readily available and simple to operate, and, as the price of cement fell, so blocks became a more attractive alternative to bricks where they were not exposed, that is, for the inner face of the wall, or for the outer face if the wall was to be rendered. But this was not simply because of the cost of the block alone. The cost of a wall depends as much upon the cost of laying the units and studies by the BRS showed that it was in the block-laying that savings were to be made.[5] The effect has been that in post-war construction bricks have become more a facing than a structural material with block most frequently used as the principal load-bearing element of the wall. An advantage that we would more readily recognize today is that many blocks offer better thermal insulation than bricks. Although breeze blocks were regarded as a cheap substitute, they were structurally quite adequate for house construction and thermally better.

Here again was a material whose properties were variable. Early regulations required walls of concrete block to be one-third thicker than those of brick. These were framed to take account of poor-quality concrete and it is difficult to be sure how the quality of these blocks may have improved. When the BRS carried out research on concrete block-making machines they observed that :

The cases where the makers had a limited knowledge of the properties of the materials and the machines they used were definitely in the minority. One or two firms took an intelligent interest in their product and endeavoured to improve the quality and output by simple research and experiments. Knowledge thus acquired was not spread, and this lack of interchange of ideas often resulted in diametrically opposed opinions being held by different firms.[6]

As this report was published in 1951 it may seem strange that such ignorance persisted, but it is an example of the poor communication in the construction industry and the apparent resilience of established beliefs in the face of scientific facts.

We need to distinguish between lightweight and dense concrete blocks. Concrete for lightweight blocks depended upon the use of either lightweight aggregates or the entrainment of air in the concrete. The former was in use from an early date in the form of breeze block, used extensively for partitions but not always accepted for load-bearing walls. The aggregate for these was a waste product of the gas industry but breeze had never been particularly satisfactory because it was quite likely to contain some unburnt material and it was far from chemically inert (see Chapter 3). The substitute increasingly used was clinker obtained from power stations, although the term 'breeze block' had by then passed into the language and continued to be used for clinker blocks. Clinker also suffered the disadvantage that it might contain unburnt material and it became increasingly difficult to obtain as the power-generating industry changed to the use of pulverized fuel which produced a fine ash rather than the larger clinker, while at the same time the demand for lightweight blocks had increased. The shortage of clay bricks after both world wars stimulated the demand for concrete blocks, but the use of lightweight blocks has become more important in recent years with the increasing concern to improve insulation standards. Thus, there has been a search for other lightweight aggregates.

Attempts in the mid-1930s to develop expanded slate based on the waste from slate quarries proved uneconomic and foamed slag was the only lightweight aggregate to come on to the market at that time going into production in 1936.[7] Expanded clay and foamed slag proved successful in post-war years even though they were more expensive than clinker block when first introduced, while pumice and vermiculite were also used as aggregates. The availability of large quantities of pulverized fuel ash (PFA) from power stations encouraged a search for ways of using this material in concrete and it was from the United States that the use of PFA as a concrete aggregate was introduced into Britain with the first plant for its production opening here in 1957.[8] Air-entrained concrete can be produced by the addition of reagents to the concrete, especially aluminium, producing what has been called 'gas concrete'. There had been earlier developments in both the US and Sweden but it was from the latter that the technique came to Britain in the 1950s even though the BRS had noted experiments with gas concrete as early as 1928.[9] Some of these blocks were of cement and sand while others used cement and PFA.

Lightweight concretes were important for other products but for blocks their success can be attributed to a combination of advantages. Light to handle and faster in laying than brickwork, they may be cut to shape easily on site, and chased out to take pipework and electrical conduits as well as providing good thermal insulation. However, they are not without disadvantages, in particular their high rate of shrinkage and they also required careful storage and on-site handling because of their high water absorption. The success of foamed concrete has depended upon the use of autoclaves in curing to reduce their shrinkage although it has been suggested (Ragsdale & Raynham, 1972) that there were blocks which did not fall within the limits for wetting and drying movements specified by BS 2028. Also, although the model by-laws did allow the use of lightweight blocks in external and party walls, some local authorities restricted their use in this way. Perhaps this may have been wise: because of the larger size, it is much more difficult to fill the vertical joints with mortar and this may have an effect on the performance of the wall. Unfilled perpends will, for example, reduce the degree of acoustic separation in internal or party walls.

As the substitution of concrete blocks for brickwork became fairly common in domestic construction, price was initially the dominant factor in the selection of the type of block to be used. On the outer leaf, their use depended upon either the acceptability of the block as a facing material, which happened only occasionally, or the use of render over the blockwork. The use of pebble dash on the upper floor of houses where exposed brickwork is used at ground floor may well be an indication that blockwork has been used above the first floor. On the inner leaf of the wall it was simply a matter of cost and, as blocks became cheaper than brick with the falling price of cement during the inter-war years, this became a more common method of construction.

Bowley has considered the factors which contributed to the relative success of different products in the post-war period, being dependent to some extent upon the position of producers within the market, but at the time she was writing, the use of concrete blocks was still developing. Since then they have become the standard method for forming the inner leaf of cavity walls with a wide range of products now available. As a result, concrete-block manufacture has ceased to

be a kind of cottage industry with the large number of small producers that there were in the late 1940s and early 1950s. At the same time there have been further developments in their design, for example, to achieve the levels of thermal insulation required, blocks have been made hollow to incorporate insulating foams.

Concrete blockwork has not been used as an external material nor as an engineered material to the same extent as brickwork even though blockwork had been shown to be feasible for use in high-rise buildings in the same way as bricks (Sutherland, 1969). Nor does it appear to have been used in the form of tall prestressed walls and its use for the external leaf of walls in housing has largely been restricted to rendered surfaces in those parts of Britain, like Scotland, where there is an established tradition of rendered walling. Where it has been used for its architectural qualities, such as in institutional buildings like colleges, one is given the impression that the choice is to provide a reflection of stone masonry in a modern form. The failure of blockwork to develop in the same way as brickwork cannot be attributed to any technical weakness but rather to an aesthetic conservatism.

Partitions

There were a variety of proprietary blocks for forming internal partitions: some clay based, some of concrete but some of other materials. The properties required were that they be light in weight in order to keep down the load on steel or concrete floor structures, and that they provide adequate fire protection. To ensure the latter, the manufacturers of several kinds of partition blocks submitted them to the BFPC for testing. Naturally, the introduction of frame structures favoured the use of these partition materials: in 1916, Specification noted that what it called 'cage construction' was becoming more common and that thin partitions were being used in place of brick internal walls.

The simplest partitions might be of straw bricks or concrete blocks made with a lightweight aggregate. Straw bricks were simply bricks in which the clay was mixed with straw which burnt out on firing to give a light brick. Hollow clay blocks were common, the companies producing these often being the same as those producing hollow clay flooring blocks for use with concrete or even patent fireproof floors (Fig. 2.8). These came in a standard 12 in. x 8⅞ in. with the range

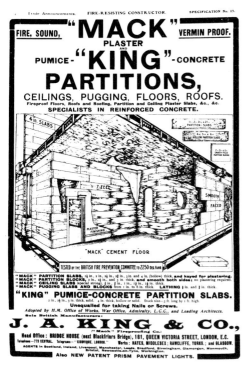

Fig. 2.8

protection between compartments while the development of different materials would have depended upon an understanding of fire performance. In the late 1930s, wood-wool slabs were developed for use as thin partition blocks while in post-war years the challenge to hollow clay blocks came from lightweight concrete blocks.

These materials were also in competition with stud and plaster partitions. Various forms of expanded metal could be fixed to studs and rendered to form a wall. The Truscon Company marketed their Hy-rib reinforcing for use in this way as an external walling for factory building and published their *Hy-rib Manual* to illustrate its use both for this and internal use. The Expanded Metal Company also produced a variety of materials for plastering and published a booklet on their use.[10] Expanded metal needed to be fixed to both sides of studwork to form a partition but between the wars, Lewis dovetail metal sheeting was available: it was rolled into a corrugated form which was then stiff enough to be fixed between light metal studs and plastered on both sides (Fig. 2.9).

of thicknesses depending upon the manufacturer. Half blocks were supplied for bonding and all had a ribbed surface to act as a plastering key. These hollow terracotta partition blocks had the advantage that they could be filled with concrete and reinforced to form lintels over openings. Of the concrete blocks available, breeze blocks had the advantage that they could take nails and in some buildings they were used for the lower courses of internal walls in order to facilitate the nailing of skirting boards. Concrete blocks could also be lightened by hollow-casting them and machines were available for this.

Rapidly constructed thin partitions could also be built using book-shaped plaster blocks. These had curved top and bottom edges, concave and convex to fit over each other, giving them their book-like appearance and ensuring a tight joint without relying on mortar. The vertical edges might be shaped in a similar way or both might be concave to enable reinforcing rods to be included in the wall.

Without the need to carry loads, this was an aspect of construction open to a variety of materials and methods. Choice between the various systems would have partly depended upon the requirement for fire

CONSTRUCTION DETAILS : Nº 59

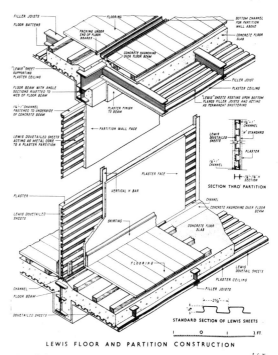

LEWIS FLOOR AND PARTITION CONSTRUCTION

Fig. 2.9

In the commercial sector the market for lightweight partitions was entered by metalworking firms who otherwise might make steel furniture or shelving. They offered part-glazed partitioning for offices, factories, hospitals and schools and in these applications it was accoustic separation rather than fire protection that became a design concern. In domestic construction the substitute for the brick or block partition came from the plaster industry. Dry linings did not have to be fixed to a masonry wall and in 1934, the *AJ* gave details of Raven Plasterboard (manufactured by Blackwells & National Roofings Ltd).[11] These were quite small coming in 18, 30 and 32 in. long, 36 in. wide and ⅜ in. in thickness, and intended to be fixed to timber studs at between 14 and 18-in. centres, scrim-jointed and finished with a skim coat, or backing and skim coat. In the post-war years this line of development culminated in complete, factory-made internal partitions comprising two plasterboard faces and an internal lightweight structure of a paper honeycomb and launched in the early 1950s.

Lime, plaster and mortar

Lime was the traditional base for both mortars and plasters, bought by the builder in the form of quicklime and slaked to produce the lime putty used as the basic ingredient of the various mixes. In this form it could be kept indefinitely and gauged as required with sand to provide the mortar. The other basic material for plastering was calcium sulphate, which has quick setting properties and is the raw ingredient for plaster of Paris and the basis of modern gypsum plasters.

There had also been a number of patent cements and renders developed during the nineteenth century, notably Martin's cement and Keene's cement. Of these, Keene's cement was still used up to the Second World War when a hard finish was required, particularly in public buildings. Grundy (1930) lists the patent plasters then available:

- Keene's cement composed of calcined gypsum plus alum or Al_2SO_4
- Martin's cement, a mixture of gypsum ($CaSO_4$) and potassium carbonate
- Medina cement, a form of Roman cement
- Parain cement, which was calcined gypsum plus borax solution ($Na_2B_4O_7$)
- Selenite cement, lias lime plus 5% raw gypsum

- Siparite, a plaster of Paris made from a gypsum which was naturally impregnated with petroleum.

Alternatively, a plasterer might used 'gauged stuff' which was simply plaster's putty (lime plaster) with plaster of Paris added to give an accelerated setting.

Like all other building materials the supply of building limes was a very local affair and the variability in the composition of the raw materials used by these local companies gave their products different properties with which the users were familiar. Plastering skills, particularly, were developed to suit the properties of these materials and plasterers would not necessarily find it easy to adapt to limes available in or from other areas. Since the turn of the century, the history of the plaster industry had been one of gradual amalgamation of rather scattered, small producers. Difficulties therefore began to arise with this gradual consolidation and the shipping of materials meant that plasterers were faced with unfamiliar materials, often sold under similar names to those that the plasterers had become used to.

The plaster industry was grouped in three main areas: a group of companies running south from Carlisle, another based principally round the village of Gotham, near Nottingham, and another in Sussex. The conditions for consolidation began when a rail connection was made with the Gotham Co. in 1903 and firms in the area were grouped together during the First World War. In the North-west the Carlisle Plaster & Cement Co. was formed in 1911 from three major firms, Joseph Robinson & Co (which had produced Robinson's Cement), John Howe & Co. and the Long Meg Plaster Co., all of which had their roots in the nineteenth century. This amalgamation was not a financial success and the company was taken over by the Gotham Co. in 1918. Later, in 1927, McGhie's, who had made the hardwall 'Thistle plaster' and who had supplied plaster to the early plasterboard company in Wallasey, were also taken over. The Cafferata Co. which possessed the best deposits of raw material remained independent until the 1930s.

Consolidation of the industry in this way was accompanied by developments in the materials being produced and so the new materials became available over wider areas. Siparite, for example, was originally a product of the Sub Wealden Co. and developed during the 1890s. It was a mixture of dead burnt and hemi-hydrate plaster which gave a gradual set popular with users. The firm amalgamated with the Kingston Gypsum Co. of Kingston-on-Stour in 1903 enabling Siparite to be manufactured in the Midlands; there was a rapid development of the Siparite trade in the 1920s. Whatever the merits of patent plaster mixes for high-quality surfaces, the criterion for normal construction was ease of use. Pearlite plaster, i.e. with Pearlite as a lightweight aggregate, was based on the discovery of a volcanic rock in Sardinia in the late 1940s. This could be expanded with heat and mixed with gypsum plaster to produce a lightweight backing coat. Although more expensive than gypsum plaster, it was a competitive material because it would go much farther and could be spread faster. While these changes were taking place the real development in construction was in the production and use of plasterboard.

Plasterboard

Unlike some other countries, where wet plaster mixes are still commonly applied to the masonry wall, now using modern machinery, plasterboard has come to replace traditional lath and plaster for internal wall linings in Britain, but this development was not initiated from within the established plaster industry. Plasterboard was invented in the US and patented in 1894. It consisted of layers of paper and plaster-of-Paris composition. The intention seems to have been to produce a board capable of taking wallpapering directly but it was soon realized that it was better to rely upon an applied skim of plaster to finish the boards on site. The size of boards were produced was only 32 in. x 36 in. but in the US production rose from 225,000 boards in 1898 to 7,085,000 in 1909. Production of plasterboard began in Britain when a plant was acquired from the US in 1916 and established in Wallasey, producing so-called 'Thistle board', presumably because it was supplied with Thistle plaster from the firm of McGhie's at Kirkby Thore. The composition of the mix was plaster, sawdust and a retarder. The new material had some difficulty in establishing itself because of the conservatism by the building industry. Architects regarded it as a cheap substitute for lath and plaster, and builders were not convinced that it would work. They could not believe that plaster would stick to the outer layer of paper and some even tried to remove this, thus negating the whole purpose of the board.

A Paramount machine was bought from the US in 1928 and the Thistle machine quickly closed down; the boards produced on this new machine having the advantage of sealed edges and a cream face for direct decoration. At this time it was still a very provincial product but grew in popularity during the 1930s with trade increasing fast. This home-based industry did not have things all their own way: in the mid-1920s the Gypsum, Lime and Alabaster Co. of Toronto began to market their Gyproc board here. The same firm was also importing Dekoosto acoustic plaster which was used in cinemas. In 1933, a plant was opened in Erith to supply the South using raw materials imported from Canada, while the Pytho Plasterboard Co. established a plant at Fauld in 1933. Gyproc had a plant at Rochester in production by 1934, and built one in Glasgow in 1938. By 1939, there were seven plasterboard factories, three owned by BPB, two by Gyproc and one each by ICI and Plaster Products.

Speculative housing builders in the 1930s enabled plasterboard to become the standard material that we know today because they realized the advantages of a dry-lining material. Bowley (1960, p. 331) has observed that this occurred while architects continued to regard the material as an inferior, cheap substitute for lath and plaster; she speculates that its first use by builders in the private sector led local authorities to use it for public housing.[12]

Mortars

Masonry construction can hardly be discussed without some consideration of the mortar used between the units and it is appropriate to do this before looking at the structural and environmental performance of the wall. The function of mortar is firstly to act as a bedding between the bricks, stones or concrete blocks, but it may also be required to transmit shear or tensile forces; moreover, the properties of the mortar affect the movement of moisture through the wall. However, the mortar's behaviour is also affected by the properties of the bricks with which it is used. Tension failure in a wall occurs by breaking the bond between the mortar and the bricks or blocks: this bond and so the strength of the wall is as much a function of factors like the absorption of the masonry units as it is the mortar strength.

Traditionally mortar was composed of slaked lime

(CaHO) and sand which hardened simply by slow carbonization as it reacted with atmospheric carbon dioxide. The mixture of slaked lime, sand and water — known as lime putty — remained in a workable state for some time. However, the presence of clay as an impurity in the raw material, and to a lesser extent, magnesium and iron oxides, had the effect of slowing the slaking action while at the same making the lime hydraulic, that is, producing a hard set by a chemical reaction with water. The quantities of these impurities varied so that limes might be termed 'feebly', 'moderately' or 'eminently' hydraulic. Middleton (1905) gives the analyses of typical stone and lias limes (Table 2.1). The principal change to brickwork mortar during this century has been the increasing use of Portland cement rather than plain lime mortar; the examples of mortar specifications given in the study by Hamilton *et al.* (1964) show that as this change was occurring mortar specifications varied widely. In the late 1930s lime mortars were still being specified, commonly with a 1:3 mix. This was used for the Senate House, University of London (1933—6), Greenwich Town Hall (1937—9) and for the pre-war parts of the Methodist Missionary Society's Headquarters in Marylebone Road. Watford Town Hall (1938—9) used a cement-lime-sand mix in the proportions 1:3:12, although the lime was an hydraulic lime. Other buildings were reported to have used Portland cement and sand mixes in proportions varying from as lean as 1:5 in some of the brickwork of the British Museum extension, to as rich as 1:2 in other parts of the same work. At the RIBA building a fairly rich (1:3) cement-sand mix was also used in facing work.

It is difficult to account for this wide variation in practice which is reflected in the range of mortars regulated for in the LCC rules for brickwork design (Table 2.4). Conventional wisdom held that, as carbonization of the interior of walls laid in lime mortar might never take place, hydraulic limes or cement lime mixes should be used for interior work. A hydraulic lime mix was used for the London University Senate House where the brickwork was load-bearing. The various editions of Mitchell's Building Construction describe the different kinds of limes and mortars but give no real recommendations on the mixes to be used in different circumstances save noting that in the construction of chimneys lime mortar might be used at the top with cement mortar used near the bottom

Table 2.1 Components of various limes

Castle Bytham Lime–a moderately hydraulic stone lime

SiO_2	14%
$Fe_2O_3 + Al_2O_3$	4.25
CaO	77
MgO	1.25
CO_2	0.9
Water and loss	2.60

Harbury Lime–an eminently hydraulic lias lime

SiO_2	17.53%
Fe_2O_3	2.87
Al_2O_3	6.83
CaO	65.84
MgO	1.00
SO_2	1.36
$H_2O + CO_2$	3.85
Insoluble matter	0.5

In addition he gives the breakdown of two non-hydraulic limes as

	Greystone lime	Chalk lime
Lime	80.24	91.22
Magnesia	0.5	1.5
Oxide of iron and alumina	4.6	0.8
Potash and soda	1.25	0.85
Insoluble silica	11.4	1.6
Combined ware	2.01	4.03

Source: Middleton, G.A.T. (1905), Building Materials, London: Batsford.

where the stresses due to wind are higher.[13] It seems likely that mortar mix specifications were one of those craft elements of design, based on that mixture of early training, personal experience and myth.

In post-war years, it has become common practice to use cement or cement and lime mortars. The practice has grown because the addition of Portland cement produces a mortar which sets hard more quickly than lime mortar so allowing faster laying of the wall: with this comes the disadvantage that it is both less porous and more brittle than lime mortar. This has two effects on the behaviour of the wall. Moisture movement through a wall laid in lime mortar would be through the mortar rather than through the less-porous brick. With the addition of Portland cement the relative porosities of the materials may be reversed so that moisture movement is in the brick rather than the mortar. As moisture carries dissolved salts this may result in a greater incidence of efflorescence on the surface of brickwork and possible eventual damage of the surface. Salts may also be drawn out of the mortar by this process. The brittleness of the cement-rich mortars also means that the wall is less able to resist movement, whether due to settlement in foundation, shrinkage in the masonry itself or long-term movements in the frame of the building.

Rather than starting with lime, slaked on site, and adding cement to improve setting as well as sand, cement mortar is seen as the basic material with lime added to improve workability. Also, the use of lime has now been simplified by the availability of hydrated lime supplied in powder form, or even mixtures of hydrated lime and sand which simply need the addition of cement. The alternative to lime to give workability is the use of various forms of plasticizers which have been developed since the war and which simplify the problems of mixing and storage on site and which achieve improved workability by entraining air in the mix. The change from lime to cement mortars has involved some change in bricklaying because the techniques for finishing the joints is different with the two materials and this does present a problem in conservation work. Lime mortars are all too commonly raked out and cement-rich mortars then used for repointing so that a hard skin is applied over the softer lime mortar behind, resulting in long-term distress in walls thus repaired. And, where lime mortars are used in repair work, the bricklayers may not be familiar with traditional techniques.

Stuccoed surfaces

Writing just after the turn of the century Sutcliffe (1902, Vol. 1, p. 122) noted that stucco was no longer in fashion in Britain but stuccoed surfaces became popular in the inter-war period with the 'modern movement' in architecture and the fashion for smooth unbroken white surfaces. Difficulties with this, now novel form of construction, and the number of failures that occurred, led the BRS to carry out a number of tests and also to examine rendering practices on the Continent. Trouble was experienced with cracking of the renders, with water penetration because of poor detailing and with a lack of adhesion. Three causes of these failures were found. The first was a high sulphate content in the brickwork. This was particularly a problem with Fletton bricks which had a higher sulphate content than other types. Water drying out from the wall caused salts to migrate to the surface of the brickwork where they reacted with the render and destroyed the adhesion with the wall. The BRS developed a simple test for magnesium sulphate which was one cause of the problem but unfortunately this did not show up the presence of calcium sulphate, which was also harmful. Second, a high moisture content of the brickwork might arise from poor detailing or because of cracking in the renders. An article in *RIBAJ* noted that what were then modern parapet designs intended for reinforced concrete walls were not suitable for traditional materials.[14] It was recommended that the back of the parapet should be left unrendered to allow escape of water. Pebble-dash produced less of a cracking problem because the large particles cause cracking to be distributed as a large number of small cracks. Third, unsuitable mixes were used for the renders. Builders in Britain tended to use renders with a higher cement content than the lime-rich renders used on the Continent. This made them more brittle and so more susceptible to cracking which allowed water to penetrate to the wall behind. The cracking that occurred was either the result of movement of the wall or were drying cracks in the render itself.

The BRS compared rendering techniques in Britain with those used on the Continent where there appeared to be fewer problems and they noted differences in craft methods which appeared to be a contributory factor. On the Continent, renders were commonly thrown on to the wall whereas in Britain it was more usual to trowel on the render. (Pebble-dash or roughcast, used in Britain was also traditionally thrown on to the wall.) Although the BRS investigators could offer no

explanation for the effect, the Continental method of
application achieved a greater adhesion between the
render and the wall. Sutherland (1981) has commented
that differences in materials and trade practices in
different countries have been a greater barrier to the
transfer of ideas rather than the differences in language.
He was referring to ideas about masonry structures but
his observation is equally applicable to other aspects of
technology, especially when we are dealing with a basic
construction technique with such a long history that we
have come to regard it as traditional. Renders were part
of this tradition and proved difficult to adapt to new
architectural forms even though the precedents on the
Continent suggested otherwise.

Brick and terracotta facing

The factors which affect the selection of the material to
be used for a building's external surface must be a
complex amalgam of architectural fashion, cost,
practicability and availability. Terracotta has been used in
conjunction with brickwork in much the same way as
stone, or artificial stone. Indeed the three may be
considered as substitutes for each other in some
instances, especially when used for the embellishment of
brick buildings rather than as the complete surface of the
wall, although the latter is not an uncommon use of
terracotta.

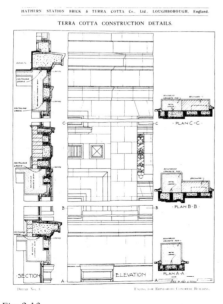

Fig. 2.10

In construction, terracotta blocks are first filled with
concrete before use although the recommendation was
'lime concrete or Roman cement; not Portland cement as
there is a danger of its being hot, expanding and bursting
the blocks'.[15] When used as a cladding over structural
steel, terracotta blocks might be fixed with cramps, not
unlike stone cladding, or might be supported in position
as a permanent shutter with the concrete poured both to
form a fireproof casing to the frame and to fill the blocks
at the same time. As the components were much smaller
than stone, and the form of decoration often more
complex, the construction was equally complex (Fig.
2.10). Hathern's of Loughborough (one of only two firms
to have survived to this day) produced a book to
advertise their products during the inter-war years which
included an example of a fixing drawing and announced
that these were supplied free of charge.[16] Of course, not
all terracotta work used complex forms; much sparer
styles imitate the form of stone masonry. Although a
decline in the fashion for terracotta has led to a decline
in this industry, brick has enjoyed something of a revival
as an architectural material after the immediate post-war
interest in reinforced concrete. The result is that it has
been used in much more complex sculptural forms and
this has necessitated the development of techniques for
its support.

Given the possibility of fixing large panels in place as
a facing, it is possible to build brickwork in this way,
making the facing units independently of the
construction of the rest of the building and then
attaching them to the structure. In this case the bricks
may also be reduced to brick tiles, a technique adopted
by Oscar Faber for a block of flats in London in the mid-
1930s (Ritchie, 1935). The wall construction comprised
a 2⅛-in. facing slab used as a permanent shutter for a 4⅞-
in. reinforced concrete wall lined internally with 1 in. of
cork insulation and ½ in. of plaster finish. Although the
eventual appearance of this building resembled load-
bearing brick construction, using this approach the
brickwork can be treated in a very free way, adopting
patterns which ignore the usual need for it to be laid in
courses. Although it has been used in this way on the
Continent in post-war years it has not been popular in
Britain for vertical surfaces where the development of
brick facings has remained within the discipline, or
limitation, of site-laid bricks.[17] Where bricks have been
used in a free way is in forming complex, three-
dimensional shapes.

The obvious way to carry brickwork over an opening is to use a lintel, honestly expressed on the exterior, but the desire for continuous surfaces of brickwork, or in some cases terracotta, requires other devices. Rather than the flat brick arches of the eighteenth and nineteenth centuries it is easier to incorporate simple steel or concrete lintels into the backing masonry. These have replaced the vulnerable timber lintels which were still being used in the early years of this century and Warland showed how 'lintels' of soldier courses might be wired back to concrete beam casings (Fig. 2.11) to present an unbroken brick surface. But modern movement ideas allowed concrete lintels, and even complete concrete window frames to be exposed. Unfortunately inadequate cover or inadequate mix specification has sometimes resulted in corrosion of the reinforcement and spalling of the concrete.

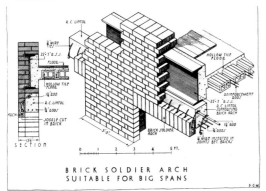

Fig. 2.11

Exposed concrete persisted into the 1960s and 1970s where brickwork was carried over opening on concrete boot lintels, a fashion which was replaced by openings with no visible support — this effect was achieved by the use of rolled T or angle sections. The durability of these is naturally dependent upon the specification for protective treatment and the standards of workmanship, neither of which have always been adequate. However, this type of construction was simplified by the introduction of lightweight steel lintels fabricated from cold-rolled sections and supplied to site with protective coatings. The ease with which these could be handled, compared with precast concrete lintels, ensured their ready acceptance especially in the house building trade in recent years.

On a different scale, the fashion for brickwork has meant that it has been treated as a sculptural material to be used in forms as varied as concrete. These forms are achieved by a combination of specially shaped bricks and new techniques to enable the bricks to be supported over wide openings and deep overhangs or deeply recessed window openings. Architects may either expose the concrete which forms the support,[18] conceal this or reinforce the brickwork itself. One means of concealing the structure has been to use brick slips as a kind of brick wallpaper, attached to the structure with mortar or with an adhesive. In this way there is little technical difference between the use of brick slips and other kinds of tile. Difficulties that have been found with tiled surfaces are the differential movements between the tiles and the backing, in the penetration of water into any cavities behind the tiles, encouraged by thermal pumping (when rain causes a drop in air pressure within the cavity, drawing in surface water) and the subsequent freezing of this water.

The other approach is one in which the forms are constructed of brickwork and hung from some supporting structure, for example, where a vertical cavity wall may be hung from some structure above by steel rods within the cavity and fixed to some supporting plate at the bottom. This technique was used for a small building at University College Oxford.[19] But the desire to have such forms as sloping surfaces of brickwork under overhangs has necessitated the use of bed reinforcement and ties back to concrete structure as well as the development of a technology of steel masonry supports, a range of which are now available as standard fixings.

Structural masonry

The function of a wall is both to support the floors and roof of a building and to provide separation from the weather — also perhaps to provide fire separation. Once the minimum thickness has been provided to achieve the last of these requirements, the principal consideration is the wall's strength and stability and regulations governing construction in brickwork have to be related to the understanding of its strength. At the end of the nineteenth century, regulations specified the thickness of brick construction depending upon the height and length of a wall. The detail of the regulations varied from place to place but the general pattern was similar. Table 2.2 shows the thicknesses suggested by

Table 2.2 Abstract of wall thicknesses

Height	Length	Thickness at base
25ft.	Any	13.5in.5in.
25–35ft.	<45ft.	13.5in.
	>45ft.	18ins.
35–45ft.	<35ft.	13.5in.
	between 35 and 45 ft.	18in.
	>45ft.	22in.
45–55ft	<35ft.	18in.
	between 35 and 45 ft.	22in.
	>45ft.	26in.
55–60ft	<45ft.	22in.
	>45ft.	26in.
60–80ft	<45ft.	22in.
	>45ft 26.5in. to within 16ft. from the top then 22in.	
80–100ft	<45ft.	26ins.
	>45ft 30.5in. to within 16ft. from the top then 16in.	

Above 70ft. there were additional requirements for piers.

Source: Knight's Annotated Model Byelaws of the
Local Government Board, London:
Local Government Publishers, 6th ed., 1899.

Table 2.3 Strength of bricks determined by thre BRS

Mild London stocks	700– 1500 p.s.i
Hard London stocks	1500–3000
Flettons	2000–4500
Wirecuts	1500–4500
Engineering	5000–15000
Hand made facings	1000–3000
but occasionally up to	8000

Source: Glanville, W. H. & Barnet, P. W. (1934),
Mechanical Properties of Bricks and Brickwork Masonry
BRS Special Report No. 22, London: HMSO.

Table 2.4 LCC regulations for allowable streses on brickwork

Class	Crushing strength lbs/sq. in.	Allowable stress T/sqsq. in.	Mortar mix cement: lime: sand
special	>10000	>40	1:0:2
1st	10000	30	1:0:2.5
2nd	7500	23	1:0:2.5
3rd	5000	16	1:0:3
4th	4000	13.5	1:0:3
5th	3000	11	1:0:4
6th	1500	10	1:1:6
		8	1:0:4
		7	1:1:6
		6	1:2:9
		5.5	1:3:12
		5	1:4:15
		4.5	1:5:18
		4	0:1:3

This table is for slenderness ratio < – the slenderness
ratios may be up to 12 with a 40 per cent reducation
on these figures.

Source: Chanter, Horace R. (1946), London Building
Law, London: Batsford

the model by-laws at the turn of the century. The first relaxation of these regulations only came with the recognition of frame construction; and hence external walls that could be non-load-bearing, but it was still some time before the design of load-bearing masonry walls could be based on research that provided some understanding of their strength.

A number of experiments were carried out at various times to determine the strength of brickwork. RIBA had carried out tests in 1896–7 which, together with tests at McGill University, were reported in Specification (1903). A load factor of 5 was suggested to allow for standards of workmanship. Here were attempts to introduce some scientific approach to wall construction but they had no effect on the form of the regulations until the work which was begun at the BRS in 1926 and published in 1934 (Glanville & Barnet,

1934). The BRS was able to establish that the principal determinant in the strength of brick walls is indeed the compressive strength of the bricks, which vary considerably, and that the strength of the mortar mix was far less important. Clearly, this was an important result because it meant that mortar specification and the degree of quality control on site would not have any significant effect on the strength of walls. It thus paved the way for regulations which accepted that walls could be designed for specific strength rather than having regulations requiring minimum thicknesses and the 1937 version of the model by-laws provided for wall design to be based on permissible pressure and the strength of the brick or block. This was the beginning of calculated brickwork. The BRS work provided data on the strength of different bricks (Table 2.3) while the London building regulations provided a table of allowable stresses for seven classes of bricks laid with different mortars (Table 2.4). However, the model by-laws issued in 1937, coming so shortly before the war, may have had little effect as the code of practice for the design of load-bearing walls was published shortly after the war.

Load-bearing capacity

There is some irony that the oldest building materials — brick and timber — seem to have been the last to attract attention as engineering materials. Perhaps masonry seemed too simple or perhaps, because it relies on rather basic trade skills and the variety of brick is so great, too uncertain to be used in ways which required some prediction of its strength. At modest heights, stresses are low compared with brick's ultimate capacity, and stability of the wall or its ability to carry horizontal loading, rather than compressive stress, is more often the limiting factor. The code of practice for the design of load-bearing walls did not appear until 1948 and was a rather slim document in comparison with those for steel and concrete. Much of it was concerned with design for slenderness and diagrams concentrated on the provision of adequate anchorage for floors which is essential for the stability of thin walls. There was little suggestion that much engineering design might be used and, although reinforced brickwork was mentioned, it was given only three pages.

Apart from BRS work on the performance of brickwork, the only sustained experimental work on its engineering performance during the inter-war years had been some rather inconclusive experiments on steel

bearing plates to be used in brick walls at points where they were called upon to carry concentrated loads. Compressive stresses in brickwork might be critical where beams are carried into the wall. So when steel beams or trusses were used in the floors and roofs of masonry buildings it was usual to incorporate York stone spreaders to distribute the loads into the wall. This was regarded as an awkward arrangement because the bearing pad was often visible in the face of the brickwork and some experiments were undertaken to see whether a steel plate could be substituted for the bearing pad. In spite of a prolonged series of tests which were reported in the Structural Engineer over a number of years no positive results were produced.[20]

In the post-war years, brick was used as the principal load-bearing element in the design of multi-storey flats by using what was called 'calculated' brickwork, a term adopted by a group within the brick industry for the promotion of the structural use of their material at a time when concrete was becoming a popular material. Even at the time when precast concrete was being encouraged by the government, and industrialization was seen as the solution to housing needs, it could be shown that, at least at certain heights, brickwork was cheaper than reinforced concrete for multi-storey flats and might even be quicker. It was apparent that the rules of thumb on which the by-laws were based were inadequate for the design of multi-storey construction and, given the possibility of increasing heights for brick structures, improved knowledge was needed for their economical design. Tests by the BRS improved understanding and showed that the failure of both brickwork and blockwork walls was by vertical splitting: as the load increases it causes some extrusion of the weaker mortar from the joints resulting in the development of tensile forces across the bedding face of the masonry units. But while the mechanism for failure was known, it was also apparent that workmanship was an important factor on the strength of brickwork: quality control measures of a similar kind to those used for reinforced concrete needed to be applied if an engineering approach to the design of multi-storey buildings was to be possible.

While mortar strength was the only variable commonly tested on-site (perhaps because a minimum strength was specified in the code), it was difficult to establish a reliable test for the brickwork itself because the testing of 9-in. cubes, which at least approximates in method to that of concrete cubes, gives a poor correlation with actual strength of the wall. A test on stack-bonded samples which gives a more reliable indication of masonry strength was difficult because of the lack of availability of suitable machines and because the samples are rather fragile. Devising a test for blockwork has proved even more intractable. The result has been that engineers in Britain have had to work with rather conservative design stresses, a position that has been compared unfavourably with that in the United States (Sutherland, 1981).

Nevertheless brickwork is, of course, particularly suited to small cellular form of dwellings, providing a stiff structure to carry wind-loading, and by the mid-1960s, there were over a dozen brick buildings in Britain of as many as 10—16 storeys relying on walls no thicker than those used for low-rise housing. A building used to publicize this form of construction was the student accommodation at Hamilton College, a 16-storey tower block using 9-in. internal walls and 11-in. external cavity walls.[21] Claiming, perhaps with some justification, that the interest in this type of structure was a result of the 1964 revision of CP 111, *Brick Bulletin* provided a worked example of the design of another hall of residence and compared its cost with that of a similar reinforced concrete frame building.[22] The design of buildings like this had preceded a full understanding of their behaviour. Research undertaken with wall-testing machines demonstrated the allowances in the design codes for slenderness were grossly conservative, but it was not simply the behaviour of individual elements of the structure that were poorly understood. Insufficient understanding of the interaction of the walls with concrete floors meant some uncertainty in the use of coupled shear wall analysis; it was to address this issue that large-scale tests which were carried out by Edinburgh University. There were also experiments on the ability of brickwork to withstand blast following the Ronan Point incident, which showed that the code requirements introduced in the wake of this incident amounted to overkill when applied to brickwork because of its ability to arch over damaged areas.

Of course research findings are all very well, but what the practicing engineer needed, if engineered masonry was to become a standard method of construction, were simple design and practice guides which were not readily available. The worked example

in *Brick Bulletin* may have helped but what probably did most to encourage the use of masonry in this way were the publications of Structural Clay Products Ltd., a consortium of brick interests which saw the commercial possibilities of encouraging the use of brickwork as a structural material.[23] The booklets which they published contained graphs and diagrams designed to help the masonry designer and showed the forms in which reinforced brickwork, or composite brick, and reinforced concrete might be used (Foster et al., 1965).

Reinforced brickwork

In buildings like factories or warehouses, large expanses of brickwork were needed which were unstiffened by intersecting floors or return walls. These sheds were commonly steel frames with an infilling of brickwork and, while this infill had sufficient load-bearing capacity to support the roof without the aid of the steel, the walls would have to be very thick to provide adequate resistance against buckling and to withstand wind loads. The result was that the steel (or concrete) columns of the frame were used to stiffen panels of brickwork between them, but economies were clearly possible if the brickwork that was being used simply as a weather screen could also be used for its load-bearing properties. This might be possible by increasing the effective thickness of the wall or using reinforced or even prestressed brickwork.

Reinforcing brickwork is one of those ideas in construction that seem to have surfaced from time to time. While there has been some progress in the understanding of the way that reinforced brickwork behaves, and so some development in its use, it has always been of minority interest. Rather than seeing a steady development in its understanding and use, progress occurred as a series of forward lurches. Brickwork in the eighteenth century was commonly reinforced with so-called 'bond timbers' to provide horizontal tensile strength between large window openings and to prevent settlement cracks. During the nineteenth century, the vulnerability of these timbers to decay was recognized and hoop iron was embedded in horizontal joints to serve the same purpose. This practice continued into the early years of the twentieth century, even illustrated in inter-war construction manuals. It was particularly used to tie brickwork walls to columns or to return walls which could not be bonded in. However, by then hoop iron was being superseded by expanded metal reinforcement.

It was realized that if brickwork could be reinforced to carry tensile forces then brickwork could be made to act as a beam in a similar way to reinforced concrete and the manufacturers of expanded metal saw possibilities in this. Sutherland (1981) says that reinforced masonry was almost unknown between 1850 and 1950 and although there were a few examples, particularly of this type, none led to any continuing development in spite of commercial intersts in its adoption. In 1908, the *AJ* reported on tests carried out on what it called 'monolithic brickwork', i.e. brickwork reinforced in the bedding.[24] Of the materials tested, Johnson's mesh proved the best with tests including accelerated ageing to examine possible corrosion of the mesh. The article illustrated its use with concrete and steel columns and reported that it had been used in a factory at York for Rowntree's. The difficulties of its use for reducing the overall thickness of walls can be imagined from an article in the *AJ* the following year which reported the introduction of a German patent system by the Fireproof Partition and Spandrel Wall Co.[25] This system used an 18-in. square lattice of reinforcement between columns but met with problems in this country because of the restrictions imposed by the by-laws.

By 1914 the Expanded Metal Co. were illustrating the use of expanded metal as reinforcement for brickwork in one of their booklets.[26] The material was dipped in Asphaltum paint to provide protection, the company warning that unpainted expanded metal should not be used for such reinforcement. In the large areas of brickwork between the steel stanchions of factory sheds, 2½-in. wide lath was laid every third course in 3:1, sand:Portland cement mortar. The 1929 edition of this booklet reported tests on reinforced brickwork which had been carried out at West Hartlepool as early as 1912. Some of these involved forming a floor as a brickwork slab reinforced with expanded metal on edge in every row, but there were other tests on beams up to 10 ft. clear of span and with 5-ft. cantilevers with reinforcing in every bed joint. These experimental reports seem to have been published to justify earlier claims that it could be used in this way since advertisements for expanded metal had already shown heavily loaded panels of reinforced brickwork spanning over openings. This kind of use

had been discussed in the 1910 edition of Specification which then described reinforced brickwork as a new development. However, no information was provided on how such beams might be designed nor what precautions, if any, were to be taken in their construction.

There was more interest in reinforced brickwork in the 1930s. Burridge (1936) published an article on the subject in the *RIBAJ* providing recommendations for construction, a theory for calculations and a worked example. He also illustrated the stand which had been built at the Building Exhibition by the London Brick Co. which had a reinforced brick canopy. Two years later the *AJ* had a small section on reinforced brick lintels giving a detailed example and referring to tests by the BRS. A larger-scale demonstration of the value of reinforced brickwork was provided by a laboratory for ICI at Manchester designed by Samuely and Hamman (architect Serge Chermayeff) where reinforcement was used generally within the walls. This unusual essay in reinforced brickwork was the work of a firm which developed a reputation for innovative engineering in a number of materials. Hamann and Burridge, members of this firm, provided a review of the state of knowledge in 1939 but reinforced brickwork had certainly not become part of the structural engineer's vernacular.

All these early experiments were with horizontal, bed-joint reinforcement but more recently there has been an interest in vertical reinforcement. The early editions of CP 111 provided little guidance for the engineer save to suggest that reinforced brickwork design should be based on the elastic theory used for reinforced concrete. Nevertheless, there were some examples of its use with the reinforcement either in a grouted cavity, within the voids formed in quetta-bonded walls (a 13½-in. wall showing Flemish bond to both faces but leaving voids within the bonding), in pockets left in the face of the brickwork, or even using specially shaped bricks to form the voids. Structural Clay Products Ltd. were interested as much in the development of reinforced brickwork as well as the promotion of unreinforced brickwork, recognizing that there are many instances in which walls may be used in conjunction with floor slabs to produce deep beams or cantilevers. This can easily be achieved in reinforced concrete but as concrete walls are relatively expensive compared with brickwork, economies could be achieved if the brick could be designed to act as the web of such beams. Work was therefore carried out to explore the behaviour of box beams formed with concrete slabs and brick walls (Plowman et al., 1966) which demonstrated that cracking due to shear forces could be reduced by some prestressing.

Prestressed brickwork was in many ways simpler in construction since it did not involve the placing and adequate grouting-up of a large number of reinforcing bars. Instead, a relatively small number of larger steel rods, given adequate protection against corrosion, could be included in the cavity of the wall. If anchored at the footings they could be used to apply an initial compressive stress to the top of the wall through a steel plate by the simple expedient of tightening down a nut with a torque spanner. Given this prestress, tall walls could be designed to resist wind loads. A demonstration of the economies that could be achieved in this way was given by the Chrysler factory at Darlington (Neill, 1966) in which the intention of the prestressing was to eliminate the secondary structure necessary to ensure stability of the wall. Eleven-inch cavity walls were constructed to a height of 24 ft. with the prestressing force from steel rods within the cavity applied through the flange of a continuous Universal Beam which formed the wall plate. This building still had steel columns to support the roof and the idea did not develop further until William Curtin & Partners used prestressed load-bearing walls. There were clear problems of allowing for the creep in the mortar joints and thus the loss of prestress under this load, but it was nevertheless a practical proposition while brickwork was still a popular cladding for industrial premises. The interest by Structural Clay Products Ltd. led to the design of a prestressed brick water-tank in the 1970s,[28] and there might have been some further development of this form of construction but for the invention of simpler structures for tall load-bearing walls.

A still more recent development has been in the formation of reinforced brickwork beams using the same kind of reinforcing as that used in reinforced concrete. This is not simple bed-joint reinforcing, nor the use of brickwork as permanent formwork, but can be seen as the substitution of bricks for concrete, the argument being that higher compressive stresses may be obtained with bricks. The use of bricks in this way has been demonstrated in the recently built Armitage building, but this was a deliberate attempt to

demonstrate the potential of the material in the offices of a brick manufacturer.

What has become popular in place of both reinforced and prestressed walls is the use of fin and so-called 'diaphragm' walls. The principal task is to prevent instability of the wall and increase its resistance to wind loading and one way of doing this without simply increasing the thickness of the wall, and hence the mass of brickwork to be laid, is to buttress the wall or increase the thickness of the cavity, providing in the latter case that the two leaves are effectively bonded together. They also avoid the complications involved in building in the necessary steel. This method was also developed by Curtin and by the time it was first illustrated in Brick Bulletin[29] the firm had already built 14 swimming pools and sports halls in this way. The finwall is essentially a buttressed wall while the diaphragm wall widens the cavity between the two leaves and connects them at intervals with diaphragms of brickwork to form a cellular structure ensuring that the two leaves act together in resisting wind loads. Using the roof structure in conjunction with the walls, the latter may be designed as propped cantilevers. This form has become popular for swimming pools and sports halls where it provides a more attractive alternative to the light clad steel shed but one of Curtin's structures was a factory in which the diaphragm wall was built with fins part-way up in order to support the rail of a travelling crane. Apart from its structural advantages, the diaphragm wall also provides a wide cavity in which services can be run or, for some circumstances, in which prestressing can be incorporated.

Failures

The development of structural brickwork has not been without its problems. There have been spectacular collapses of tall walls which were inadequate to resist wind loading; less spectacular but more insidious has been the failure to appreciate the effects of movement in brickwork, which expands over time to an extent which is difficult to predict with any certainty. (The bricks appear to be affected by the temperature of firing.) This problem is compounded because the movement of concrete, whether concrete block or concrete frame, is in the opposite direction. Concrete blockwork shrinks on drying out while concrete frames exhibit creep under load so that columns shorten appreciably. While the majority of the movement in the brickwork may be early in its life, the effect is nevertheless a long-term one and failure may occur after many years. Compressive stresses slowly build up in the brickwork, most probably in a single-brick skin, eventually resulting in buckling failure or even crushing of the bricks in some cases. Where concrete floor slabs were brought through the cavity to support the outer leaf of brickwork and brick slips used to cover the face of the slab, a growing compressive load on these slips forced them off.

The need for movement joints was brought to the attention of designers in a technical note by the Clay Products Technical Bureau (CPTB) (K. Thomas, 1966) and discussed in more detail by Lenczner (1973). Apart from making an allowance for vertical movement in the design of walls when used in conjunction with frames, it has now become standard practice to include horizontal movement joints, which can be closed with mastic pointing, in long runs of brickwork. An obvious question is why such failures were not observed in the 1920s and 1930s when brickwork was being used in association with frame buildings. Horizontal expansion of brickwork did occur in parapet walls of flat roofs; the relatively unrestrained parapet brickwork slid over the damp-proof course and the movement became only too apparent at the corners, but the effect of vertical expansion has not been seen in the same way. Sutherland (1981) suggests that this was because steel frames were used which did not have the creep problems of concrete frames, so that there was less differential movement and so less compressive stress developed in the brickwork.

In contrast, sand-lime bricks shrink after laying, with the unfortunate result that they often develop large vertical or diagonal cracks, which not uncommonly include bricks that have been ruptured by the tensile forces developed. The cause here is simply that the mortar mixes specified (or simply used) have been too strong. Mixes weaker than the bricks should have been used; that they were not implies a failure to appreciate that additional control is needed where less common materials are being used.

Environmental performance

Two important improvements in the performance of walls could be achieved by the adoption of damp-proof courses at the base of the wall to prevent rising damp from the foundations, and the adoption of cavity construction to improve both weather-resistant and thermal properties. Both of these were known at the turn of the century but by no means in universal use. The former was a clearly recognized improvement but its adoption depended upon the quality of the building. While damp-proof courses were being incorporated into buildings of any substance at the beginning of the century, working-class terrace housing of the pre-First World War period was normally built without such a refinement. Damp-proof courses at that time can be simply categorized into bituminous and non-bituminous. The former comprised Russian Tallow, bitumen sheeting, asphaltic lead and mineral asphalt, while the latter include vitrified stoneware blocks, slate, waterproof cement, lead, a course of slates or even an impervious brick. Vitrified stoneware blocks laid as a complete course were illustrated by early building manuals (Fig. 2.12) but they do not appear to have survived very long. In 1933 *Building* gave comparative prices of the different kinds of damp-proof courses then available (Table 2.5); the price of materials varied according to the thickness or quality of the material used. The disadvantage with asphalt was that it had to be applied hot and that it might be squeezed out in hot weather but bitumen products were available from an early date and, like lead, had the advantage of flexibility so that they could be used both vertically and horizontally. Lead-cored bitumen was also available. Slates formed a reliable damp-proof course if laid in more than one layer (breaking joints) and continued to be used at least to the end of the inter-war period. They were specified for use in the construction of Watford Town Hall in 1939 but demonstration houses built after the war had damp-proof courses of bituminized felt, sheet copper or sheet lead.[30] In the 1970s and 1980s, improvement work carried out with government grants

VENTILATING DAMP-COURSES.   85

against damp, they afford continuous and constant ventilation to the space below the floor, and so help to prevent the decay of the wood. Special slabs are made for salient angles.

Fig. 29.—"Broomhall" Vitrified Stoneware Ventilating Damp-course, 1¼, 2¼, and 3 inches thick, with Open Joints.

Fig. 30.—Doulton's Vitrified Stoneware Ventilating Damp-course, 1¼, 2¼, and 3 inches thick, with Tongue-and-groove Joints.

Fig. 2.12

Table 2.5 Comparative cost of damp-proof courses		
Price per sq. ft.	From	To
Bitumen	3.5d.	4.75d.
Slate	10.5d.	
Asphalt	4.3d	7d.
Bitumen with lead core	6d.	11.25d.
Lead	1s. 2d	1s.5.5d

Source: Building, 1933, p. 345.

normally included the injection of chemical damp-proofing materials into a course of brickwork below the ground-floor joists.

At the top of walls not covered by a roof, that is, parapet walls, it would be considered normal practice to place a damp-proof course under the coping, though in their inspection of a number of buildings Hamilton *et al.* (1964) found that these had often been omitted. Where roofs abut against walls and chimneys, flashings are needed to waterproof the joint. Before the introduction of modern plastics, lead became the established material for this, although copper has sometimes been used. The development of plastics has made a dramatic change in this area construction. Bitumen, naturally a popular material because of its flexibility, has now been replaced by plastic material which is supplied in rolls in the same way. Not only can plastic material be used in the same way as bitumen, but it is possible to preform such components as cavity trays and flashings simplifying the skills needed for fixing and the degree of site supervision required.

Cavity construction

The other damp-resisting function of the wall is to prevent damp from penetrating from the outside, whether this be the external soil against a basement wall or rainwater penetration. Damp in a cellar may be acceptable if it is not possible to waterproof the wall but it is essential to ensure that the floor joists are sufficiently dry to prevent the development of rot. To achieve this the best construction set the ground floor

joists on a ledge, rather than building them into the wall, and ensured that the space below was well ventilated. Damp-proof walling could be built using a filled cavity. This comprised two 4½-in. leaves with a ½—⅜-in. cavity, subsequently filled with a rock asphalt composition between them. Specification clauses for this state that the filling should be done every four courses. Because solid walls remained common in multi-storey building (see below), measures were needed to prevent the possible migration of water through the wall. Penetration of damp through the wall to the construction behind, possibly a steel frame, was a matter of concern and so a waterproof paint, commonly a bitumastic paint, would be applied to protect the structure. Similarly, where stone was backed with a brick wall the back surface of the stone was painted with a damp-resisting paint to prevent staining from alkali leached out of the mortar by movement of moisture from inside to outside.

The simple solution to the problems of moisture movement through the wall is cavity construction, which came to be regarded as the standard, providing both improved weather resistance and greater thermal insulation than solid masonry walls. The use of cavity walls had already been suggested by the turn of the century and illustrations showing this form of construction appeared in the earliest volume of *Specification* in 1898. However, the idea took a considerable time to gain acceptance and until 1914 the majority of brick walls were still solid. The mythology is that there was a rapid acceptance of cavity construction following the First World War so that it was universally used by the 1930s, but this is by no means true. Although cavity construction became increasingly popular, solid brickwork continued to be used right up to the Second World War. Indeed, as late as 1937, Warland was discussing the possible advantages of cavity walls in his book on construction and still illustrating solid masonry as an alternative.

In 1935, a pair of houses were built in Hampstead which had externally rendered 9-in. solid brick walls built of Flettons, and these were by no means cheaply constructed dwellings.[31] When Yorke produced his *Modern House in England* in 1937, nearly all his examples of brick construction had cavity walls. However, one by Gropius used a solid 9-in. wall and they were not only used in small house construction. A number of blocks of flats illustrated in the companion work on flats (Yorke & Gibberd, 1937, 2nd. ed.) had solid walls, all dating from the late 1930s. A number of flats and institutional buildings were described in the journals which had solid walls, and because these were multi-storey buildings 13½-in. walls were used. It may not be surprising that solid walls were used in municipal flats in Brixton in 1938 where we might expect low-cost construction to be used, but they were also reported in use for private flats built in Regent's Park in the same year.[32] Solid 13½-in. external walls were used in combination with frame construction, in spite of the fact that this load must have unnecessarily increased the steelwork sizes, because of the regulation which required that when a wall was carried by a steel frame, two-thirds of the thickness of the wall must be carried by the beams. Thus, until the introduction of brick slips, the simplest way to achieve this and carry the wall past the outside of the frame was to use a solid wall in this way.

There were difficulties with the introduction of cavity construction. It was regarded as possibly harbouring vermin, a perhaps not unreasonable fear because during the inter-war period there was a serious concern about the problem of bed-bugs in dwellings. (The bedbug is a parasite that does not live on the host but within the construction of dwellings; cavity construction may have been assumed to aggravate the problem). The other hindrance to the use of cavity walls was that there was no knowledge about the strength properties of such walls. The London building regulations required that where cavity walls were used there should be no reduction in the thickness of the thicker leaf below that required for solid walls, which meant cavity walls were more expensive than necessary.

Building a cavity wall requires some means of closing the cavity at window and door openings and in such a way that damp is not conveyed from the outside to the inside of the building. The 1937 edition of Jaggard and Drury simply suggests the use of non-absorbent bricks, 'such as blue bricks, pressed facings or engineering bricks laid in cement mortar' to form the the sides of the openings or 'If common bricks only are available they are occasionally coated with tar on the cavity side and on the surfaces abutting against the sides of the opening ' (Vol. 2, p. 23) This approach did require the opening to be positively closed by the brickwork as is common practice today. The alternative technique, illustrated in Mitchell's Building

Construction (12th ed., 1934, p. 32), was to simply stop the brickwork at the opening and close the cavity with slate. Of course, this was only possible if the wall was rendered externally so that the render could cover the slate and it would be desirable to use metal lath over the slate to form a key for the render, as shown in an inter-war window catalogue (Fig. 2.13).[33] These practices were to change with the use of concrete blocks forming the inner leaf and closing the cavity and the introduction of flexible damp-proofing materials.

If a wall is to be constructed of two leaves of masonry then some means must be found to joint them together, and at first there were two ways of doing this.

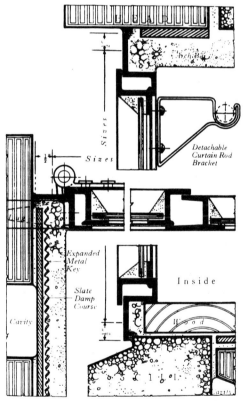

Fig. 2.13   15

One method was to use a special vitrified clay unit which spanned the cavity and was built into the brickwork at either side (Fig. 2.14). The simpler method relied on metal ties, which has now been universally adopted. Although there were initially a

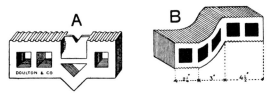

Fig. 2.14

wide variety of these, as one might imagine, the
simplest and cheapest were to prevail over the more
complex. All that was wanted was sufficient metal to do
the job, shaped to prevent any water which might have
been driven through the outer skin, and hence be
running down its inner face, from being carried across
by the tie to the inner leaf of the wall. Sutcliffe
illustrated both cast- and wrought-iron ties in use at the
turn of the century (Fig. 2.15). By the end of the 1930s
the flat twisted steel tie had become the standard form
although later the much lighter twisted wire 'butterfly'
tie was to become more popular.

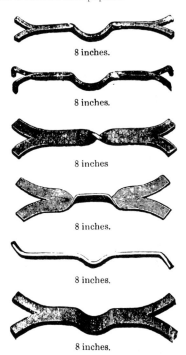

Fig. 2.15

After the Second World War two concerns were to
emerge. The first was an aspect of that perennial issue,
site workmanship. Cavity ties had to be at a sufficiently
close spacing but it was difficult to ensure that they had

been placed correctly once the wall had been built, and
from then on impossible without special equipment to
know what condition they were in. In 1974, a large
section of the outer leaf of a wall of a comprehensive
school at Newnham collapsed revealing a complete
absence of ties over a considerable area. This may have
been an exceptionally bad example, but in 1983, a
much larger section of a wall at Plymouth Polytechnic
collapsed due to corrosion of the cavity ties.

The longevity of ties depends upon their zinc
galvanizing, the critical variables being the thickness of
the galvanizing and the harshness of the conditions of
service. The first British Standard for cavity ties was
published in 1945 and this specified the thickness of
galvanizing for both wire and flat mild steel ties. The
performance of these ties appeared to be satisfactory, so
in 1964, throwing caution to the wind, the Standard
was revised and the thickness of galvanizing reduced.
This turned out to be a mistake and by 1979 there had
been sufficient cases of corrosion that the BRS
published an information paper (IP 29/79)
recommending methods for replacing the ties; in 1981
there was a further revision of the code which raised
the level of protection required.

Methods have had to be devised for the
replacement of corroded ties but unfortunately the
corrosion problem cannot always be solved simply by
their replacement. While corrosion of the thin butterfly
ties may simply lead to separation of the two leaves of
the wall, corrosion of the more substantial flat metal
ties is more serious. They have such bulk that the
formation of iron oxide, being of greater volume than
the parent iron, exerts sufficient pressure to lead to
cracking of the wall along the mortar joints in which
the ties are placed, cracking which may be visible on
both faces as it cracks the plaster on the inside.[34]

To those who learned their trade in the post-war
era, cavity walls were the basic form of construction
which provided a defence against driven rain and coped
with the problems of interstitial condensation. All that
was required was to ensure that damp-proof courses
were provided in the right places, that there were
sufficient weep holes to allow water within the cavity to
drain out and to make sure during construction that the
cavity was not bridged by mortar lodging on the ties or
falling to the bottom. Lightweight blockwork would
provide better thermal performance than a brick inner
leaf and, if the wall were to be rendered, might even be

used for the outer leaf. In recent years, however, the required standards of thermal performance have been increased and this simple form of construction is no longer adequate. At present there are still a number of competing methods and we are still to see the end of this development. However, the trend appears to be towards a separation of the insulation from the load-bearing wall, placing the former within the cavity. Methods were even devised for doing this to existing houses and the use of blown-in vermiculite fill or foamed polystyrene enjoyed a brief vogue until there were concerns about the bridging effect which they had and the appearance of damp. It is now common to use fibreglass bats held in place by special wall ties.

No-fines concrete

Advances in masonry construction have largely been incremental developments on forms that were already in existence in the nineteenth century, changes in the materials used, improved understanding and the introduction of damp-proof courses and cavity construction. In this century the revolutionary invention in the construction of walls, particularly for domestic building, has been no-fines concrete. This was introduced into Britain from Holland as a method for building house walls by the firm Corolite Construction Co. Ltd, which built a small number of houses in Edinburgh in 1923 using clinker as an aggregate. In the next few years, more were built for local authorities in London, Liverpool and Manchester. However, no-fines concrete's later development in Britain was the result of pioneering work carried out by the construction manager of the Scottish Special Housing Association (SSHA) which was set up in 1937.

The organization's objective was to build houses in areas of high unemployment as a means of providing jobs, and no-fines concrete construction was a method that was suitable for unskilled labour. About 900 houses were built by the SSHA on different sites in the Scottish lowlands including a number for the Admiralty. This method of construction was particularly suitable for Scotland, where the initial developments took place, because the country has almost no clays suitable for brickmaking. Construction involves casting a solid wall from a concrete which comprises just coarse aggregate and cement, using ¾-in. aggregate and a mixture ratio of between 8 and 10:1. The voids within the concrete

give a better level of thermal insulation than solid concrete of the same thickness and prevent the capillary action that would lead to damp penetration. Walls are finished externally with a rendering, normally roughcast.

During the war the SSHA used no-fines concrete construction for a commission to build facilities for the Post Office serving the fleet at Scapa Flow. It also seems to have attracted considerable interest as a likely method for the construction of houses after the war. As well as reporting favourably on the houses that had already been built of no-fines concrete, *Post War Building Studies No. 1*, House Construction (1944) included an extended appendix describing the method and providing recommendations for design and the specification of materials and workmanship. It commented that the lack of fines within the concrete prevented capillary action with the result that it was 'highly resistant to moisture penetration', although there were to be some problems here. The SSHA started using no-fines concrete again in 1950 when building 250 houses in Dundee. Also after the war, the system was taken up by George Wimpey for local authority housing and this firm made a number of changes to the method of construction used.

The early development which the SSHA made was to use dense stone aggregate rather than clinker because of the variability of the latter. The early buildings had been cast one floor at a time using timber-framed shuttering faced with expanded metal. The shutters at this time were built in small sections, suitable for manhandling when labour was readily available, but in the post-war development, at a time when there was a labour shortage, there was a move to large shutters to be handled by crane. The system adopted by the SSHA was to use two-storey-high internal shutters with the external shutters forming separate storey-high panels. As expanded metal became difficult to obtain, woven wirecloth was substituted. In the early post-war years the shutters were still timber-framed but these tended to warp with use and the facing material was not stiff enough to give a flat surface, which increased the quantity of material needed for external rendering and internal plastering. There was also concern to find substitutes for the finishing materials then used: plasterboard was difficult to use because of the unevenness of the internal surface.

There was therefore a move to all-steel shutters, in

spite of objections that this would limit flexibility. The shutter developed was a steel plate welded to a light steel frame, the plate being solid on the outside shutter but perforated for the inside. Shutter panels were bolted together and designed so that after the no-fines concrete had set, the outer shutter could be jacked out $1^1/_2$—2 in. to provide a gap into which a sand-and-cement finishing material could be poured. This complex method for forming the outer finish did not prove completely successful but the perforated plate provided a sufficiently flat surface to receive both internal and external finishes. An advantage of the perforated plate shutter was that it was possible to see the concrete as it was poured. Once the initial investment had been made, the considerable life which these shutters gave resulted in a dramatic reduction in shuttering costs per dwelling. In the early 1950s the use of three-storey-high shutters was also found to be possible for low-rise flats.

Attempts to improve productivity in no-fines concrete led to two quite separate developments in floor construction which have since been more widely used. An alternative to the poured concrete floor was sought and while precast floors were the obvious solution, the 14-in.-wide floor beams then available were lighter than the capacity of the cranes being used to handle the shutters. The Bison 'wide slab' was developed initially to use this crane capacity in no-fines flats. Where timber floors were used with two-storey pours, the intermediate floor joists were initially carried on timber bearers bolted to party walls. The notched joists resulted in splitting and so a steel bracket of folded galvanized plate, the joist hangar, was developed as an alternative.

Before tall blocks of flats could be produced, a method of quality control had to be devised to ensure adequate concrete strength. Cube tests, originally based on German experience, were devised for no-fines concrete. Germany had also showed that flats of over ten storeys was possible and, in 1955, a ten-storey block was built by the SSHA at Toryglen, Glasgow. This used rubble as the basis for the aggregate, and ordinary reinforced concrete floors. Problems with dampness in these tall flats were traced to penetration through the roughcast under conditions of prolonged driving rain. This was solved by changing the detailing at floor intervals and improving the specification for the roughcast while at the same time leaving a small area below window sills unrendered to allow some ventilation of the wall. Condensation was tackled by using plasterboard linings to improve the standard of insulation.

Summary

At the turn of the century brickwork was the basic structural material, the epitome of a traditional method of construction, but its behaviour was poorly understood. Some experimental work had been carried out to try to understand its properties but this had hardly any effect as the ways in which it was used, even if rather inefficient by present-day standards, had been proved by long experience and enshrined in building regulations. Today there is much better understanding upon which much more rational design may be based so that a range of different structural forms have been developed which make use of the material. And yet this development has not been the result of a steady process and a gradual series of experiments and developing design. Indeed if it had been, we might have been spared some of the failures which occurred during the post-war years as a result of designs which failed to take full account of the material's behaviour.

Looked at as an overall process, what we see, apart from a few attempts to use masonry as an engineering material in the inter-war years, is its virtual abandonment as a structural material with the appearance of frame structures and its rediscovery in the 1950s and 1960s. In the meantime what had been developed was the engineering profession and a much more scientific approach to the design of structures. One could argue therefore that its rediscovery took place in quite a different engineering climate and that this led to the comparatively rapid development of load-bearing masonry for high-rise dwellings and the later rapid acceptance of diaphragm walls. Given the more rational approach to design, there were no longer the restrictive, tradition-based, building regulations. It also seems likely that in the immediate post-war years, when there were shortages of building materials, engineers were encouraged to seek more efficient methods and as this mood infected the profession it seemed only sensible to explore the structural possibilities of what was often an essential cladding.

Nevertheless, the progress of brick structures may well have been hindered by the pressure for precast concrete and other forms of industrialized building. It might also suffer from being too familiar as a material. Sutherland has pointed to the higher stress values allowed in the United States. There, where it is not the common material of building, it may be easier for brick not only to be seen as a rather special architectural material but being treated as something more easily handled as an engineering material, because US brick builders are not working against common trade practices.

Notes

1 'Sand-lime bricks & the bye laws', *RIBAJ*, 42 (1934/5), p. 541.

2 'Construction Details #31 Suggested construction for schools based on Board of Education circular', *Building*, 8 (1933), p. 61.

3 'Materials — hollow clay bricks', *Building*, 34 (1959). p. 202.

4 *Specification*, 27 (1925), p. 50.

5 *A Work Study in Blocklaying*, NBS Technical Paper No. 1, (1948), HMSO: London.

6 *Concrete Block Making Machines*, NBS Special Report No. 17, (1951), HMSO: London.

7 BS 877: 1939, Foamed or expanded blast furnace slag lightweight aggregate for concrete.

8 'Aggregate from pulverised fuel ash', *Concrete*, 52 (1957), pp. 255—6.

9 Chairman's Report, 1928, p. 98.

10 Expanded metal lathings for plasterwork (1910 with editions of 1914 and 1929)

11 AJLPI Information sheet 169 (1934).

12 The economic development of the plasterboard and other lining materials is discussed in detail by Bowley (1960), pp. 323—63.

13 3rd edition, 1925, p. 319. This in the volume described as the 'Advanced Course'.

14 *RIBAJ*, 43 (May 1937), pp. 710—14.

15 *Specification*, 6 (1904), p. 275.

16 *Modern Practice in Architectural Terra Cotta, with construction details.*, The Hathern Station Brick & Terra Cotta Co., Ltd, (n.d.), Loughborough.

17 Brick panel prefabrication was discussed in *Brick Bulletin*, March 1967 and November 1972.

18 See for example 'The Warwickshire Masonic Temple', *Brick Bulletin*, March 1972.

19 Wier Common Room, Architects Design Partnership: see *Brick Bulletin*, 9 No.11, July 1973

20 'A report on bearing plates for girders', *The Structural Engineer*, 10 (1932), p. 84; 'Interim report on bearing pressures on brickwork', *The Structural Engineer*, 11 (1933), pp. 379—85 and 417—21; 'Report on bearing pressure on brick walls', *The Structural Engineer*, 16 (1938), pp. 242—68.

21 CPTB Technical Note, Vol. 1 No. 11 and Brick Bulletin, 6, No. 7, November 1966..

22 *Brick Bulletin*, 7, No. 8 January 1969 featuring Castle Leazes Hall of Residence.

23 There were five brick companies involved with Harris and Sutherland carrying out the engineering work.

24 ' Monolithic or reinforced brickwork', *AJ*, 27 (1908), p. 194.

25 *AJ*, 28 (1909), p. 358.

26 The company earlier produced a number of booklets describing the use of its products. Pamphlet No.1, (1910) and Pamphlet No. 2 (1910) both titled, *Expanded steel for reinforced concrete construction*; Pamphlet No. 3, *Expanded steel in plaster, concrete etc. including fire resisting and other building construction*, (1910).

27 AJ., 88, p. 107.

28 See *Brick Bulletin*, 10, No. 7, (1974).

29 *Brick Bulletin*, 12 No.2, (1977).

30 *Your New Home*, House Building Industries' Standing Committee, (n.d.)

31 '*Houses in Highgate* by J. Cruikshank and D. Grant-Coollie', *AJ*, 81 (1935), p. 774—5.

32 AJ, 87 (1938), pp. 57 and 204.

33 *Hope's Standard Steel Windows*, (1926), London: Henry Hope & Sons Ltd.

34 For a more complete discussion of this problem see de Vekey (1986) & BRE Information Paper 28/79, 4/81, 4/84, 16 & 17/88.

3 Steel and concrete floors

It may seem a statement of the obvious to point out that in most buildings, apart from single dwellings, the floor structure serves as a fire separator between storeys as well as a load-carrying element. Obvious perhaps, but it is this requirement that has determined the design of floors as much as the need to span between supports and provides the reason for this separate chapter. The term 'fireproof floors', no longer in common use, comes from the nineteenth century when this type of construction was first employed and so indicates the original reason for the development of brick, concrete and prefabricated flooring systems. Of course, the latter subsequently became important because they simplified and/or accelerated the construction process and it is this development that we shall follow.

As it is impossible (and perhaps not very useful) to chronicle every type of floor it is sensible to ask what issues a discussion of floor structures might address. This type of structure may be approached both from practical and historical points of view. Practical questions are asked by those dealing with historic buildings today, concerned with identifying and assessing the performance of an existing floor, while historical questions are associated with understanding the development of the technology or the structure of the industry associated with that technology. What, for example, were the factors that contributed to the development and the success or otherwise of particular designs or design types? Both practical and historical questions often require much the same data for their resolution and what will be attempted here is a review of the evidence. This also provides an opportunity for exploring, albeit briefly, some of the issues involved in the historical exploration of building technology. Floor construction is a good subject for this because, while the basic task to be performed by the structure is relatively simple, and is essentially the same for all buildings, the nature of the loading and the degree of separation required between floors may be different
in different building types, providing some variation in design.

It is sensible to preface this discussion with a brief review of the kinds of historic question that may be asked and of the sources available to answer them. If we ask how a particular floor was designed, this has two possible meanings. We may be asking how they were designed by their inventors or how they were designed as part of the building process. Both are legitimate questions, the first being concerned with the state of building technology at the time, while the second concerns the structure of the industry and the relationship between designers and suppliers. Only partial answers to both may be attempted given the limited evidence available.

Sources

Descriptions of some floor systems, presumably the more popular of them, can be found in contemporary journal reviews. *Concrete* published such a review in 1908 and again in 1936. *Concrete* also published a regular review of new patents which naturally included new floor systems but it is not certain that any of these were extensively used. Other journals also announced the introduction of a new system of flooring, doubtless based on companies' press releases because of the variations in the descriptions provided. In some cases tables of loads and spans are produced in these accounts, while for others there is no such information. Apart from these reviews, advertisements in annual catalogues and *Specification* occasionally provide more information, while brochures of a few companies have survived in collections like the Science Reference Library or the RIBA Library.

The position is much better for floors produced after the Second World War because in 1964 the BCSA produced a handbook of manufactured floors suitable for use with steel frames. This was revised in 1965 and again in 1977. The editions of this book were more consistent in their reporting than earlier reviews, providing a drawing of each floor, some indication of the safe loads and spans, and data on their fire ratings.

It is possible to obtain some idea of the companies

involved in some precast floor production from the listings in the *Concrete Year Book* which divided member companies by the services they offered or the products that they produced; unfortunately, the information is not complete. At one time flooring firms were listed together; such listings included not only manufacturers of precast floors, but also agents for those manufacturers who only provided a supply and fix service, and also companies who provided flooring surfaces of the granolithic type. It was only later that precast floor manufacturers were listed separately.

Floor and ceiling treatments

As the first function of the floor structure — to support the wearing surface — is the first consideration in design, this must inevitably be affected by the nature of that surface. In factories or warehouses a hard, jointless, concrete-based surface may be acceptable, but for commercial premises at the turn of the century timber was the standard flooring and any structural system had to take this into account. Boarded wooden floors needed to be nailed down and an advantage of coke breeze concrete (which was commonly used) was that it could take nailing. However, as the harmful effect of this was realized, the practice fell into disfavour during the inter-war period. An ingenious way to overcome this problem was used in some LCC flats in the 1930s in which filler-joist floors (see below) had the top of the concrete scooped out to allow for a topping of coke breeze concrete to provide a top surface to which a boarded floor could be nailed.[1] More usually, however, some grounds or battens were provided for the boards to be nailed to and these might either be laid over the floor or set into a concrete screed.

The alternative to boarding was a floor finish laid on to or fastened down to the concrete. The concrete surface itself could not be used unless some surface treatment was applied to prevent its dusting. Granolithic concrete and terrazzo were used as hard flooring surfaces and in the 1930s the use of oxychloride floors became popular. Thermoplastic tiles did not appear until after the Second World War but rubber floors were used in the inter-war period. The use of carpeting over a simple screeded floor would have been unheard of in offices until relatively recently, dependent as they are upon the development of cheap synthetic fibres and the manufacturing technology to weave these.

Another function of flooring is to provide acoustic separation and attention was turned to this in the 1930s. A building board might be placed over a simple concrete floor on which battens and boarding could then be placed. Warland (1937, p. 141) suggested 1¼-in. thatch board for this purpose. Alternatively, compressed cork could be used (the method recommended by the BRS), or a double layer of boarding, each layer separated from the other and from the concrete with a resilient blanket. Horace Cullum advertised their hollow-tile floor for its soundproof properties. It was a fairly conventional hollow-tile floor, over which was laid rebated timber joists to carry boarding. The joists were spaced at 14-in. centres on rubber isolators (also at 14-in. centres). The critical feature of this floor was the use of loading slabs which were rested on the rebate of the joists and so reduced the sound transmission.

Post-war commercial buildings have almost universally used suspended ceilings, which both clothe the structure and conceal any services which may be run under them. However, the prefabricated systems used for such ceilings is a post-war development. Before the war, suspended ceilings might be formed with wet plaster on metal lath and while this would be suitable for covering ventilation ducts, it did not provide the ready access to lighting services that we are used to having today. Moreover, rather than the structure providing the flat flooring surface with a separate ceiling below, the position before the war was often the reverse and this could produce a complex section. In steel construction, for example, rather than having the top flange of floor joists level with that of the girder supporting them (as we would assume today), the steel could be fixed so that the bottom flanges of the joists and supporting girder were aligned, with concrete then cast at the ceiling level.

In 1906, an article appeared in the *AJ* providing details of fireproof floors which could be constructed using broad-flange beams produced by the Grey process.[2] This used a combination of a concrete slab and secondary joists at the level of the bottom flange of the broad-flange beams. This construction was then used to support timber bearers for tongue-and-groove boarding. Of course, the small joists did not need to be at the bottom of the broad-flange beams (Fig. 3.1). Such an approach was not confined to steel-based floor construction: the floors of Senate House, London

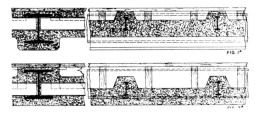

Fig. 3.1

University used a hollow-tile concrete floor in association with steel beams in much the same way, with a rather complex system of support for the floors above. Truscon developed precast U-shaped units to form the ceiling surface and sold them as a standard system.

Design and selection of the flooring systems was thus determined by a range of factors as well as the need to support the load and provide fire separation. Also, before the common use of suspended ceilings the long-term appearance of the construction could be a factor. When concrete and clay-tile floors were used, a problem presented by simple plastering of the ceiling structure was the pattern staining that eventually appeared on the finish as a result of the different thermal properties of the two materials. There were attempts to prevent this by attaching building board to the undersurface of the slab before plastering. The so-called 'Aerodrome floor' was an early approach to the prevention of pattern staining. By using an inverted U type of construction and a suspended ceiling below it, a continuous layer of air was introduced between the ceiling and the structure so avoiding the temperature differences which produced the staining.

Fireproof floors

Fireproof floors date from the nineteenth century, when they were developed for use with cast-iron frames in mill construction, but many were used in association with load-bearing walls. By the beginning of this century a similar technology had been extensively developed in the United States to provide the fireproof construction of city-centre commercial buildings, a development stimulated by the Chicago fire of 1871. There was a considerable variety of such systems in use in the US by the end of the nineteenth century, which were reported in some detail by Freitag (1895, 1912).

These were largely based on the use of hollow terracotta components, since a major concern for the designers of the much taller US buildings was to keep the self-weight of the floor to a minimum.

In Britain, a wide range of floors also existed at the turn of the century and for all those that were in use many more had been patented. Potter (3rd ed. 1908) pointed out :

within the last twenty years the number and variety of floors adopted and patented in this country is beyond calculation. Some have died a natural death for want of fitness for the object in view; others have been kept alive by means of advertising and persistent push, irrespective of merit; some from gushing descriptions of huge buildings in America and elsewhere where no other system but the advertiser's was used, and none comparable therewith... In the course of time matters will adjust themselves, and Darwin's theory of the survival of the fittest probably applies to concrete floors as well as to human kind (p. 201).

This comment nicely demonstrates both the characteristics of manufactured products and some of the consequent problems of tracing their history. When a need is perceived, a number of possible solutions will be devised and marketed, but Potter's Darwinian assumptions do not seem to have had the result that he assumed. There is nothing as prolific in nature as the spontaneous acts of human invention — someone writing half a century later could have made the same observation as Potter. With many products in use it is difficult to assess their relative success. A published description of a floor is no guarantee that it was extensively used nor patent records an indication that a system even went into production. All that such sources show is the extent of engineering ingenuity, how many of such devices have been proposed — rather than how many have been used in practice, or over what period. The same would be true of any product (even if fireproof floors are an extreme example of many patents and few products in actual use) so that some engineering judgement must be used in reviewing this form of construction.

Hamilton (1958), in his review of fire protection methods, described a number of systems but only dealt with floors used with steel frames, and even for these did not consider their performance in any detail. Neither did he discuss contractual arrangements, methods or standards of construction, nor the geographical distribution of particular systems, and since his book, there have been a number of major developments. While some modern floor systems closely resemble examples that were in use at the turn of the century, others are the product of newer technologies. The so-called 'house floor' in use today is similar in some respects to the Armoured Tubular Floor being marketed well before the First World War, while systems using prestressed concrete and welded reinforcement depend on recent post-war innovations. As floor construction is the issue here, rather than simply fire protection, a wider range of types will be considered and it is useful to attempt a division of the various types into some recognizable categories as a preliminary step in considering their evolution. The order in which these are placed does not imply a particular line of development, although some chronology will be attempted.

Filler joists

The simple approach to providing a fireproof floor in a steel-frame building was to encase closely-spaced steel joists in concrete producing the 'filler-joist' floor which was in use for some time. This had the advantage that it needed no clay or concrete components, although it did of course require shuttering, though there is the possibility of some confusion in terminology here because Warland (1937) called the joists used in a King-tube floor 'filler joists'. Filler-joist floors were a common form at the end of the nineteenth century, possibly because of their simplicity, and Twelvetrees (1875—89) illustrated a floor of this type which he called Fox and Barrett's floor (Fig. 3.2) in which timber laths were laid on the bottom flange of the joists to support the concrete. Variations on this arrangement provided support for the wet concrete but the simplest, which eventually prevailed, was to use temporary shuttering and nothing more than the steel joists and concrete. *Steel Construction* claimed in 1927 that the filler joist had enjoyed a virtual monopoly in fireproof floor construction until 1909, regretting that as a result of their becoming almost a form of building vernacular, the theoretical understanding of their behaviour was neglected.[3] The concrete was clearly intended to carry some of the load because, while the floor might often be no deeper than the joists, in other cases there might be two or three inches of concrete above the top flange.

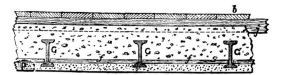

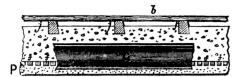

Fig. 3.2

Specification recommended that joists be 3—5 feet apart, depending upon the load and span (although it did not say what the relationship should be), and provided clauses which gave the proportions of concrete mixes for different uses to be used in such floors recommending: 'The concrete should be made with coke breeze, broken brick or other similar porous material, so as to combine as far as possible the qualities of lightness, strength and resistance to fire.[4] A problem with floors of this type that has become apparent in the years since their construction is that they were so often built using concrete with the coke breeze aggregates recommended. These concretes caused severe corrosion of the steel, so that there may be little of the original joists remaining today.

The claim for a virtual monopoly for the filler-joist floor seems hard to credit, in view of the large number of patent floor systems that were on the market before 1909. According to the writer of the 1927 article, its relative advantage changed after 1909 because of the requirements of the LCC (Steel Frame) Act, which favoured reinforced concrete floors. To remedy this, Redpath Brown commissioned the NPL to carry out a series of tests which were reported by Andrews (1925) and Scott (1925). However, it seems unlikely that building designers ever troubled to do calculations for such floors themselves because steel manufacturers included safe-load tables for filler joists in their handbooks and continued to do so until 1950.

Variations on the filler-joist floor, marketed as a Fawcett's Monolithcrete floor and Lindsay's floor, included reinforcement between the joists, allowing them to be further apart. In the Fawcett floor, the joists had holes punched out of their webs so that a form of reinforcement, consisting of a twisted flat bar, could be threaded through them. Fawcett also made a hollow-tile floor, and thus it is difficult to tell which floor is being referred to in many of the reports. A Fawcett floor was reported in use for the White Star offices in Liverpool in 1897[5] and was still in use in 1930. Neither is it known on what basis this was designed, but load and span tables were given in the *Architect's Standard Catalogue*. Lindsay called their version a 'trussed fireproof floor', and it seems to have been more complicated since, in at least one version, short lengths of bar were fixed to the joists taking a form rather like herringbone strutting. Such floors would appear to be more labour intensive than a simple filler-joist but the intention, according to a Lindsay advertisement, was 'In case of fire any portion of concrete perished by the extreme heat will not fall away from the girders and joists, as in ordinary floors, permitting the flames to pass through, but is held in position by the trussed rods.'[6] The system was also used for mansard roofs, that is to form the sloping surfaces ans well as the flat part of the roof between the steel framing.

In situ concrete systems

Although it is natural today to think of reinforced concrete as a general system of construction, there were several early systems simply intended to be used for floors. Of the British firms, one of the better established and more successful by the turn of the century was Homan and Rogers who not only made a number of patent floors (see below) which were produced until the Second World War but had devised some early systems of reinforced concrete in the 1860s and 1870s. One system used 3-in.-deep rolled joists set at 1-ft. centres in a 6-in.-deep concrete floor, relying upon the concrete to carry the compressive forces. This was essentially a form of filler-joist floor, but the company also marketed a floor whose reinforcement comprised a combination of rolled joists at 4 ft. 6 in. centres with tension bars at right angles to these, rather like the Fawcett and Lindsay floors. They had a concrete floor based on T irons at 3 ft. centres, and in 1906 they

introduced their 'Waved-Tee' reinforcement which, as the name suggests, had T-bar reinforcement but with the stem of the T taking a wavy form (Fig. 3.3), possibly with the intention of increasing the bond between the steel and concrete. There were four depths offered — $2\frac{1}{4}$, 3, $4\frac{1}{2}$ and 6 in. — and their brochure provided safe-load tables rather than a method of calculation for their design. The effectiveness of these floors was proved in a number of disastrous fires,[7] and the firm was a frequent and prominent advertisor in the *AJ* 'Fire Supplements' (referred to in Chapter 1).

The Columbian floor was an American import based upon rollings which were in the form of a cruciform or double cruciform section. This was a form of reinforcement intended to be used with steel framing. In their standard form, these bars were supported on steel saddles which sat over the top flange of the steel joists and had holes of a matching size and shape to retain the bars in place. This type of floor seems to have been favoured by Mewes & Dawson, or possibly by Bylander, for it was used in their Ritz Hotel

5. The Homan & Rodgers Waved-Tee Bars are simply rested on the joists without stirrups being required (Fig. 18). If desired the web of the **T** can be cut and the flange riveted or bolted to the joist.

Transverse Section through Lintels.
References: *A*, joists; *L*, lintels; *Z*, ribs.

FIG. 18.—**Homan Waved-Tee Floor.**

6. In Homan & Rodgers' (London) Hollow Brick System, between the lower flanges of steel joists hollow triangular bricks are placed. Over these is laid concrete to the required thickness. The steel joists are placed about 18 in. apart, and

FIG. 19.—**Homan & Rodgers (London) Hollow Brick Floor.**

the special bricks are grooved on the lower surface, thus affording a good key for the plaster, and the lips are so formed as totally to cover the lower flanges of the steel joists. No centering is required.

Fig. 3.3

and Morning Post buildings. In the latter, an unusual form of double floor construction was adopted with a slab to form the ceiling separated from that forming the floor. A mixture of clinker and ash several inches thick was used to form the surface on which the floor slab was cast and this was subsequently dug out through holes that were left. In this construction the bars for the ceiling slab were simply cranked to sit on the lower flange of the steel beams.

In addition to loose bar systems, a number of types of steel fabric were in production quite early and the advertisements for them suggest that these were largely conceived for use with steel beams. Various forms of expanded metal were used to dispense with formwork by placing it over the top flange of the joist and casting the concrete on to it. The expanded metal could be prevented from sagging under the concrete's weight by temporary timber bearers carried on the lower flange of the beam — although if profiled types like Hy-rib were used even this might not be necessary. A feature of Johnson's steel mesh, which was produced simply as a concrete reinforcement, was that rather than laying the mesh flat, it was draped over the top of the steel joists to hang in a catenary. As it was supposed to take this form after the placing of the concrete, it is not clear how they ensured that it did indeed do so. Friedman (1995, pp. 101—3) discusses the development of what he terms 'draped mesh systems' in New York and comments on the structural behaviour of these which differed from simple reinforced slabs.

Steel joists and hollow clay

The first patent fireproofing systems used hollow ceramic pieces shaped to span between the iron or steel beams and to cover their lower flanges. The material used was variously described as 'terracotta' and 'fireclay', which we would regard today as different materials, and it is not clear whether this difference existed in the products or if it was simply a loose use of the terms. In this chapter the word 'clay' will be used to cover all these products. A disadvantage with clay systems was the variety of sizes of components that were often needed to cope with the different spans and sizes of rollings and Hamilton suggested that the Kleine floor was one of the most successful because of its simplicity. In the same category are the King 'tube floor' and Homan & Rogers' A-type floor. Both of these comprised clay units which were slotted at their ends

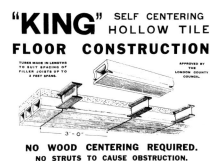

Fig. 3.4

so that they could be supported by the lower flange of steel joists, both affording complete protection to the steel and giving a flat soffit. The King tube floor (Fig. 3.4) was an unusual example of the type because the units were designed to interlock. In a later version of this floor, instead of the slotted ends to fit over the flanges of joists, the units were supported by precast beams of inverted T section. Homan & Rogers was a direct competitor of the King tube with their A-type floor and was even more curious in its design (Fig. 3.5). Again the clay units were slotted so that they could fit over the lower flange of the beam but they were triangular in cross-section so that more concrete would have been needed for the same depth of topping and

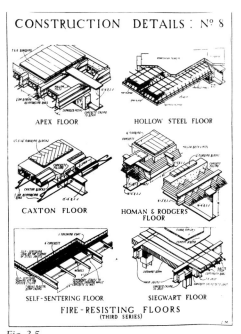

Fig. 3.5

the weight of the floor would have been greater. Tables of spans and loads were published by Homan & Rogers for their floor, and these systems were still in use in 1930.[8]

An indication of the range of floors used at this time can be seen in Fig. 3.5. Following simple reinforced concrete floors, hollow-tile floors must be seen as the most important type because hollow clay tiles placed between the reinforcing bars in a reinforced concrete slab lightened the floor and so reduced the self weight which the structure had to carry. As a result, hollow-tile floors became very common. The production of hollow clay tiles was already part of fire protection technology for structural steel so it was possible for a number of patent systems designed simply for reinforced concrete to be sold from an early date. Hollow tiles were also used as an internal walling material and there is some indication that even before reinforced concrete became firmly established there were some experiments to reinforce hollow tiles to form floors. In the Tower Building, Liverpool, flat bands of steel were set edgeways between hollow bricks to achieve spans of 7 ft. and 12 ft. between steel joists with the floor then covered with wood blocks.[9] Steel bands were also used in the walls of this building with the banding every fifth course. The bands used were 2 mm. wide and 30 — 36 mm. deep depending upon span and this appears to have been an early version of the Kleine floor (Fig. 3.6)

Once reinforced concrete was an established method, the idea of reinforcing brickwork or hollow tiles could hardly have been attractive. Of the designs then developed the Caxton, Cullum and Kleine floors had the simplest reinforcement, much as it might be done today, with bars between the tiles, one or more of which was bent up to provide some continuity over the steel beam. Both Cullum and Kleine floors used 10-in.-

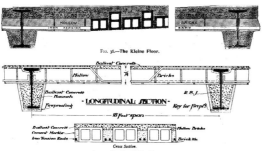

Fig. 3.6

wide rectangular section tiles with 3-in.-wide concrete between. The Cullum floor had tiles which were unusual in being chamfered, so that they did not fit tightly together. The drawing of the Kleine floor shows that the recommended practice was to hook the bars over the top flange of the steel beam, although it is doubtful that this could have been done effectively and at least one writer at the time deprecated this practice. The drawing also shows that while the topping was of concrete the infill between the blocks was specified as mortar.

The Caxton floor was one of the more ingenious designs of this type. If a floor is designed to be continuous over the supporting beams — and all were — then there will be some hogging moment and the small concrete rib will be in compression rather than in tension. This is nearly always the critical condition for the floor, since these bending moments will be greater than those in the centre of the span where the larger area of concrete in the top of the floor carries the compression. To mitigate this effect, the Caxton floor used a special shape of tile, one which was far from rectangular in cross-section, and which gave the reinforced concrete ribs an I-beam shape. More importantly the tiles were unsymmetrical and could be inverted near the supports, in order to increase the area of concrete in the rib and so keep the compressive stress in the concrete (due to hogging) within acceptable limits.

The Diespeker system used rectangular tiles, but the reinforcing bars were suspended from the blocks by V-shaped wire hangers hooked over at the top. The intention may have been to locate the bars more accurately. Continuity over the steel beams was provided by separate bars rather than bending up the bottom steel, although, curiously, it was bent down to the bottom of the concrete ribs — suggesting that the intention may have been as much to carry shear as to provide anti-crack steel. A version called the 'Big Span Floor' had 10-in.-deep (rather than 6-in.) tiles.

The Dentile floor is not one that would seem to recommend itself to a practical builder even though buildings were illustrated using this type of floor. The hollow tiles came in different types: 'Mitre', 'Bridge' and 'L' tiles. The Mitre tile comprised four pieces, triangular in plan, which were assembled to form a series of square boxes so that steel could be laid in both directions between them to form a two way spanning

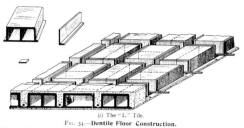

(c) The "L" Tile.

FIG. 34.—**Dentile Floor Construction.**

Fig. 3.7

floor. This must have been a labour-intensive operation. Bridge tiles formed a conventional hollow-tile floor, while the L tiles were used with the bridge tiles to make a two-way system (Fig. 3.7), perhaps less labour intensive than using the Mitre tiles.

All these methods of construction involved the placing of small components, reinforcement and in situ concrete on to temporary formwork which needed propping, and any system that could eliminate or simplify any of these operations would have an advantage. The Sidéolith floor, for example, which was being marketed as early as 1908, used a form of prefabricated reinforcement that was pressed out of a flat strip of steel to provide both top and bottom steel at the same time, an approach which was to re-emerge after the Second World War. This was used in conjunction with hollow tiles (Fig. 3.8) although the reinforcement was also marketed separately (see Chapter 5). Greater savings were possible by eliminating the formwork and its attendant strutting which was the method adopted by Smith's Fireproof Floors. This used telescopic centering (which was part of the system) to support the blocks during construction. Introduced in 1934, this method used concrete blocks made on site rather than clay tiles. In spite of this kind of development, the hollow-tile floor lost popularity in the years after the Second World War, as they were supplanted by precast and prestressed floors.

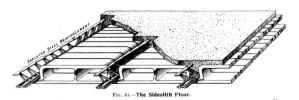

FIG. 61.—**The Sidéolith Floor.**

F.

Fig. 3.8

Formers

In the 1920s the Weston-Reuter Co. produced a hollow floor that was formed using light wood lathing boxes.[10] Clearly a hollow floor can be manufacutred from anything which takes up space which would otherwise be occupied by concrete, is sufficiently inexpensive, and is simple to place. After the war, wood-wool slabs were the obvious material to use for this and a number of companies marketed this in the 1960s. These can be regarded as alternatives to hollow clay tiles, acting as formers for the concrete.

Hollow tiles can be seen as a kind of permanent shutter, since the object is to reduce the quantity of concrete by producing a series of ribs, but there have also been systems in which some kind of metal former was used to produce much the same effect. In some cases these were reusable moulds but there have also been floors in which the steel former acted as a permanent shutter. The British Reinforced Engineering Co. Ltd (BRC) called its system of steel formers a Steel Tile Floor. Truscon's T-rib floor which used removable steel formers to make the ribs was designed to be used with their Kahn reinforcing bar and the Economic floor anticipated the post-war 'waffle slab'. This last system had steel domes acting as temporary centering. The domes had a 15-in.-square base, slightly tapered sides, and a vaulted top. Two-way steel was then placed between them, and was claimed to produce a floor of great lightness. A 6-in.-deep floor weighed only 45 lbs per sq. ft., compared with 72 lbs per sq. ft. for a solid span. At these depths the floor was intended for modest spans and there are reports of its being used in flat construction.[11] It was also pointed out that the ceiling would be sound-diffusing. Since the war, plastic formers have been used to produce the same effect, but with a wide range of sizes available to cope with different spans and loads.

Precast systems

Many of the floors in use during the first half of the century were based on precast concrete, a flooring type that became even more important after the Second World War when prestressing improved its performance. Precast systems were developed remarkably quickly and were commonly used in association with steel frames. Handling of the floor units has depended upon the availability of cranes, but even at an early date this presented no problem, as the practice was to erect the structural frame and then to put a fixed-leg derrick on top for lifting building materials into place. Some precast systems were designed so that the manufactured components alone carried the load, while others were designed to have some composite action with in situ concrete. The floors also used a variety of components in combination with the precast beams.

Beam and block

Perhaps the most obvious type of precast system is the beam-and-block type, that is, floors in which either hollow clay tiles or (more commonly) hollow precast concrete pieces span between precast concrete beams with an *in situ* topping that can be cast over the whole. These have the great advantage over simple hollow-tile floors that they require no centering, although some systems might be designed so that the beams need some temporary propping at mid-span during casting. Possibly the earliest of the precast floors was that by the Armoured Tubular Flooring Company (Fig. 3.9) which was certainly in production in 1907. Originating in Germany, it was also called Herbst system. The earliest description of the system is in *Concrete* of that year [12] but a company brochure of 1908 which survives in the Science Reference Library illustrates the manufacture of both blocks and beams and makes it clear that the latter were designed for composite action with the topping. The brochure also gives details for calculating the strength of floors but, as it also provides a table of loads and spans, it is not clear if the designer of the buildings was expected to design the floor himself. It seems more likely that this would be left to the supplier while the calculation method was provided simply to engender confidence in the mind of the buyer for what was at the time a novel device.

A number of companies produced this flooring system under licence or acted as selling agents (it is not

clear which from their advertisements), but it was clearly a simple design that could be produced by other manufacturers assuming that patents were not infringed, for example the Apex floor, made available in 1930. There were also some variations possible. In some designs the precast beams might be doubled in order to carry heavier loads or cope with longer spans. Broadmead Products produced a variant on this design in which a hollow space between the beams was formed from two flat precast units set on to ledges on the sides of the beams, effective in using less material but more labour intensive. Flooring Contracts (London) Ltd. manufactured the H.B.S. (hollow block self-centering) floor, in which the precast beams had corrugated sides and an inverted T shape to carry rebated tiles shaped to give a flat soffit; in a variation on this, a ribbed floor was produced by using asbestos sheets sitting on the beam rebates to carry the in situ concrete topping.

Precast beams

Site operations and the delivery of components are simplified if the precast units alone form the complete floor or the complete ceiling. The simplest precast beam floor, although by no means the earliest, was the Rapid floor. The beams simply took the form of a precast concrete I beam but with the top flanges formed so that they overlapped each other, enabling a screed to be placed over them. When the design was first introduced in 1933, a fully illustrated article in *Concrete* described their manufacture in some detail.[13] In a highly mechanized operation, a stiff mix was placed into steel moulds and the description gives some idea of the level of investment and mechanization that might be used in precast concrete factories at the time — in contrast to the primitive on-site casting that was used for some other systems. When the *AJ* subsequently reported the introduction of this type of beam it pointed out that one disadvantage of precast floors which the design overcame was the difficulty of accommodating service runs in the floor, as the Rapid floor beams had holes in the webs for piping.[14] The design may appear to be rather heavy and apparently less efficient in its use of concrete than some of the designs described above but presumably it lived up to its name. The placing of the beams would surely have been easier and quicker than placing beams and blocks, and in domestic construction (for which it was used)

fig 3.9

the weight would have been little disadvantage. It would also have been easier to cast than the hollow-beam systems described below. In the event the design was successful and it survived into the 1960s.

U-shaped beams were marketed by Truscon, which provided a flat ceiling. Today we would more likely think of using these in an inverted form to provide a flat floor, but these beams were designed to carry bearers within the U to support timber joists to which a floor could be nailed. With the troughs laid side-by-side, the system required no site concrete and this type of floor was still on the market in the 1960s. In the 1930s, Bison were offering an inverted U which was closed by a separate casting to form the ceiling soffit. The same company also produced a floor with essentially the same cross-section as their inverted U with its separate closer, but in this case cast as a single hollow unit.

Hollow beams, that is, a series of rectangular tubes laid side-by-side, possibly with a screed over the top, provide both a flat soffit and a flat floor surface. Siegwart's was an early and successful version of this type, originating in Luzern, Switzerland, and first reported in Britain in 1907. At that time there were five sizes of casting forming hollow boxes 10 in. wide, from 3½—8¼ in. deep and up to 22 ft. long. They were reinforced in each bottom corner with two rods while in the top was a 'transit' rod, presumably to provide sufficient strength for transport and handling. Siegwart noted that it was possible to increase the floor strength by setting the units apart and forming a cast in situ rib between them, but this would have been possible with any such designs. In 1925, it was reported that the firm began to make these with rapid-hardening Portland cement and carried out load tests on their floors made with 'Ferrocrete'. There were production advantages if the concrete strength could be developed more rapidly and, while the use of this cement may have been satisfactory, later developments of this kind were to prove problematic.

Constone's Corite Hollow Beam Floors and the Indented Bar Co.'s Hollocast concrete floor were more substantially reinforced. Although the Corite beams had ordinary bar reinforcement in the sides, they were also reported to contain 'a core of sheet steel which give additional resistance to impact and prevent the beams being damaged in transit' while Hollocast beams which were introduced in 1923 had a 'permanently embedded perforated steel core' which appeared to be their only reinforcement.[15] The Hollocast wet floor used the same perforated steel formers to make an in situ concrete floor, producing a floor which will look as if it is solid from below.

Research into this type of construction attracted the attention of the Building Research Board in its early years when it carried out some tests on floors with hollow blocks, although little seems to have come of this.[16] In 1936, *Building* was comparing the costs of various floors, while much later during the war, and with a number of systems on the market, Glasgow Corporation used several different types in housing which it built in an attempt to compare their costs.[17] The Springbank, Girlingstone, Invictus, Rapid, Hy-rib, Unicon and Siegwart systems were all used but the records of this experiment have not survived.

Post war developments

The importance of the prefabricated floor can be gauged by the fact that the position during the 1960s and 1970s was much the same as in Potter's day. In the mid-1960s and later during the 1970s the BCSA published a catalogue of 'concrete' floors for use with steel-framed buildings, listing over 70 manufacturers — some producing several different types of floors, a large proportion of which were precast concrete.[18] However, not all of them were precast concrete systems, and between the catalogue's two editions there was a definite shift in the technology being employed. By the late 1980s, precast flooring had ceased to have the same importance and the Precast Flooring Federation now has less than a dozen members. Precast concrete has been far less popular for floors in multi-storey framed buildings in recent years, but it has become more widely used in house construction.

Far from producing conditions which killed off those species less fit to survive, the post-war rebuilding programme provided opportunities for yet other species to appear and to find a niche in the market. Moreover, technical developments applied to the production of floors produced types of product that had not been possible before. Any consideration of the technical innovations which contributed to the developments during this period cannot be confined to the manufacturing process alone. The introduction of tower cranes in the 1950s improved *on-site* handling and so facilitated the use of heavy manufactured components.

The Bison Broadslab has already been noted (see Chapter 2); the other distinctly post-war development has been the Double T floor, providing flat top and supporting ribs in a single casting. The development of road transport, with the increasing capacity of lorries — partly a result of the wider use of articulated vehicles — enabled larger components to be transported. Such factors affected the small site as well as the large.

Prestressed floors

The most significant post-war development was the introduction of prestressing. Reinforcement is used in concrete because concrete itself has a very low tensile strength and is therefore unable to resist the tensile stresses induced by bending. The alternative is to apply an initial compressive stress larger than the tensile stress that would be produced by bending. This is the prestress which can be produced in two different ways. One of these is to put a number of steel strands into tension and to cast the concrete round them. Once the concrete has reached an adequate strength, the tension in the strands is released but, gripped by the concrete, they are prevented from returning to their original length and the concrete is thus put into compression. This technique is called pre-tensioning because the steel strands are tensioned before the concrete is cast. The other technique, called post-tensioning, involves casting the concrete with ducts within it to take the steel strands. These are then stressed against end anchorages after the concrete has been cast.

The idea of prestressing had been developed in France by Freyssinet in the years before the war. It then attracted considerable attention in Britain in the 1940s and 1950s but was first used here in what Bowley (1960) called an ersatz innovation because, although it had the potential to both improve the performance of precast products and reduce costs, it was first used to replace timber railway sleepers during the war. Freysinnet had used prestressed concrete to manufacture transmission line poles. After the war there was still a shortage of reinforcing steel, and its use was restricted, but with no similar restrictions on prestressing steel there was a natural incentive to develop this method of construction. The Intergrid school building system, for example, was designed to use no reinforcing steel relying upon post-tensioning to hold together cast concrete pieces. However, pre-

tensioned precast systems were more attractive for general use because they produced a structure that could be used by contractors with no specialist skill or knowledge. Although there were some production problems to be overcome before pre-tensioning could be used extensively, the first production began with the opening of a pilot plant in 1948. From then on, the development of the industry came about largely through developments within companies which were already precasting other products.

The first firm to go into production in Britain was Concrete Ltd. with its Bison system in 1949. *Concrete* when describing the factory at Iver, Bucks. called it a concrete bonded system, that is, pre-tensioned.[19] The beams were cast into timber moulds with regular testing of the concrete's consistency. Concrete Ltd. were soon producing a range of products because prestressing enabled forms to be used that had not been possible in reinforced concrete. Wide, thin units could be made light enough to handle and be transported, thus reducing the labour of placing, but strong enough to form a floor slab or beam when acting together with site-placed concrete. Hollow units could be extruded. This firm not only proved to be one of the most successful but also the one producing the greatest range of products.

It was also realized that prestressing was not only applicable to concrete. In 1953 Costain opened a factory near Glasgow which claimed at the time to be the largest of its kind.[20] The factory produced the Stahlton floor which, originally developed in Switzerland, was a more complex product than precast prestressed concrete and comprised a number of small clay units with grooves for prestressing wires. After stressing, the wires were grouted in so that on release the clay units were prestressed together. The advantage was that beams could be made in any length to order and eliminated the need for shuttering. The prestressed units formed a series of shallow planks on which hollow precast concrete units were placed on site, the whole being completed with an *in situ* topping to provide composite action with the planks.

Prestressing was adopted by a number of companies so that by the mid-1960s the BCSA could report a wide range of floors made using the method. Pre-tensioned precast concrete was the most popular method, but post-tensioning of precast flooring was also possible if not very common. In 1955, Raphcon

Ltd was founded by a number of firms specializing in concrete work to market such a flooring system. It comprised hollow precast beam units manufactured by extrusion in a long line. These units were laid on supports on site with gaps between their ends, allowing cross reinforcement to be placed between them. They were then prestressed to separate precast anchorage blocks at one end only, with the wires being passed round semi-circular end blocks at the other.

Filigree reinforcement

By prefabricating the reinforcement, some skilled work may be removed from the site to the factory. The bottom bars of this reinforcement might then be cast into a thin concrete slab. The effect is to form reinforcement and a permanent shutter for site concrete in one piece. The product is light to handle, simple to erect, eliminates formwork and produces a flat soffit, either by placing such units side-by-side or by combining them with preformed hollow blocks. All such floors need is a cast *in situ* topping. In 1956, Omnia introduced a similar kit of parts for site precasting.[21] The reinforcement was made of sheet steel 'supplied in strips 40 feet long cut to the required pattern and opened out on the site by a hand operated machine to form the lattice shape'. There was a clip to which a bar forming the bottom flange reinforcement was attached. The intention was for the beams to be precast on site, which was possible using very simple forms with the floor completed with hollow precast blocks.

This seems like a reincarnation of the Sidéolith floor which had been on the market some 50 years before — but such a system hardly seems to recommend itself, given the degree of work required on site to form the reinforcement. A more satisfactory design for preforming the reinforcement used welded-wire reinforcing. A German system was imported in the 1950s in which wire was bent to shape and welded together to form a reinforcing cage, on to which a plank of concrete was cast so that the Kaiser floor which was formed in this way was a largely *in situ* floor. This approach seems to have enjoyed some popularity in post-war years. Another development used a wide shallow concrete plank with two or three rows of such reinforcement incorporated into it.

High-alumina cement

It would be wrong to leave the subject of precast floor and roof systems without touching upon the problems which occurred in the 1970s. What has been presented so far is a picture of a lively and successful industry, lively in the sense that there was no shortage of innovations, and successful because a wide variety of products were available to the designer many of which long continued in production. But the use of any prefabricated product raises issues of both adequate specification and of quality control in manufacture, whether for off-the-peg products developed for sale in a wide market (as most of these systems were) or for bespoke items specially designed for particular situations. Two examples illustrate the issues involved.

In 1973, the roof of the assembly hall at the Camden School for Girls collapsed. Fortunately this occurred at night when the school was unoccupied, so that although the collapse was complete — and catastrophic — there were no injuries. Less dramatic, and so less well reported, was the collapse of three roof beams at the University of Leicester which had occurred only the day before. In the following year, part of the roof of a school's swimming pool in Stepney collapsed. On this occasion the building was occupied but a pupil noticed fragments of concrete in the pool and drew this to the attention of the instructor. As more fragments were seen falling, and a crack was seen to be developing in a roof beam, the building was cleared. Shortly afterwards one of the beams failed at mid span and later that same day a second beam collapsed.

The construction of these roofs was not the same. The Camden school roof had rectangular prestressed beams 390 x 100 mm. @ 610 mm. centres, supporting corrugated asbestos which formed a permanent formwork for an *in situ* structural topping of lightweight concrete. A castellated top to the beam and projecting bars ensured continuity between the beam and topping. These beams were supported on an L-shaped edge beam. The Leicester building was similar, with prestressed I beams at 1600 mm. centres — somewhat closer — but both spanned a little over 12 metres. The Stepney roof was made with standard Pierhead prestressed roof beams supporting wood-wool slabs.

A similarity of detail in the first two collapses initially suggested that too small a bearing as a major contributor to both: 'Although [the Leicester design] differed in detail from the school hall at Camden, it was the same sort of thing. The same principle was involved.'[22] What struck some observers was that the apparent weakness seemed self-evident: 'Prior to this collapse, I have never in my life seen such a detail — that is, the connection of the 12 m. beam to the edge member. I cannot believe that engineering training in this country is such that this type of thing is common.'[23]

In the eventual report, a number of contributory reasons were suggested for the collapse at Camden, and there was some similarity in the details of this building and that at Leicester (Department of Education and Science, 1973). Both incidents had in common the use of high-alumina cement (HAC). The danger with this type of cement is that hydration of the cement results in a metastable form and, given the necessary conditions, there is subsequent conversion to a more stable form which has a lower strength. Whether or not conversion occurs depends firstly upon the initial curing conditions of the concrete and then upon the conditions in service, in particular the temperature and humidity. Curing at high temperatures results in conversion to the lower-strength form and it gradually became clear to all concerned that this would also happen in service. The Stepney collapse was due to slightly different circumstances because conversion also leads to increased porosity of the material which in this case had allowed chemical attack from the gypsum plaster applied to the ceiling.

These failures raised considerable concern for the safety of many other precast concrete structures which were known to have been built of similar components. Testing methods for the presence of HAC and its conversion needed to be devised and many checks were eventually carried out on existing structures. The Building Regulations were also modified so that HAC was no longer 'deemed to satisfy' the regulations. The development of these test methods need not concern us here, more instructive is to ask how this situation had arisen.

High-alumina cement was by then in regular use by precast concrete manufacturers, largely because of its early gain in strength, a property particularly valuable to manufacturers of prestressed components. This was in spite of the fact that its susceptibility to conversion in adverse conditions was already recognized and

caveats against its use contained within the relevant codes of practice.[24] Davey (1933) and Lea (1940) had both noted the effect of high temperatures on the material before the war, and both had repeated their findings after the war (Lea & Davey, 1948—9). Moreover, Neville (1963) had already drawn attention to the possible dangers in the use of this material.

When Neville presented his paper on HAC he was emphatic about the importance of low temperatures during casting and of the need for a low water:cement ratio. He also noted that subsequent conversion could occur with temperatures as low as 25°C. In the discussion which followed, contributors fell neatly into two camps: the representatives of the prestressed concrete manufacturers, and the consulting engineers and government laboratories. Masterman, director of Pierhead and Babrowski — who had been the engineer to the same firm — took an optimistic view of the material, as did Sykes, an engineer with Sir Robert McAlpine. In contrast, Crosthwait of Freeman Fox & Partners reported that his considerable experience of the material had nearly always been unfortunate. CP 115 first noted that HAC should only be used with the engineer's approval, that is, the prestressed concrete manufacturer's engineer. However, it is difficult to imagine that he would always be aware of the conditions in which the manufactured components would be used.

Engineers using the material in Britain should not have been unaware of experience on the Continent. HAC was used at an early date in France but in 1943 its use was forbidden in public works.[25] Restrictions were also placed on the material in Germany in 1960 and a comprehensive ban was imposed in 1962 following a series of failures.[26] The material was also banned in Scandinavian countries: in Norway from 1962 and in Sweden from 1960. Neville, responding to the comments on his paper quoted a letter from a correspondent in Germany who said: 'As I learnt, in England the conclusion has been drawn that HAC concrete can be used in prestressed concrete when the precautions are observed; one will only allow for possible loss of strength in the design calculations. I fear that in England . . . this will lead to serious consequences' (Neville, 1964, p. 84).

Shortly after the first act of the HAC drama the rehearsals began for another problem of precast concrete quality and, although in this case the problem occurred in supporting columns, it is still worth discussing here. In 1976, signs of corrosion were noticed in the structures of schools built with the Intergrid system, briefly mentioned above, and investigation traced the cause to the use of calcium chloride in the mixes used.[27] It was already known that calcium chloride, used as an admixture to concrete, caused steel corrosion and its use was prohibited by many engineers. In this system, the use of any admixtures was prohibited in the specification, but the developers of the system clearly failed to exercise sufficient control over the manufacture of components to ensure that the specifications were being complied with. The proprietors were the builders Gilbert-Ash — who originally made the components and erected the majority of the buildings using them — but manufacture was contracted out to other companies. It has been estimated that components were eventually made by at least 18 manufacturers, operating from 24 works.

There is a greater incentive to improve the curing time for prestressed concrete, because more time is needed for the concrete to reach a sufficient strength for the prestressing forces to be applied, longer than that needed before ordinary reinforced components can be taken out of their moulds. This system used prestressed columns to support the floors and roof and it was clearly in the interests of the manufacturers to use some form of accelerator to increase the rate of concrete set and so achieve greater productivity. Calcium chloride was the most readily available. No doubt it would have been possible for Gilbert-Ash or their consultants to have instituted some system of quality control to prevent the licensees from doing this, had they suspected that it was occurring, but the absence of any such control allowed many defective frames to be used in building, the effects only appearing some years later.

Profiled steel floors

In recent years the popularity of precast systems has declined considerably. From over 50 manufacturers listed by the BCSA in 1965, the Precast Flooring Federation now has only a handful of members producing a much more restricted range of products. In part this may be accounted for by the process of natural selection suggested by Potter, although it seems to have taken a long time to take effect. Of course, during this time the transport of products has also become much

easier — but such factors are not the only explanation. The use of precast concrete has also been affected by the increasing popularity of profiled steel as the basis of the floor structure.

Profiled steel may be used to form the structure of floors in two different ways. Either it forms the complete structure or it is used as permanent shuttering, and possibly the reinforcement, for a concrete floor. The first seems the most obvious, even if used with a concrete topping to provide the level surface, and in 1904 Birkmire illustrated Pencoyd corrugated flooring in use in America. This comprised U-shaped sections laid alternate ways up and overlapping, much like sheet steel piling, and riveted together to support either a concrete topping or boarding. The lightness of such floors is obvious, and the advantage of this in the American market has been commented on above, but such floors would be more economical to construct if wider rollings or a more rapid method of joining were possible.

In September 1937 *Architect's Journal* reported the construction of a small block of experimental flats built by the British Steel Association (BSA) in Battle Bridge Rd, Kings Cross, almost underneath the gas holders there. These were two-storey brick-clad buildings so that it was not obvious that they had a steel-framed structure. They also had a novel form of floor, formed of sheet steel units which were 2 ft. wide and spanned 12 ft. The top and bottom of the units were of profiled steel, with flat steel sides, and were assembled by spot welding. The floor was completed by laying more profiled sheets over this, at right angles to the span, and covering it with a screed. The overall depth was 6 in. but the floor only weighed 21 lbs per sq. ft. Later the BSA produced a small booklet on sheet steel, citing the Council for Research on Housing Construction and the Sheet Steel Marketing Development Committee and illustrating these cellular floor units.[28] The timing of this innovation just before the outbreak of war was hardly propitious, but a subsequent *AJ* article considered the suitability of this type of construction for the building of air-raid shelters.

When F. R. Bullen (1957) described the construction of the new Binns Store, Middlesborough (1954—7), he reported that 'normal precast concrete floors with encased steel beams' had been rejected because of weight, and that instead a troughed steel decking had been used. This, he said, was an American technique being used for the first time in Britain. With profiled steel available in wide sheets, it was possible to weld two together (attaching the peaks of one to the troughs of the other) to form a series of box section beams which provided the basis for a floor over which a concrete finish could be placed. Rather than form what was essentially a rectangular box, it was simpler to use two deep profiled sections and connect them together directly, that is, at mid-depth. A concrete finish could then be placed over this. This was the basis of the Robertson Thain 'Q floor', essentially a steel floor with a non-structural concrete topping (Fig. 3.10).

As has been pointed out elsewhere (Friedman, 1995, pp. 133—4), this construction method had the advantage that the steel acted as permanent formwork for the concrete, eliminating the need for temporary forms, but had the disadvantage that the steel was vulnerable to fire and needed some form of protection, perhaps sprayed-on asbestos or a separate suspended ceiling. What was required was something that provided the advantages of this kind of floor but with fire protection as well. The Pratt Rectagrid was an example of a type in which the steel formed the reinforcement for the concrete but suffered the disadvantage that some form of shuttering was still needed. Much more satisfactory was the Holorib composite floor, in which a profiled steel sheet acted as permanent shuttering. Using profiles like this as the basis of a floor was not a new idea, but one which had failed to take off in the same way during the inter-war period. Just as metal lathing — which was used as the basis for lightweight plastered partitions — was used to form both permanent shuttering and the reinforcement in floors, another metal partition material was also used for floors. This was Lewis dovetail sheeting, which was on the market before the First World War and which could be used as a basis for both partitioning and concrete floor construction (Fig. 2.9).[29] It was only in post-war years that a similar type of structure has been marketed as Holorib flooring which forms both a permanent shutter and reinforcement for the floor. An additional advantage of this method was that it suited the use of composite steel and concrete construction and with the increased popularity of steel frame structures in recent years it has now become an almost universal method of construction for the floors of multi-storey buildings.

The pattern of development

It is difficult to present a complete indication of the state of the industry at any given time; although a large number of firms can be listed, it is difficult to trace the precise production period of all the different products. Even knowing when a particular firm was trading does not provide a complete picture because it may not indicate that particular products were still being made. Neither would such information show the relative popularity of the different systems or types of construction nor the geographical area over which they were supplied. Nevertheless, we may make some tentative observations based on the descriptions given. Clearly, the Darwinian pattern of development expected by Potter so early in the century does not apply to flooring systems — or at least not in the way in which Potter assumed that it would. Certainly, there were some systems which have proved to be ill-adapted to the construction environment and soon died a natural death. Nevertheless, new types continued to appear, some from firms who were already substantial players in the market and who were adapting to meet new demands or take advantage of new technology, while others were completely new inventions.

One of the factors which would have encouraged the development of new systems was the appearance of new markets, created either by changing circumstances within the industry or by external factors. The various products would not all have been competing directly for the same market although there may have been some overlap in their customers. For example, while the BCSA booklets illustrated flooring systems which could be used with steel frame, this did not mean that they were designed for that part of the market. The Pierhead floor is included in these booklets but when it was first marketed it was seen as a reinforced concrete system intended to provide a flat ceiling. An early drawing of it in *Concrete* showed the precast units being carried by a broad flat reinforced concrete beam no deeper than the floor.[30] Similarly, we have already seen that the Bison Wideslab was developed for the construction of tall flats of no-fines concrete rather than for steel-frame buildings although it could also be used for the latter. Just as this floor was devised for use with high-rise load-bearing wall construction, rather than for frames, so prefabricated floors were also used in association with low-rise masonry buildings, both circumstances where self-weight had little or no effect on the structural design. Thus, the Rapid floor appears better suited to house construction than to frame construction.

This last example shows how circumstances outside the industry may affect the relative of particular systems. The comparison made by Glasgow between different floors would have been important at the time because during wartime domestically produced concrete would have been preferred to imported timber. Another example is the recent popularity of precast floors in the domestic market to an extent that one type of floor, the beam and block, is now marketed as a house floor. This may be linked to an increasing use of sloping sites and consequent need for suspended ground floors rather than the solid, slab on grade, ground floors which were possible and popular with flat sites.

These changes may be thought of as overall changes in the climate of building but there are changes in the details of construction that would have shifted the balance in favour of certain types of floor. The move away from timber as a flooring surface, for example, simply made some types of construction obsolete. This applies to the arrangement of steel joists shown in Figs. 2.9 and 3.1 and, although the Truscon U-shaped flooring units were still being marketed in 1965 when the second edition of the BCSA booklet was issued, it was the only floor structure where the use of timber was even suggested. By the time the BCSA's third edition was published in 1977 Truscon had ceased to exist. The increasing use of suspended ceilings in the inter-war years has already been considered and there may be other factors. An advantage that profiled steel-based systems offered was not simply their very low weight compared with precast concrete but possible ease with which electrical services could be run. Illustrations of these floors show how trunking could be fixed to them and cast into the floor screed and that ceiling hangars could be easily fixed at the same time. This essentially post-war flooring type appeared coincidentally with the growth in demand for electrical services. Of course, that growth has outstripped the capacity of such built-in trunking and the adoption of service floors, stooled up from the structural slab has removed this potential advantage.

The overall reduction in the number of floor types may be partly attributed to the operation of market forces in a climate where developments in

transportation made it possible for companies to compete nationally. But the competitors cannot be seen as a homogeneous group: some were essentially precast concrete companies, possibly as a branch of their other concrete contracting activities, some were in the fireproofing business, some were steel-based and some seemed to have no other business than floors. Given this wide spread of interests the fortunes of some flooring system may have been as much affected by the success of the company as a whole rather than by their ability to compete in this particular market. To explore this issue in detail is beyond the limits of the data presently available and beyond the scope of this essay.

Another way of looking at this issue is to consider it from the point of view of the building designer who

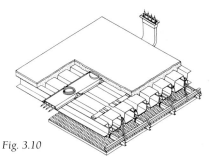

Fig. 3.10

has the task of selecting the right floor for the job. How was this done, what choice was available and who was responsible for the structural design? If the last of these questions is asked first the answer might well depend upon the kind of building. At a time when load-bearing construction was handled within the architect's office, selection of the flooring system might well have remained with the architect, with the detail of the floor delegated to the supplier. Either that or the selection was made on the basis of safe-load tables which the manufacturers sometimes provided in their brochures. Where such data has not survived it may either be because published information has been lost, or because it never existed. If a building designer relied upon the contractor to provide an adequate floor who in turn relied upon the flooring system supplier, there would then be no need for safe-load tables. Where safe-load tables do exist it need not mean that they were actually used by the customer: they might have been published for guidance only. We can imagine different design methods and different contractual arrangements and it is likely that several were in use at the same time depending upon the particular manufacturer. It is not even clear from some of the early literature whether a range of sizes was available to suit different loads and spans, in the way that we expect with modern products, or just one product produced, presumably with a limiting span.

In assessing the strength of a floor today it may be useful to know how it was designed in the first place. Assessing the capacity of a floor known to have been purpose-designed for each particular situation will be different from that of a floor that was sold in a single size whatever the load and span. If the floor was designed by the producer from first principles, then it may be possible to compare its predicted behaviour at the time with that predicted by modern methods of computation — assuming that we know something of the properties of the materials used. The brochure for the Armoured Tubular Flooring Company gives details of the design methods used. On the other hand, if a product was literally 'proved' by test loading then are the test results available?

These are all issues which remain unanswered. Some have practical implications while some are simply historical questions but there are two aspects of the fireproof floor which have implications on other aspects of building history. Floors were one of the early examples of prefabrication in construction, although curiously ignored by writers dealing with this subject who have been more concerned with complete building systems; they were also a part of the building which favoured the use of sub-contractors from an early date. If for no other reason than these the history of the floor deserves more attention than it has received in the past.

Notes

1 'LCC Flats, Oaklands Estate, Clapham Park', A & BN, 145 (1936), p. 395—9. In the article Fig. 6 shows this detail.

2 5 Dec. 1906, *Concrete and Steel Supplement*.

3 Etchells (1927) edited this, the unidentified author of the article on 'Joist-Concrete Floors' having the initials WBS.

4 *Specification*, 6 (1903), p. 259.

5 *The Builder*, 8 May 1847, p. 421.

6 *Specification*, 7 (1904), p. 296.

7 For details see *AJ*, Concrete and Steel supplement of 19 October 1906, p. 76.

8 See 'Construction details', a series of articles in *Building* for that year.

9 'Reinforced brickwork in Tower Buildings Liverpool', *The Builder*, 99 (1910), p. 45.

10 Described in 'New method of hollow floor construction', *Concrete*, 18 (1923), p. 41.

11 'New methods of construction', *Concrete*, 30 (1935), p. 19.

12 'Characteristics of the chief systems of reinforced concrete applied to buildings in Great Britain', *Concrete*, 1 (1907), pp. 427—44.

13 'Precast concrete floor beams', *Concrete*, 28 (1933), pp. 321—8.

14 'Trade notes', *AJ*, 79 (1934), p. 261

15 'Types of concrete floors: descriptions of special Systems', *Concrete*, 31 (1936), pp. 79—93.

16 DSIR, Experiments on Floors , HMSO & reported in *Concrete*, 19 (1924), p. 443.

17 'Wartime housing in Glasgow', *Building*, 17 (1942), p. 32.

18 BCSA, 1964

19 'A factory for prestressed concrete members', *Concrete* , 44, (1949), p. 131.

20 'A large factory for prestressed concrete products', *Concrete*, 48 (1953), p. 197.

21 'A new system of flooring', *Concrete*, 51 (1956), p. 558.

22 'Urgent checks on schools after new roof collapse', *Guardian* , 16 June 1973.

23 F.W. Gifford, *New Civil Engineer*, 28 June 1973, p. 13.

24 For example, CP 114 (1957) Clause 201 'High alumina cements are sometimes unsatisfactory in warm moist conditions'.

25 Ministère de la Production Industrielle et des Communications, Secretariat General des Travaux et des Transports. Circulaire Série A no.1, 5 Jan. 1943.

26 Ministers fur Landesplannung, Wohnungsbau und Offentuche Arbeiten Nordrhein-WestfalenVerwedung von Tonerdeschmelzement Publication IIB2 2.323 No 179/62 Ministerialblatt NRW, Issue A15, No. 95, 31 July 1962, p. 1413.

27 Building Research Establishment (1978), The structural condition of Intergrid Buildings of prestressed concrete, HMSO.

28 'Trade notes' *AJ*, 88 (1938), p. 1035.

29 *Specification*, 12 (1909—10).

30 'A new type of floor', *Concrete*, 52 (1957), p. 290.

4 The steel frame

Introduction

A relatively late introduction to Britain, the steel frame had been developed in the US, particularly in Chicago and New York, in the later decades of the nineteenth century where the technology for its fire protection had occurred in parallel with the expanding use of steel frame for commercial buildings. The disastrous Chicago fire of 1871 had demonstrated the efficacy of terracotta claddings as a means of providing fire resistance so that by the end of the century a number of tall, fire-protected steel-framed buildings had been constructed in the US, first in Chicago and then in New York. The significance of this development for Britain was that Freitag (1895, 1912) published two books on the subject which would have been available to engineers in Britain; the earlier of these, *Architectural Engineering*, considered the whole range of issues concerning steel construction and ran into several editions. Steel was already used in building structures in Britain, in floors for example, and there were iron and steel frames contained within load-bearing masonry walls. Indeed, there was a sufficient use of iron and steel in construction for Twelvetrees (1900) to publish a book describing its use and for *The Builder* to run a series of articles on the subject in the same year. However, the development of complete steel-frame buildings independent of external masonry walls was hindered by regulations, especially by the 1894 London Building Act which governed construction there and which had failed to recognize the possibility of framed buildings. Its drafting had enshrined both the tradition of load-bearing masonry wall construction and a system of firefighting from external ladders that made framed construction uneconomic and limited the heights of buildings to 80 ft.

Steel structures in Britain developed from the use of an iron frame within a masonry box, the form of construction that had been used for mills and warehouses, just as they did in the US; and the difficulty of tracing this development in both countries is the confusion of terms that was used to describe the different possible construction types. During the years when construction methods were changing, writers were not always clear about the terms used and so it is not always possible to know what kind of frame was being described. Of those which might be called frame buildings we can distinguish the following types:

- A building with load-bearing masonry external walls with an internal frame of iron or steel supporting the floors, essentially the form used in nineteenth-century mills and warehouses. This form had changed little, except that wrought iron and steel were being used instead of cast-iron beams.

- A building with framing members in the external wall which were designed to carry the floors but where the wall itself was self-supporting. While a masonry external wall may have been wanted for architectural reasons, or to comply with regulations, it was not necessarily load-bearing. It may have been economical to put up a steel frame first and then clad it in masonry but, if self-supporting, it had to be substantial enough to carry its own weight. Moreover, the different thermal expansion rates of masonry and steel would result in some differential movement between the two. It was therefore advantageous for the wall to be supported by the frame.

- A framed building, with an external masonry wall but where the load of that wall is carried by the frame, is a true steel-frame building because none of the masonry is self-supporting. However, it may not be possible to tell, without extensive opening-up of the building or even demolition, whether or not the frame supports the masonry. Indeed, what is now recognized to be the first true steel-frame building in Chicago, the Home Insurance Building (1884—5) by William le Baron Jenny was, until its demolition in the 1930s, thought to have been constructed with self-supporting walls.[1]

- A frame without masonry external walling. These are clearly framed buildings but there are also examples of buildings which may have external masonry walls on some but not all elevations; the connection between the

Fig. 4.1

structure and the masonry wall of the principal elevation may still not be clear. An excellent example of this is Canada House, Manchester (Fig. 4.1).

Thus, the early development of the steel frame has to be seen within this rather confused picture and, like the Home Insurance Building, the exact form of construction may not be apparent until demolition, unless contemporary design drawings survive.

Materials
Cast iron

By the turn of the century, wrought iron had been almost entirely superseded by mild steel but there was still some use of cast iron. It continued to be used for columns; Twelvetrees (1900) reported that cast steel might also be used. R.A. Skelton and Co. were showing the properties of their standard round cast-iron column sections up to the opening of the First World War and they were still covered by regulations in the 1930s.[2] To some extent this reflects the continuing use of 'mill' framing but when Adams discussed their design in an article as late as 1927 he noted that cast-iron columns were often used in supporting the 'bressumers' (his word) of shop fronts.[3] His purpose was to provide a method for the design of these columns because, as he pointed out, the safe loads given in different section books varied for the same section. This was presumably because they were based on the different column formulae, which he compared in his article, and he recommended the modified Gordon formula.[4] Although rather more than a shop front, cast iron columns were used in 1929 for the front of Martins Bank, Liverpool, where stone cladding was threaded over the cast iron (Fig. 4.2).

Cast iron was also important as a decorative material. In some cities, complete cast-iron fronts were erected, with well-known examples surviving in

Fig. 4.2

Liverpool and Glasgow. McFarlane was still advertising these in 1914 and, although in London they were forbidden by the 1894 Act as a structural material, there was some use of cast iron in forming parts of external walls. Gloag and Bridgewater (1948) illustrated a number of buildings which used cast iron as a major feature of the elevation, as window surrounds and the spandrels between stone columns. Selfridge's warehouse in London (1924) was reported as the first all cast-iron front there.[5]

Rolled steel

Freitag (1895) claimed that mild steel had replaced wrought iron for building structures in the US because its higher strength made it more economical in spite of its higher cost. The transition which he described there was a gradual one, with some buildings using a combination of wrought iron and steel depending upon the span of the beams. However, he was describing development in a country where the steel frame had been developed earlier. In Britain, Twelvetrees, in 1900, reported that wrought iron was almost completely obsolete as a material by then. By the time the steel frame was introduced, mild steel was the basic structural material and the facility with which designers could use frames was to some extent determined by the availability of steel rollings. The rolling of structural sections had begun in the first half of the nineteenth century with quite small simple sections, but by the end of the century a fairly wide range of I-section beams had become available. Each company rolled their own sizes so the designer was faced with a wide choice, but standardization of these sizes began with the first issue of BS 4 in 1903. This gave a range of sizes for beams varying between 3 x 1.5 in. to 24 x 7.5 in. although manufacturers naturally continued to roll their own sizes for a period. This standard remained unchanged until 1921 when a revision was issued which not only increased the range of standard rollings available but improved the efficiency of the existing sizes by changes in their geometry. (For tables of rolling sizes see Bates, 1984.)

Simple rolling mills were unable to produce broad-flange beams whose production depended on the use of the Grey process (see below). As there were no mills of this type in Britain, broad-flange beams were not covered in the British standard but they were being imported from the Continent and marketed by the

Skelton Company certainly as early as 1906. No tables are available for the properties of these sections before 1921 although it seems unlikely that the earlier sections would have been different.

There seems to have been some differences in the way in which the working loads for these structural sections were determined, so that it is difficult to know how any particular structure may have been designed. Although the standard work on construction of this period is Twelvetrees (1900), an article in *The Builder* by Dawnay (1901) also gives a good indication of the practice of the day. In part, differences in design methods existed because there was no standard specification for steel quality. Dawnay suggested that steel quality might vary considerably between Bessemer and open hearth steel and made reference to loading tests used to distinguish different qualities of joists. Twelvetrees suggested calculating the strength of beams from the modulus of rupture and applying a safety factor — he suggested that 5 might be an appropriate value for this. Although there were different approaches to design, the effect may not be significant because, as *Specification* noted, 'Some authorities prefer to take the elastic limit as the basis of design rather than the ultimate strength of the material; but as they employ a proportionately smaller factor of safety, the result is practically the same.'[6]

Specification probably represents the most common practice giving the allowed working stresses for the materials used at the time (Table 4.1) with sections dealing with cast iron, wrought iron and steel. By 1904, makers' catalogues not only showed the sizes and weights of joists kept in stock, but in some cases included tables of the safe distributed loads over various spans for each joist. However, they did not state

Table 4.1 Safe stresses for iron and steel			
Safe loads in T./sq in.	Cast iron	Wrought iron	Steel
Tension	1.5	5	6–8
Compression	8	4	6–8

Source: Specification, 7 (1904), p. 283

the breaking stresses assumed in determining these values or, if they did, they did not add the factor of safety which was used to determine the safe working stress. The position became clearer with the publication of BS 15 in 1906 which specified a yield stress between 28 and 32 T/sq. in. The higher figure was raised to 33 tons in the 1912 revision and these figures remained throughout subsequent revisions of this code until it was replaced by BS 4360 in 1968.

No official values for the loads to be assumed in design were available until the 1909 Steel Frame Act and so designers had to decide for themselves the safe working load for each case. Some designers determined the dead loads coming on to particular components of a structure while others simply made an allowance in the overall loading. Bates (1984, p. 47) has discussed the possible margins of safety that there might be in existing structures and points out that at the time designers might have used load values given by the *Encyclopaedia of Architecture*, the *Dorman Long Handbook* or some other published source. While the figures given by these for different types of building are of the same order, they are by no means identical.

Building frames at the turn of the century were still closely related to the mills and warehouses of the nineteenth century. Frames were set within load-bearing masonry shells which provided some stability to the structure. In its first issue *Specification* provided the construction details of Salisbury Hotel (Fig. 4.3) which had masonry walls with all iron framed interior.[7] Cast-iron columns, 12 in. in diameter, stood on York stone bases with Portland cement grout in between. At each

floor, there was an octagonal cast-iron box section attached to the top of each column to form the junction with the beams. Machined faces on both the flanges of these box sections and on the column ends ensured a close fit between them. At the periphery of the building the beams were supported on the masonry walls although the plan was such that some cantilevers were required and these were achieved by plating to top flanges of the beams at the supports.

Although the Steel Frame Act was to make this type of construction seem rather old-fashioned, its use persisted into the inter-war period. In 1924, *Concrete* illustrated the construction of a building in Leicester, in order to show a new type of concrete floor in use, but the photographs show clearly that, in spite of the novelty of the floor, the basic structure of the building used brick masonry walls and round, and therefore cast, columns.[8] The persistence of this type of construction is an example of the inertia frequently seen in design although it might be explained by its simplicity.

Early detailing

Dawnay (1901) discussed the method which a designer might have used at the time. He noted 'In selecting joists the first thing to determine is whether one third or one fourth of the ultimate is to be adopted, then adopt about one twenty-fourth of the span for the depth of narrow flange joists' and 'For the wide flange joist it is safe to work to one twentieth to one thirtieth of the span...' (p. 385). For the design of compound girders he refered to the work of Kirkaldy[9] and to Fairbairn's constants, an indication of the lack of development in Britain during the intervening years. Based on these, he suggested that for a girder carrying an internal wall $1/12$—$1/16$ is proper proportion for depth/span. He also suggested a deflection limit of $1/40$ in. for each 1 ft. of span.

With no large rollings produced at that time, it was necessary to form larger sections by plating the flanges of standard joists or by combining two joists together with plates. This was sufficiently common that section properties and safe-load tables were published by manufacturers to include these and examples of such tables have been reproduced by Bates (1984). In addition to these standard compound sections, it was necessary to make up deep plate-girders for the larger

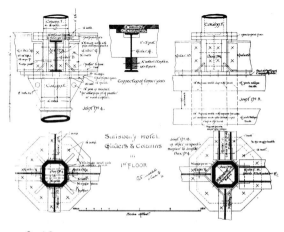

fig 4.3

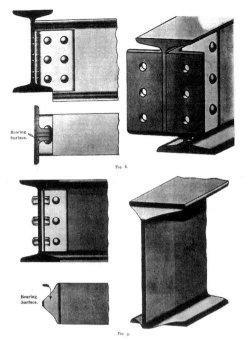

Fig. 4.4

bear on the beam flange (Fig. 4.4). Dawnay said that this 'notched joggle is only suitable for light work,' while 'the forged set up joggle [one in which the web itself was cut away and the flange bent up] is the most approved method for good work' (1901, p. 388).

One reason for the continuing popularity of cast iron for columns was because otherwise it was necessary to form columns by combining a number of sections together to obtain the required properties. This must have been an expensive operation as Freitag (1895) showed by comparing the relative assembly cost of different column designs for US construction. As the iron columns were replaced by steel, similar floor-

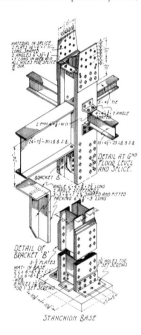

Fig. 4.6

spans and loads. Sections were assembled by shop riveting and Twelvetrees (1900) gave a number of typical details for these, observing that web stiffeners might be formed simply by bending angle sections or by cutting, bending and welding. There were similar differences in the detailing of beam connections. Where joists were fitted to beams their lower flanges might be joggled to fit over the beam flange by grinding away the lower flange so that the web of the joist was brought to

level junctions could be used with the columns terminating in a cap to carry the beams and column above. This kind of joint was illustrated by Twelvetrees for use where cast columns were used in conjunction with rolled section beams (Fig. 4.5) but it was more convenient for steel columns to be carried above the floor and spliced there (Fig. 4.6), leaving the beams to be carried on cleats. Of course, at that time, Twelvetrees was drawing largely on American experience.

Before steel frames were used, fabricated steel structures were being used in buildings where long spans were required or where heavy loads needed to be carried. Deep trusses or plate girders reminiscent of

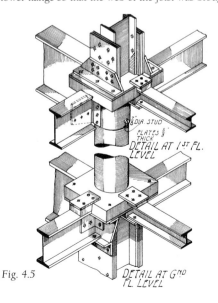

Fig. 4.5

bridge construction were incorporated into large hotels or theatres. The use of deep trusses like this in buildings to support floors was hardly new: timber trusses had been a routine feature of buildings since the seventeenth century. However, the ability to fabricate deep-riveted plate-girders instead of trusses reduced the depth of such long spanning structures and the availability of universal plates, which made edge planing unnecessary, facilitated the fabrication of these by the mid-1920s.

Frame buildings

There have been a number of claims for the first steel-frame building in Britain and although this is hardly a significant historical event, as it followed the American lead by some time, these claims indicate the growing use of steel frames in the first years of the century even though the type of construction used may not always be clear. Bates (1984, p. 63) reports a claim that the first steel frame was a furniture store in Stockton on Tees built by Redpath Brown in 1900, while Bowley (1966) cited a factory in Sheffield built in 1907 which had stanchions cased in terracotta externally and concrete and steel lathing internally. Saint (1977) has staked a claim for Norman Shaw's Royal Insurance Building in Liverpool which is certainly an early example and one which deserves some consideration, not simply for its claim to be the first but because of the details which we have of it from a contemporary publication (Hetherington, 1904). Shaw's earlier White Star offices in Liverpool (1894) provided a dramatic expression of the use of iron with exposed box stanchions supporting riveted plate girders which in turn carried jack arch floors, but the building did not have a steel frame. Shaw was only able to expose the iron construction in this way because of the fairly relaxed building regulations in Liverpool. Following his design for this building, Shaw became the assessor for the competition for the Royal Insurance Building through Thomas Ismay, who was director of both companies. Embarrassingly, this was won by his partner J. Francis Doyle but the design was changed by Shaw to incorporate a steel frame as a means of improving the space on the ground floor.

Its construction was described by Hetherington as classic style 'freely adapted to modern requirements'. There is certainly little to suggest that the building has a

steel frame from its external appearance, which is of Portland stone on an Aberdeen granite base. Building began in February 1897 and was completed by the middle of 1903. Steel construction was used in this building because the client required an uninterrupted general office at ground-floor level. Shaw achieved this by removing the ground floor columns of Doyle's design and hanging the floors above from steel arches. Columns in the external walls support transverse arches at 34-ft. centres at the third-floor level from which the first and second floors were hung. Having columns in the external walls to support the floors seems to justify a claim for this to be the first steel-frame building in England although Hetherington's drawings do not show clearly whether or not the walls are carried by this frame.

Shortly after the construction of this building, architects' attention would have been drawn to the possibilities of steel frames for more modest buildings. In 1904 the *Architect's Journal* described a warehouse in Manchester which had a steel frame with terracotta cladding to form the external walls.[10] As this was a novel form of construction it appeared as a series of photographs illustrating the weekly progress of the construction. It is worth noting that the building had precast concrete floors by Fram — precast floors were to be commonly used with steel frames. A photograph of the interior of the completed building showed that again there was no fire protection to the steel columns and it is not uncommon to find buildings from this period with frames that remain unprotected to this day.

What inhibited the development of framed buildings, at least in London, was that regulations governing the construction of external walls implicitly assumed that they would be load-bearing and specified minimum thicknesses dependent upon their height and length (see Table 2.2). If walls had to be this thick, whether they were load-bearing or not, there was no advantage in their being non-load-bearing and so no economic advantage in using complete frame buildings. The London Building Act of 1894 was out of date as soon as it became law because it failed to recognize the possibility of steel-frame building even though this form of construction had been in use in the US for some time. Such regulations were common to many cities, although not all authorities may have been so conservative in their enforcement and it is clear from the above examples that steel-frame buildings were being put up in some cities before they were fully recognized by the regulations.

It must have been clear to all involved with building that the regulations were in need of revision and in London attempts were first made to recognize steel framing in the 1905 amendment to the London Building Act. However, when the bill was published there were objections to it because it failed to give clear guidance to designers. Discussions then began on the drafting of regulations and the possibility of steel framing was officially recognized in London four years later by the 1909 Amendment Act — the so-called 'Steel Frame Act' which laid down design rules.

New practice

The first essay in steel-frame building in London was the Ritz Hotel, erected 1904—5, whose structure was designed by Sven Bylander and was said to be based on American principles. Although the building was designed as a steel frame, the walls still complied with the requirements of the 1894 Act. Bylander later commented that bolts had to be used rather than riveting, normal in the US for this type of construction, because of a requirement in the London regulations for slotted holes at the ends of beams. However, the photographs published at the time do not show bolts. Freitag reported that, in the US, bolted connections were found to be unsatisfactory. While the Ritz Hotel is regarded as a landmark for the steel frame, it was not the first steel building in London by very much, because Bylander was also involved in the design of the smaller Wardorf Hotel, and a number of other large buildings including the Morning Post building (1907) and the RAC Building (1911). Describing this period of activity some years later, Bylander (1937) pointed out that his buildings built in the period immediately after the 1909 Act would have been designed before it appeared and so might not be complete steel frames. He noted that Australia House was his first building designed after the Act.

The introduction of steel-frame design involved changes in practice which Bylander was keen to point out. He wrote a number of articles describing the design and construction, first of the Ritz Hotel and then Selfridge's store which was built in 1909 (Lawrence, 1990). Apart from pointing out the advantages that could be derived from this form of construction, he was careful to discuss the way in which the designer and contractor had to adapt to its needs. First, there was a

need for some form of quality control at each stage of the production process, beginning with inspection of the steel at the rolling mills. Second, there was an increased workload for the drawing office because schedules had to be produced for the cutting and drilling of all the components. It was also important that these components be marked up carefully so that there should be no confusion when they came to be assembled on site. A consequence of the use of steel frame was that once work had begun there could be no change of design without considerable difficulties. One cannot help feeling, from the considerable number of articles that Bylander produced for the architectural press describing the process of design, detailing and the supervision of the erection of the steel frame, that he was implicitly making a case for the employment of a consulting engineer. It must have been attractive to be able to delegate not just the design but also the management and supervision of this new form of construction to specialists. Nevertheless, the journals for architects continued to carry articles explaining the working of the steel-frame regulations and providing methods for the design of steel members.

It was not just changes in the design office that were needed; the contractor also had to devise new means for erecting steel frames. Building had suddenly ceased to be an incremental process: the frame dimensions established the dimensions of the construction that followed, so it was essential that the frame be plumb, the floors level and the dimensions correct. Later, in the 1930s, writers were to comment about the difficulties of 'creep' in the erection of large frames by which they meant the increasing dimensional errors that tended to occur in the erection of large frames. Jackson (1913), writing in the *RIBAJ*, recommended levelling the frame by erecting the steel as far as the first set of floor beams and then trueing the structure by wedging up the foundation grillage to bring these floor beams level, rather than by trying to plumb the columns which he said was a more difficult and less reliable method.

Jackson's article described the design of steel-frame buildings following the 1909 Act and was a combination of practical approaches to design and criticisms of some of the provisions of the Act. Both the article and the discussion which followed it provide some insight into the limitations of the Act and the opinion held of it in profession circles, while at the time it may have given some warning of the difficulties to come. His principal criticisms of the regulations were those governing the design of beams which produced some curious results. If the span/depth ratio was less than 24 then design was governed by the allowable stress of 7.5 T/sq. in. Above that ratio, the deflection was limited to l/400. The result was that beams only just within the 24 limit might have very large deflections. He was also critical of the regulations governing the coupling of twin beams which required top flange stiffening when the span/flange width was greater than 30 (Jackson, 1913, p. 415).

It was not just the provisions of the Act that incurred Jackson's displeasure. He was also critical of some commonly used details and noted 'It is not uncommon to find the webs of plate girders kept ⅛ to ¼" short of the backs of the main angles' (Jackson, 1913, p. 417). It must have made erection simpler to have the beams a little short but he regarded this as especially poor practice where only a single angle cleat was used to support the beam and recommended that angle cleats supporting beams be packed out with a piece of plate to bring the load of the beam down on to the stem of the angle, the standard detail later recommended by Cocking (1917) and illustrated in Redpath Brown's handbook (Fig. 4.7).

His discussion took in the design of concrete in floors and opined that the safety margin on reinforced concrete floors was likely to be less than that of the frame supporting them because of the brittle nature of concrete. (One wonders whether this reflected a general prejudice against reinforced concrete.) He suggested

Fig. 4.7

that filler joists should be continuous to reduce their depth and hence the weight of the floor, and he showed an economical system of lapped joists. Steel mesh was used in the top of the concrete to control cracking where it was in hogging over the beams. He deprecated the practice of hooking bars over the top flange of steel beams to obtain anchorage because of the difficulty of ensuring they were tight. In Jackson's opinion the cheapest construction was achieved by using simple rolled joists whenever possible. Pairs of rollings might be used for heavier loads although this created a problem when a beam formed in this way trimmed another beam. He recommended that in such cases one of the joists had to be made strong enough to carry the whole load of the beam so trimmed.

Some of his criticisms did not go unchallenged in the discussion that followed the presentation of his paper. The most interesting contribution came from Etchells. Referring to discussions about the mens for connecting twin girders, he compared different drafts of the regulations and pointed out a number of instances where the state of regulations was unsatisfactory because the original draft had been changed at the insistence of what he referred to as 'the opposition' (Jackson, 1913, p. 483). It is clear from this that the drafting of the Act had been the result of some compromises.

It is questionable how much effect the Steel Frame Act had in its first years. An article in *The Builder* even went so far as to call it a dead letter because little advantage had been taken of it, although, as this was only written in 1911, it hardly seems to have given the Act much of a chance to take effect.[11] The article suggested that the apparent lack of interest in frame buildings was because of possible delays in obtaining approval for designs because the surveyors needed time to check the calculations. The stresses allowed were also thought to be too low and the article noted that fire protection requirements are not always observed. The conclusion was drawn that steel frames were fine for the better class of buildings but for ordinary quality building it was cheaper to use brickwork.

Without the kind of changes made possible by the use of a steel frame which occurred in American architecture, that is, the opening-up of the elevation with large windows, 'mill' construction provided just as much advantage in planning as a complete steel-frame building. Unless the designer wanted some lightening of the outer wall the only advantage of using a frame was to speed construction. Freitag (1895) had shown how the frame might do this because it was no longer tied to the pace of the walls, and he described how a frame might be carried to the top floor and the cornice fixed before the wall beneath it was built. Later, Etchells (1927) was to illustrate much the same advantages for using steel frame in London. Once the frame had been erected as far as the roof beams, possibly over only a part of the complete plan, a crane could be built on top of this structure and used for the erection of the rest. Moreover, scaffolding for the masonry walls was simplified because it could be suspended from the steelwork. While the erection of a frame could speed the building process, this advantage might be lost if there were delays in obtaining approval of the design and this alone might account for the comments in *The Builder*. Delay in obtaining approval would have less effect in large buildings where the advantages in construction would be that much greater.

Inter-war steelwork

Although the 1909 Act finally enabled steel frame buildings to be constructed within the London area, it was far from perfect and the Act incurred criticisms from the very beginning. There were some discrepancies between its provisions and the ideas of practicing engineers and there were also ambiguities within it . As may be imagined, the method of employment of the district surveyors (see Chapter 1) led to differences in its interpretation by surveyors in different districts. Because of difficulties over the meaning of some of the requirements of the (1909) Act, a joint conference was held between RIBA, the District Surveyors Association and the Concrete Institute. This met in the early days of the First World War but its report was delayed until 1922 when it was issued by the chairman, F. R. Farrow, in the journal of the Concrete Institute. When it did appear the Joint Conference Report was seen to act as 'a useful relief from some of the most onerous provisions of the Act'.[12] Unfortunately, as details of the regulations for steel were contained within the Act itself, it was not possible to amend the regulations as they were found inadequate or as understanding of the behaviour of structures improved.

An example of the problems which occurred concerned the design stresses given for columns.

Columns within a building structure were clearly not fixed at both ends and yet, even if they were assumed to be so, the stresses allowed were rather low compared with those given by reliable formulae. Conditions were therefore established under which columns might be assumed to be fixed-ended for design purposes:

a) be continuous with joints near beam level,
b) have splice plates to flanges at joints $\frac{1}{2}$ in. thick,
c) be connected in the direction of the radius of gyration by a beam with cleats above and below $\frac{1}{2}$ in. or $\frac{1}{4}$ in. less than the rivet diameter with two $\frac{1}{4}$-in. rivets in each leg of the cleat.

Rules were also laid down for determining the area of rivets and eccentricity of the support reaction which was to be assumed, depending upon the detailing of the cleats. By taking a worked example from Cocking's textbook (1917a), Andrews (1922) showed how the new rules resulted in a reduction in the size of columns. The 1909 Act did make provision for the LCC to grant waivers from certain of its requirements, but because the clauses referred to had little effect upon the design of steelwork there had been few applications for such waivers. However, in 1923, the General Powers Act which followed the conference extended the power of waiver to all the clauses of the Act and a number of applications were then made.

Building form and structure

The Joint Conference Report contained a number of appendices dealing with practical design issues; one of these showed how to calculate the stresses in mansard roofs which was an important feature of building regulations in London. (Other appendices discussed the dimensions and stresses of rivets and the design of splice plates.) The London building regulations allowed two attic floors above the 80-ft.-high cornice of the building. It was common to frame these as mansards with dormer windows to obtain the maximum usable space within the regulations. To obtain this space, additional framing was needed which both formed a sloping (mansard) roof and supported the intermediate attic floor and the flat roof above. A simple way of doing this which was satisfactory for a single-storey attic was to stand columns on the beams at cornice level, set back from the eaves and under the ridge of the mansard. The mansard slope and dormer windows might then be formed in reinforced concrete. A better

MANSARD

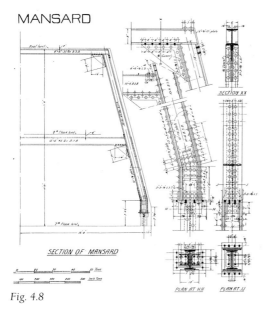

Fig. 4.8

arrangement, which could be used for two-storey attics, was to have the main steel framed to the shape of the mansard roof using sloping columns. In some cases these were brought down on to the main column line but the common alternative, where a parapet and concealed gutter were used, was to set them back so that they were carried by the beams forming the upper floor (Figs. 4.8 & 4.9). Although an attic floor seems to have been defined as one lit with dormer windows, Sullivan (1932, p. 605) pointed out that 'Nothing in the Act limits the length of a dormer' and produced

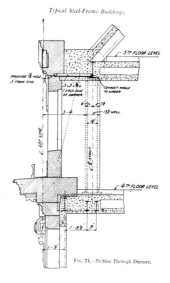

Fig. 4.9

analytical drawings to show how it worked. This observation paved the way for a change in the shape of attic floors, eliminating the sloping mansard.

Commercial buildings were given two quite different elevational treatments. Many architects continued to treat the external wall as if it were load bearing with windows set within a masonry wall. The alternative architectural treatment was to express the non-load-bearing nature of the wall by cladding only the columns in stone and using metal spandrel panels between the windows. If the window wall was then set back to line up with the back face of the columns it followed that the floor structure needed to be similarly set back to allow uninterrupted panels. In 1922, *Architect's Journal* provided details of an office building where it claimed that this form had been adopted to provide the maximum amount of light.[13] The elevation had glazing and metal panels between brick piers, with the exception of the first-floor level where there was a strong horizontal band of brickwork. At each floor, including the ground floor, the concrete slab was brought to a transverse beam set back behind the elevation. A second, lighter beam was set in the plane of the elevation at sill level to carry the glazing and between the two was a short sloping section of ceiling (except at first-floor level where a pair of beams were needed to carry the brickwork).

In the 1930s, architects began to adopt the style of the modern movement which required a horizontal rather than a vertical treatment of the elevation. Reports of the use of this style on the Continent had appeared in articles by Howard Robertson who wrote regularly for *Architect and Building News* and who emphasized this horizontality, particularly in his 1928 article on Dutch architecture. The desired elevational effect could be achieved by using contrasting colours in the spandrel panels between the windows of successive floors and between adjacent windows on the same floor. This might be done with contrasting brick colours or by continuous bands of rendered brickwork. A much simpler way of providing horizontal emphasis was to use concrete string courses above and below the windows. Adopting any of these devices presented no problems for the structure which could still be set within the plane of the wall, but a more dramatic effect was achieved with continuous bands of glazing, in which case the structure had to be set back. There was also a practical advantage in the use of set-back columns, which simplified the running of heating pipes, where radiators were used under windows, and so might have commended itself to commercial architects for that reason, but no doubt much of the pressure for this form of construction was an architectural fashion.

It might seem simplest to form cantilevers in concrete frames, but while to the modern eye many of the forms associated with this style of architecture may appear to lend themselves to the use of reinforced concrete, they may well have been constructed of steel. In his book on the modern house, Yorke (1937) showed how the desired appearance, the white box, could be obtained in steel or masonry as well as in concrete. The truth-to-materials tenet of the modern movement was not always followed in practice and the same was equally true of larger buildings. Marine Court, a block of flats on the seafront at Hastings, has semi-circular ends that suggest concrete, but it is a steel-frame building and the circular-shaped balconies of the Freemasons Hospital in west London, which also give the appearance of concrete construction, were in fact framed of steel (Bylander, 1932). There is no clear sense in which the form followed from the choice of material, or vice-versa; steel had established itself as the more common framing material and so it was used to produce these styles. A simple way of forming a cantilever in steel was to use double beams passing either side of the front row of columns. This arrangement was adopted in the Peter Jones Store, London in 1932 (Fig. 4.10), but more commonly the cantilever was formed by planting a section on to the column.

Improved detailing

There were some improvements in detailing during the inter-war period. Beam-to-column connections were commonly made by simple angle cleats top and bottom, although Crabtree (1933) pointed out that the weakness of the former was that they could easily deform under load and recommended using Ts cut from I sections to provide a more effective top-fixing where resistance to wind-loading was required. This kind of detail was illustrated by Goodesmith (1933) in the *Architectural Review*, suggesting that architects were still taking some interest in structural details. Riveting was the standard method of making connections but the 1932 Act allowed black bolts to be used for site connections. This had the effect of reducing the noise on construction sites, although riveting continued to be used for shop fabrication because the joints were more effective and cheaper. It should also be noted that very large fabrications were sometimes used.

Articles in journals and standard works on construction discussed the relationship between the masonry skin of the building and the supporting structural skeleton (Warland, 1928). Features such as cornices often required secondary structural steelwork for their support (Fig. 4.11) The main structural steel

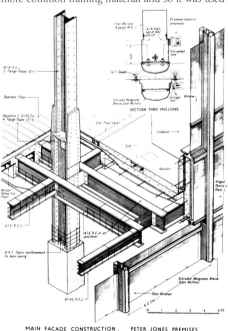

MAIN FAÇADE CONSTRUCTION . PETER JONES PREMISES

Fig. 4.10

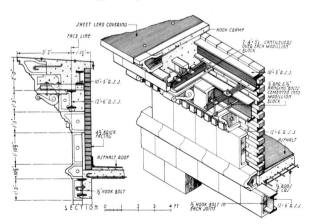

Fig. 4.11 TERRA-COTTA CORNICE

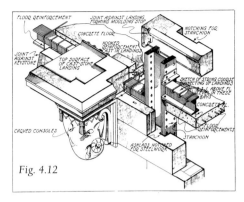

Fig. 4.12

could be treated in two ways: the steel members could be encased in concrete and the masonry added as a decorative covering to this, or the masonry could be cut to be fitted round the steelwork (Fig. 4.12). In the former the concrete provided protection to the steelwork against corrosion but in the latter, the degree of protection provided was as much a matter of workmanship as of specification. It was recommended that the steel be protected by grouting in the joint between the two materials but this would not have been an easy operation. Steelwork was naturally susceptible to corrosion unless protected and it was common practice to specify some protective treatment to exposed structural steel and specifications called for either a paint treatment or just a cement wash to be applied. A coat of Portland cement wash seems to have been the common form of protection used in Britain in the early years of the century,[14] and it is difficult to tell how long this practice persisted, even after protective paints came into use. RIW Protective Products Ltd made a Marine Cement Damp-proofing composition which was to be used with prepared felt paper, burlap or other, and could be used to protect the outer surface of spandrel beams when used in conjunction with solid walls.[15]

The common form of fire protection in this country was to case the steel in concrete, but this could also be a source of corrosion problems because of the use of coke breeze as an aggregate. It eventually became apparent that the sulphur content of the coke breeze caused corrosion of the steel (Brady, 1930). Even internal steelwork was at risk because the breeze tended to absorb water from the atmosphere and, although Bylander set an early date for the change from breeze to stone aggregates, it seems to have continued to be a problem long after the harmful effects were noted.

The crisis in steel design

While the LCC General Powers Act continued to govern steel construction throughout the 1920s the regulations were still regarded as rather restrictive by practicing engineers. At the simplest level the design loads that were to be used were too high. This was pointed out by J. F. Baker who, having visited the US, reported on the regulations there and consequently recommended a reduction of floor loads in Britain (DSIR, 1931, Table 3, p. 18). Work had been carried out in the US to assess the actual loads on floors and, while office floor loading was 100 lbs per sq. ft. in London, the load being recommended in the US was only 50 lbs per sq. ft. Given this difference, a proposal for a reduction to 80 lbs per sq. ft. in London seems very modest.

Regrettably, the London Building Act of 1930 did not make any major changes in the design rules but simply consolidated previous Acts and amendments. Reliance was still being placed on waivers to enable design to take account of advances being made but this placed the designers in a difficult position since they would not know in advance whether or not a waiver would be granted. Following a petition organized by Lord Ebury, the LCC set up an advisory committee in 1931 to consider the 1930 Act. This committee issued a code of practice for steel and other materials for buildings which was published in 1932 as the rules by which the authority might grant waivers.[16] This placed the LCC in the curious position of publishing a manual on how to avoid the provisions of the Act which it was itself administering. But this tinkering with the rules would not do, as the pressure for a reduction in the design loads for floor made only too clear. Such pressure for change was natural because it was the simplest way in which savings in steel structures could be made, but those concerned with the regulations were aware that, because the design loads were only one part of an interdependent system of assumptions and working practices, change could hardly be made in this piecemeal fashion. Taken together they had provided safe, although possibly rather inefficient, designs. The critical problem was that the overall assumptions on which design, and design regulations, were based were, in effect, irrational and a complete radical revision of the whole system was required.

Assumptions used in steel-frame design were mutually contradictory. In order to simplify the design of beams they were assumed to be simply-supported at the columns, that is, any degree of fixity provided by the connections was ignored. Moments applied to columns from the beams were simply taken to be the product of the supporting reaction and its assumed eccentricity at the connection. Of course, if a frame did behave in this way it would have no resistance to wind loading; to provide this resistance, designers had to assume that the connections were rigid. It is questionable whether wind-load calculations were routinely carried out. The only references to wind-load stresses by Cocking (1917) are to those on roof frames and his model calculations for a five-storey warehouse contain no reference to wind loading. The Steel Frame Act allowed a 25 per cent increase in the permitted stresses due to wind loads and for the modest heights allowed this would have hardly have required much steel to carry wind-induced moments.

During the early development of steel frame building in the US it had been assumed that no special provision need be provided to resist wind loading and that stability of the frame would be ensured by internal masonry walls. It was only the experience of the effect of high winds that demonstrated that some form of bracing was required and several types were described by Freitag. However, no assumption of the stiffening effect of walls could be made under the 1909 Act which required the frame alone to carry the applied loads.

It was also assumed that the greatest stresses occurred with the full loading on the frame which might not always be the case. Greater bending is produced in a column when the live load is applied to the beam on one side only and particularly when alternate sides are loaded on alternate floors so that columns were likely to be under-designed.

In 1929, the DSIR established the Steel Structures Research Committee (SSRC) as a response to the general dissatisfaction with the regulations. This committee was given the task of finding a more rational approach to the design of steel structures which might form the basis for revised regulations. The British Steel Association provided some funding for a period of five years and the work was carried out under the direction of Stradling at the BRS. The committee divided its work into a number of divisions. The first, under B.L. Hurst, looked at the codes of practice in a number of other countries and was the first official acknowledgement that the LCC regulations were out of step with those

elsewhere, where design loads were generally lower. But the most important divisions were those involving experimental work. If the new design rules were to bear some relation to reality, some investigation was needed of the true behaviour of structures under load and this was investigated in several ways.

A three-storey test frame which could be subjected to a variety of loads was built at the BRS and the resulting bending moments in the members assessed from strain gauges attached to them. The committee was also fortunate enough to be able to monitor the behaviour of actual buildings by attaching strain gauges to their frames. The first of these was the extension to the Geological Museum in South Kensington which was then under construction. The advantage of using such a frame was that it enabled its behaviour to be measured both before and after the protective fire casing was added so enabling some assessment to made of the stiffening effect provided. The disadvantage of using this particular structure, however, was that its casing was much heavier than that normally used in either domestic or office structures. The committee then monitored two other buildings — an hotel and an office block being erected by the Dorman Long Company — which provided examples of different stiffnesses of floors and which had column casings of more usual construction.

These experiments were not only sufficient to show the fallacy of the design assumptions but also that they resulted in some disturbingly unrealistic stresses. As the design method for vertical loads assumed that the beams were simply supported, the designer had to select an appropriate eccentricity for this load as applied to the columns, which depended upon the detailing of the supporting cleats. The eccentricity for flange cleats, for example, would be half the depth of the column section plus an allowance for the cleat. Web cleats would produce a much smaller eccentricity which might be as little as two inches. By ignoring the moment that was transmitted to the column by the connection, this method seriously underestimated the stresses on the columns. At the same time, the beams were being designed for larger moments than those actually occurring in practice. In reporting the results of the experiments on the structure of the Geological Museum, Oscar Faber (1933) reduced the moments which the beams transmitted to the columns to an equivalent eccentricity for a pin-ended support. The effect was that the effective eccentricity of beams needed to be much larger than the size of the supporting cleats to produce the moments measured in the experimental structures. While the cleat size might suggest an eccentricity of two inches, the moments generated by the fixity required the equivalent eccentricity to be nine inches..Today, this use of an equivalent eccentricity probably seems like a curious way of looking at the behaviour of the structure but at the time it was a way of fitting the actual behaviour of structures into the existing conceptual framework. It was the way of looking at the structures that needed to be changed.

The behaviour of bare frames was naturally affected by the addition of concrete floors and fire casing. The floors and the fire casing of the beams must increase their stiffness and so reduce the moments in the columns. While the casing of columns increased their stiffness, and thus the moments which were developed in them, the effect on the stress in the steel was shown to depend upon the nature of the casing. Heavy casings which increased the effective section of the column might result in a reduction of stress while light casings increased column stresses. But just as casing affected the moments so did the design of the fixings. Moments in columns due to concentrated loads were reduced because of the floor slab's continuity but at the same time the opposite effect was produced by the casing round the connections which increases their stiffness.

Column-to-beam connections were neither pinned nor fully fixed and if a rational method of design were to be produced, some account had to be taken of their actual behaviour. Therefore, experiments on the behaviour of connections was carried out at Birmingham University by Professor Batho in parallel with the tests on full-scale structures. The relative stiffness of different assemblies was measured and tests were also carried out to determine the effects of workmanship so that the results could be used in design. Comparison was also made of the behaviour of riveted and bolted connections. The experiments showed that the behaviour of connections was complex. They were not elastic but, although some yielding of the fasteners occurred, the loads to failure were far greater than those they were called upon to carry in practice. It was unreasonable to treat columns as pin-ended because they were continuous at each floor level with some restraint provided by the beams. The design problem was therefore to assess the degree

of restraint provided by the construction and thus the effective length of the column.

While the experimental work allowed a much fuller understanding of the behaviour of steel structures, the difficulty lay in translating this into an acceptable design method. Baker suggested alternative methods of analysis that were possible. In a lecture to students (Baker, 1932) he drew attention to the then recent work of Hardy Cross (1932) and suggested that moment distribution might be used for the analysis of frames. This would not have described the behaviour of steel structures because it had long been recognized that the connections in the frame could not be considered as rigid. Some slip occurred as loads were applied and a method of design which represented the true behaviour of the structure would need to take account of this. Baker devised an ingenious method of model analysis in which connections represented the slip that occurred in real connections and which gave results close to the actual behaviour of the structures, but it was hardly the kind of method that would recommend itself to practicing engineers. Although the required models could be made fairly simply, the method of measurement involved the use of instruments that were more appropriate to the laboratory than the drawing office. Its principal value was the use made of it in the analysis of the experimental frame at the BRS.

The report of the committee (DSIR, 1936), having demonstrated how irrational existing methods were, and that they led to unreal stresses, proposed alternative methods of design to take account of the findings. Unfortunately these led to more complex calculations without any noticeable improvement in the economy of steelwork. Neither were the methods now proposed completely rational. Objections to the SSRC's recommendations are probably best summed up by comments made when J. F. Baker (1935—6) reported on his work to the Institution of Civil Engineers. In the discussion of Baker's paper, M. B. Boxton was concerned that the method of calculation proposed by the committee would be too complicated for the 'ordinary engineer employed in the industry' and wanted to know if Baker could offer a method that was less complicated (pp. 215—16). At the same time he noted that there was no allowance for the contribution made to the strength of columns by the concrete casing and suggested that some increase in the allowable stress might be made to take account of this. Even a modest contribution of the concrete was not to be recognized in regulations until 1948.

Manning's objections were rather more fundamental (Baker, 1935—6, pp. 216—20). He pointed out that dimensional changes in the structure could be caused by such factors as settlement of the foundations or differential temperatures within the building and that the effect of these would be to introduce significant moments into the frame which were not taken into account in the design method which was being proposed. Indeed, the committee's own work on the experimental structures had shown how this could occur when unexpected stresses near the foot of a stanchion were traced to inadequate tightening of the holding-down bolts and poor seating. Manning was also concerned that the stresses to which designers were working were still within the elastic range of the material and so less than half of the total available range if the ultimate stress were taken as the basis for design. What he was looking for was a method of design based on the ultimate load which the structure might carry. In asking for a method which represented the behaviour of the structure at this ultimate load he was anticipating Baker's later work on load-factor design.

Bowley commented that the result of the objections to the SSRC's proposals was that, rather than producing a new and rational approach to design, the structural principles of the ancient Greeks continued to govern the design of steel structures until 1948. Perhaps so, but it was an understandable position. Designers need a method which will ensure the safety of a structure, which provides a reasonable level of economy and which is not expensive in design time. For all its irrationality the method which they were using provided this already. While reinforced concrete designers were forced into using much more sophisticated methods of design by the nature of their material, there was no pressing need for steel designers to follow suit. Is not this a likely explanation for the popularity of the material among engineers?

Welding

When the SSRC was formed, welding was in its infancy for building structures but there was representation from one firm, who offered some financial support for work to be done in this area. The committee

approached other firms with an interest in this subject for additional support enabling some work to be carried out. The Welding Panel was formed in 1930 and the intention was to have a series of tests carried out at the NPL from which statistical data could be obtained. Unfortunately there was some delay in this because of disagreements over the testing method to be used and the work was not started until 1934 with results obtained too late for the main SSRC report in 1936. The welding panel eventually reported separately in 1938 (DSIR, 1938), although a British Standard had appeared in 1934[17] and welding had already been used in building structures before that date, both in small elements of the structure and for complete buildings.

At its simplest level, welding may simply be seen as a substitute for riveting or bolting, that is, the designer may use much the same structural forms, simply changing the method of making connections. Under these circumstances there is little advantage in welding over riveting. Although some early examples of welded construction used the technique to its best advantage it seems that other engineers were slow to adapt and the approach which simply substituted welding for riveting was slow to die out. Hajnal-Konyi (1945) complained about this and showed comparative connections, one treated as a welded version of a riveted joint, with the other designed for welding. He pointed out that there is little saving of metal unless the joint is designed from the start to be welded. Welding eliminates gusset plates and both the angles needed to connect sections together and the complex riveting patterns associated with them are avoided. In this way welding can be used in the controlled conditions of the fabricating shop to simplify the design and construction of heavy plate-girders and trusses.

Greater advantage could be taken of welding if it was seen as a completely new approach to the design of structures. Welding could allow the designer to adopt forms less easy to construct by riveting because high bending moments occur at the junctions, the obvious examples being the portal frame and the Vierendeel girder. It could also be used in the construction of light frames, making them even lighter by allowing the designer to form sections that could not be achieved by rolling. Before the availability of rolled hollow sections, pairs of angles could be welded together to produce a light box section or they could be connected together

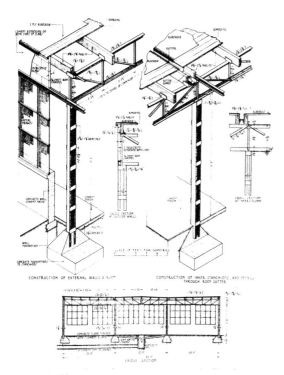

Fig. 4.13

European shoe company, based in Czechoslovakia, and the factory was an exact copy of their works at Zlin where their engineers claimed an 11 per cent saving in steel by using welding. Columns, built up from pairs of channels connected by small plates were supported on lattice girders built up from Ts and angles.

Felix Samuely and Partners, the engineers for Simpson's store and the De la Warr Pavilion (see below), published a number of articles on the topic in 1935 (Helsby et al., 1935a, b). Much of this work was concerned with the welding of large sections but they also had some early experience with light steel-welded structures and in 1937 designed a factory for Steel Ceilings Ltd (Samuely, 1937). This factory's roof structure was formed from Lewis dovetail sheeting which the company made, with the sheets welded together to form three-pin tied-arch trusses. The dovetail sheeting was a cold rolled $1/16$-in. metal section and the roof was supported internally on $1/8$-in. box section columns. This was a sufficiently novel design for it to be one of the few building structures in the journal *Engineering*.

by small steel plates to form an open box section, in either case being lighter than an equivalent I section. Not many engineers used this method but it came into its own where light frame construction was required. Welded frames of this kind were suggested for school buildings in the 1930s, buildings which were exempt from local authority by-laws and so where experimental structures could be more easily used.[18]

These schools were single-storey buildings; the other common single-storey structure where welding was used was the factory frame. Matrix Welding Process Ltd put up an all-welded factory for themselves at their Ferry Lane Works, Walthamstow in 1932. *Building* noted at the time that it was possible for them to do this because of the sympathetic approach of the local building inspector.[19] Since welding was the company's business, this can only be seen as an early experiment. In the following year the Bata Shoe Company put up an all-welded factory at East Tilbury (Fig. 4.13). Again *Building* commented on the foresight of the district surveyor in allowing welding to be used.[20] This building was an example of a manufacturing company importing a building technology with which they were familiar in their home country. Bata was the largest

Fig. 4.14

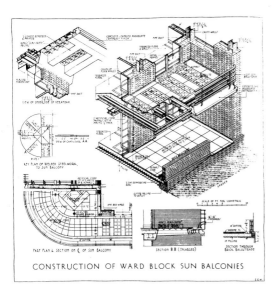

Fig. 4.15

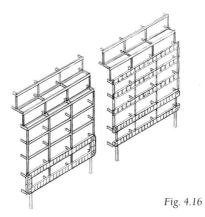

Fig. 4.16

Bylander was an early enthusiast for welding and demonstrated its possibilities in the structure of the balconies for the Freemasons Hospital in west London. This was an example of a structure which would have been difficult, if not impossible, to achieve without welding and he described (1932—3) the design of this structure in some detail. Superficially the balconies appear as if they might be of concrete construction (Fig. 4.14) but the construction details show that this was formed by a welded steel frame (Fig. 4.15). (For a detailed description of this steelwork see Bylander, 1932—3.) More ambitious were Felix Samuely's designs for large building frames. Welding offered the possibility of using radically different structures in buildings and a small-scale example of this was seen in a welded Vierendeel girder bridge used to connect two buildings at the Building Centre, New Bond St. Welding facilitated the use of this type of structure because high bending moments are produced at the connections. A Vierendeel girder was also used in the construction of the RIBA building which was completed in 1934.21 Welding might have resulted in a novel structure for Simpson's store in Piccadilly (1935) which, but for the objections of the LCC surveyors, might well have gained a reputation as a significant early all-welded steel frame. The intention was to bring all the columns on the front elevation down on to a pair of girders above the shop window at first- and second-floor levels. Sufficient strength was to be provided by connecting

these girders together at their ends so that they acted together. Unfortunately the design was objected to by the LCC and instead they required a much less efficient structure with girders to carry each floor load separately (Fig. 4.16). This involved a late change in design and as the fabricating company did not have the welding capacity to produce these girders at short notice, they had to be riveted while the remainder of the structure was welded.

The De La Warr Pavilion (1936) has been credited with being the first steel frame building in Britain (White, 1966) although, as we have seen, this reputation is undeserved because of the all-welded factories built earlier. Perhaps it is simply that, according to Pevsner's criteria, it is the first all-welded work of 'architecture'. The building has been described in some detail (White, 1965) while at the time of its construction it was regarded as sufficiently novel to warrant several articles in *The Welder* and *The Builder* (see White, 1966). It was not originally designed to be a steel frame but was an example of steel being used as a substitute material for reinforced concrete, which was the material intended by the architect. The planning of the building meant that it was not possible to support the roof from columns and in the event it was decided to hang the second-floor beams from plate girders at roof level. These plate girders were made up by welding with hangers welded to their webs and passing through their lower flanges. In addition to this, the channel sections used to form the curved front of the restaurant balconies had to be stiffened by welding on plates in order to resist the torsional moments. Box-section columns were made up by welding and the welded frames of the auditorium allowed Vierendeel girders to be created over the ground-floor doors and windows. This innovative structure was needed as a result of the architect's failure to work within the limitations of his chosen material and was the kind of construction that would have been far more difficult with riveted assembly.

Samuely, whose firm was responsible for this design, had already produced the first volume of a text on building construction (Samuely & Hamman, 1939) and it was their intention to produce a subsequent book on welded structures. The manuscript for this was prepared but it seems as if the intervention of the war prevented its publication.[22] In the immediate post-war years, Samuely was to deal with welded structures in a series of articles for the *Municipal Journal* which discussed the official Steel Bulletin and considered the economies which could be made in structural materials.

The Second World War and after

Efforts in the 1930s may have been directed towards the improved design of steel structures but the changes which took place in the post-war period owed far more to improvements in production methods and developments in methods of fabrication. During the war, the allowable stresses for steel had been raised and the shortage of steel both during the war and afterwards naturally encouraged methods which would reduce the quantities of steel used. Thus, it has been welding, in combination with developments which were able to make use of this technique, that have had the greatest influence on the use of steel, but not so much on the design of multi-storey frames. In spite of the pre-war interest in welding, and the eventual appearance of Baker's load-factor methods of design, which would have facilitated the design of all-welded steel frames, the conditions of a normal building site and the need for weld inspection hardly encouraged its use as the normal method for such frames. Instead it became a method used mainly for shop-fabricated structures, proprietary building components and light-weight frames.

Beams

Of the various methods suggested by Creasy (1949) for achieving economies in the use of steel, one of the simplest for engineers to adopt was the use of castellated beams. This form of structure had already been referred to by K. Hajnal-Konyi (1945) when it was called the 'Boyd Beam'.[23] For most of the span the web of a steel beam is doing little more than holding the flanges apart

and much lighter sections can be achieved by removing some of this metal. The same effect was achieved by making a zig-zag cut through the web, moving the two halves of the beam apart and along by 'half a wavelength' and then welding them back together again. The resulting beams, being deeper, were stronger in bending than the sections from which they had been cut and some compensation could be made for the resulting weakness in shear by welding pieces into the holes in the webs where they were needed near the supports. These beams quickly became a standard building component, particularly for such applications as roof beams where there were long spans and light loadings and where they were an alternative to the lattice trusses which had also been developed.

Lattice trusses depended upon a combination of cold-rolled sections and welding for their fabrication. Spans and loads were limited as the production method depended upon the use of small sections but they were ideal for supporting flat roofs of low-rise buildings and quickly came into use for the construction of schools where they were commonly combined with light-weight prefabricated roofing components, such as wood-wool slabs. Often such trusses were left exposed with the underside of the slabs above simply painted, but the incorporation of timber fillets into the top and bottom chords enabled ceilings to be nailed to them where required.

Welding was to make obsolete the single-storey shed, built of angle and gusset-plated trusses standing on I-section columns, through the adoption of two different types of construction. The first was the welded portal frame. Work had been carried out on this structural form during the war years, with both experimental work on the behaviour of the welded knee joints and publications on the analysis of such frame (Wallace, 1941; Gray, 1950; Hendry, 1950). The advantage that they offered was not just a simpler frame but also improved space within the building and when BCSA produced a publication on welding in 1960 it was concerned entirely with the design of this type of structure.[24] Its simplicity also enabled it to be marketed in the form of standard prefabricated buildings which were in direct competition with the precast concrete portal frames which had developed at much the same time. While the roofing was at first commonly of asbestos sheeting, the fragility of this material hardly recommended itself as a wall cladding and such frames were commonly clad in brickwork. Today, profiled steel has replaced both asbestos sheet roofing and the brickwork walling and cold-rolled sections are used for both purlins and sheeting rails instead of hot-rolled angle sections.

The development of these cold-rolled sections as purlins has led to a change in design methods, which in turn has necessitated a new approach to load assessment. Safety has been built into structural design both by ensuring that the design loads are higher than the working loads and by providing a margin of safety in the ability of the structure to carry the design load. The overall safety of the structure thus depended upon two independently applied factors: the margin of safety in the assessment of load and that in the assessment of the strength of the structure. The development of new structural forms, particularly the introduction of thin-walled cold-rolled sections has made the calculation of the failure loads more difficult. Their behaviour is more complex than hot-rolled sections and because the prediction of their performance by calculation has been more difficult, design has returned to the methods used in the nineteenth century with performance determined by proof-loading rather than by computation. However, such testing is now carried out by the manufacturers of the components who provide designers with safe-load tables. The result is that the failure load can be predicted more accurately by this method with the paradoxical result that safety margins have been correspondingly reduced. This has resulted in failures in cases where the roof design load was set too low (Pidgeon et al., 1986) and stimulated a better understanding of the behaviour of snow on structures. It has recently been realized that the behaviour of snow on complex roof forms is more complicated than had been assumed and that some allowance must be made for drifting. The use of light-weight claddings more susceptible to wind loading has also called for improved understanding of local wind effects.

The other change has been brought about by the availability of tubular sections which can be welded together. A tube provides better resistance to compressive forces than an angle or I-section of equal weight and so offers the opportunity to make savings in the weight of steel used in roof trusses. Thus while the portal took over from the truss in the design of pitched roof sheds, welded tubular steel trusses made the single-storey flat-roofed shed a structural possibility.

Developments in frames

There was no universal rolling mill in Britain until the end of the 1950s. Mills in which the steel is passed between pairs of parallel rollers are limited in the size and shape of the sections which they can roll, and to produce broad flange beams requires additional rollers at right angles to these. A rolling process to do just this was invented by Grey who built a 4-roll mill at Differdange, Luxemburg in 1902. This rolled sections up to 1m x 300 mm., which was large for the time, and it was from this mill that broad flange beams were first imported into this country. This mill was rebuilt in 1912 and again in 1930. Another mill was built in Germany and five in the US giving in total seven mills of this type by the early 1930s. It was not until the late 1950s that Dorman Long built a mill using the Grey process at their Lackenby steelworks in Britain (Barlow & Foster, 1957), which was the first since the last mill had been built in 1930 in the US. The design was based on the American range of sizes, rolling sections from 6 x 6 in. to 36 x 16$\frac{1}{2}$ in. A feature of this kind of mill was not simply that the width of the flanges could be increased but also that the taper on them could be reduced, in this case from 8° to 2°52' with a consequent improvement in the efficiency of the section. The new mill also included a splitting facility to produce structural T-sections and this opened up the possibility of welding plates between the T-sections to form deep beams ('Autofab' beams intended for bridge work rather than for buildings) and also the possible use of the T-sections to form lattice girders.

Steel fabrication was improved by the use of high-tensile steel bolts. A US specification for high tensile steel bolts was published in 1951 and they came on to the UK market in the mid-1950s.[25] Their use was discussed by Lewis (1957) and a British Standard (BS 3139) was published in 1959. A brief discussion of the action of connections is necessary to understand the importance of these. A simple model of a bolted or riveted joint between two pieces of metal simply assumes that the connector is loaded in shear. According to this model, joint capacity can be determined by calculating the shear load on all the fasteners and the bearing loads between them and the components being joined. However, a hot-driven rivet shrinks as it cools and clamps the pieces together producing friction forces between the components which contributes to the strength of the joint. For this reason, a riveted joint's capacity is greater than that of a simple bolted joint. High-tensile bolts now provided the clamping force of rivets while having the advantages of bolts for site fabrication.

To be effective these bolts clearly need to be tightened to their correct load and this presented problems of quality control. They could be tightened by a load-indicating spanner, but how was the engineer to be confident that this had been done correctly? The solution came in the form of a number of load-indicating devices which were part of the bolt itself, or at least part of the assembly. Projections from under the head of the bolt or on the washers could be designed to be squeezed flat when the bolt had reached its correct load so that the problem of inspection was reduced to ensuring that this had been done. Of course this did not prevent a larger load than necessary being applied (Jones & Baker, 1961). A rather more ingenious device was the Torshear bolt which made the application of the correct load automatic. The bolt was designed to be gripped at the shank while tightening and was made in such a way that this part sheared off as the correct load was reached.

There had been calls before the war for some allowance to be made in regulations for the stiffening effect of concrete casing on steel columns but the first concession within the code of practice only came in 1948 when, in BS 449 (Clause 18b) an allowance was made for an increase in the radius of gyration for the weak direction in cased I-sections. The effect of this was to increase the calculated stiffness in the design of columns but the advantage which it gave was small and it was still unrepresentative of the true behaviour of columns because the load still had to be assumed to be carried by the steel alone. Proposed amendments in 1955 were an improvement but Faber (1956) thought that these were not generous enough. A change to allow the concrete cladding of columns to carry load appeared in the 1959 revision of BS 449 and before long, steel handbooks were including the load capacities of cased columns in their safe-load tables. However, by this time a move towards lightweight methods of fire protection had already started.

Another change that occurred in this revision of the code was the recognition of the contribution which the floor structure might make to the stability of the top flange of the beam with the recognition that frictional resistance between the floor and the top flange

provided some lateral restraint to the beam. Load-sharing between the steel and the concrete was also possible in beam design. While the SSRC had examined the stiffening effect of floors on steel beams and the resulting affect on the distribution of moments between beams and columns, floors could only add stiffness if they also contributed to the load carrying. As a simply supported beam deflects and its top flange goes into compression so must the floor slab which it is supporting. The resulting stress distribution is not as simple as beam theory suggests for the beam acting alone. The neutral axis must be above the mid-point of the beam with compressive load shared between the top flange of the beam and the concrete slab. Recognition of this behaviour was only possible in design if engineers could be sure that the necessary horizontal shear forces would be generated between the top of the beam and the floor slab. This became possible with the introduction of shear connectors which were welded to the top of the beam. They were first introduced during the early 1960s with a Code of Practice (CP 117) published in 1965.

The adoption of this type of construction was facilitated by the use of Hollorib permanent shuttering, one of a number of steel-based floor systems that were being introduced (and discussed in Chapter 3). When the BCSA published the first edition of its booklet on floor systems for use with steel frames in 1964, most of the systems were precast concrete. This was still true of the later 1977 revision but by that time a number of steel systems had been introduced.

Fire protection

Even though the 1948 edition of Warland's book on construction was still illustrating precast concrete and hollow tile casings for beams and columns, the normal method of providing fire protection for structural steel during the pre-war period was to encase it in concrete. In 1940, after trials were carried out by the BRS and the Fire Offices Committee, *Building* reported the introduction of sprayed asbestos for fire protection, seen at the time as protection for both steel structures and concrete floors.[26] A stanchion was tested with a 2-in. covering of the asbestos, the same thickness as that required for concrete, and this was sufficient for it to give the two hours' protection required. What the journal wanted to know was how little of the material was needed to satisfy this requirement but such data was not available at the time.

The 1950s saw the development of sheet materials as fire cladding (Johnson, 1961), with Turners Asbestos publishing its manual Fire protection of structures in 1958. By the early 1960s other forms of lightweight fire protection were sufficiently common for them to be considered in the Structural Engineer (Makay, 1960). Development was rapid because a BCSA booklet published in 1961 needed revision in 1963 to accommodate the developments that had occurred. The adoption of these new methods of protecting steel had become sufficiently widespread that the Association of Structural Fire Protection Contractors and Manufacturers was formed in 1975.

There were several methods then in use. Briefly these might be divided into preformed casings and those applied in situ. The preformed casings might be shaped to fit round the steel sections or be simple flat components held in place by clips which were part of the system. The materials used for this were plasterboard, mineral fibre board and, in some cases, a lined sheet-metal casing. Those which were formed in place were either placed on to some form of metal lathing or sprayed directly onto the steel. Vermiculite plaster was used on metal lathing while asbestos or intumescent coatings went on to the steel directly. The great advantage of all of these systems was not simply that they were lightweight but the effect that their use had on the building process by dispensing with the need for concrete shuttering. However, the in situ systems and in particular the use of sprayed asbestos did raise questions of quality control.

Notes

1 *Architectural Record*, 76 (1931), pp. 116—7.
2 *Architect's Standard Catalogue*, 1914—17.
3 *AJ*, 66 (1927), p. 52.
4 This was given in the *Engineers Handbook*, Waverley Book Co. as P = f/{1+m/nq(l/d)2}, where m = 1 for a pin-ended column, n = 0.75 for a solid cylinder, q = 3750 for mild steel, l & d are measured in inches.
5 *AJ*, 61 (1925), p. 584.
6 *Specification*, 7 (1904), p. 308.
7 *Specification*, 1 (1898), pp. 126—32.
8 'New type of floor construction', *Concrete*, 19 (1924), p. 124.
9 'Kirkaldy on Compound Girders', *The Builder* , March 1866, pp. 147—8. Kirkaldy reports a test on Mssrs Philips patent girders which were 8 in. deep and had 2.5-in. flanges.
10 *AJ*, 19 (1904), p. 153 ff.
11 'The prospects of the steel frame building' *The Builder*, (1911), p. 648.
12 'Steel frame buildings — an explanatory note upon the Joint Committee's report', *AJ*, 56 (1922), p. 875. This explanatory note was available from RIBA.
13 'Architects Working Drawings, Messrs Hamly's Premises, 27—8 Kingley St (Regents St.)' *AJ*, 55 (1922), pp. 508—9.
14 In 1905 a note in *The Builder*, 89, p. 695—6, discussed the merits of this form of protection citing the opinion of E. O. Sachs.
15 See 'Spandrel beam damp-proofing', AJ Library of Planned Information No. 363, 4 June 1936.
16 'Code of practice for the use of structural steel and other materials in buildings', London Building Act 1930, London 1932
17 BS 538: 1934, Metal arc welding in mild steel as applied to general building construction. Replaced by BS 1856: 1952.
18 'Construction Details No. 34', *Building*, 8 (1933), p. 213.
19 'An all-welded building', *Building*, 7 (1932), pp. 368—71.
20 'The Bata shoe factory, constructional details of an economical welded steel building', *Building*, 8 (1933), pp. 216—18.
21 'The RIBA New Building — XI The structure', *RIBAJ*, 42 (1934), pp 73—7.
22 Samuely Archives, Felix Samuely and Partners, London.
23 See also AJ Library of Planned Information, Sheet 837. Sheets 826—94 refer to structural steelwork.
24 *The use of welding in steel building structures*, BCSA Black Book 14 (1960).
25 See 'High tensile bolts in structural steelwork', AJ, 122 (1955), p. 29 and High *strength friction grip bolts* , BCSA Black Book, No. 26 (1965).
26 'New Materials Sprayed "limpet asbestos"', *Building*, 15 (1940), pp. 23—4.

5 Reinforced concrete

Origins

Reinforced concrete is a product of the closing decades of the nineteenth century: a number of scattered experiments in both Europe and North America which attempted to combine steel and concrete in a number of ways, not all of which we would recognize today as reinforced concrete. The use of iron or steel to provide some tensile strength and so enabling concrete to be used to make a beam or a floor slab was a simple enough idea, and one that had occurred to a number of people, but the exact form which this metal reinforcing might take was the essence of any invention. It was not enough just to embed steel bars into the wet mass of concrete before it hardened. If the bars were to resist the tensile forces they had to be placed correctly and adequately bonded to the concrete. While bars clearly need to be placed in the bottom of beams and slabs to resist bending stresses, less obviously, substantial tensile forces are developed by the shear which occurs near the ends of beams and unless some reinforcement is provided to resist these forces a beam will simply break off at its supports. How much the behaviour of reinforced concrete was actually understood by the inventors is a moot point given the variety of different forms that were put on to the market.

Not all the tensile steel in the various patents taken out for the different reinforcing methods took the form of simple round bars, and there were equally many different ideas for providing shear reinforcement. Inventors also differed in the extent of their ambitions: some limited themselves to the relatively simple problem of designing reinforced concrete floors, while others took the more general problem of designing reinforcement for beams and columns and so provided the basis for the design and construction of complete frames. By the end of the nineteenth century, a number of companies were promoting various patent systems, and whether for complete frames or just for floors or roofs, they may be just as important to the history and development

of the material. The attraction of concrete was its fire-resisting properties, and while reinforced concrete shared this advantage with the filler-joist floor which relied on small rolled joists to provide the structure (see Chapter 3), combining the concrete with some form of bar reinforcement reduced the quantity of steel that was needed. It also enabled lighter floors to be formed using hollow tiles. Much of this early development has been ignored by historians whose interest has been principally in the development of the concrete frame (see Saint. 1991) so that many of the early systems have failed to attract the attention commensurate with their importance at the time simply because they were designed as flooring systems.

Reinforced concrete was already widely used for building floors before the formal acceptance of concrete frame construction was established by the publication of regulations governing its use in 1915. Reinforced concrete floors were used in some load-bearing masonry buildings and many articles in early issues of *Concrete* report the use of reinforced concrete floors with steel frames. The alternatives to the poured in situ reinforced concrete floor were the various forms of prefabricated flooring, based on precast concrete or terracotta, which had been developed as fireproof flooring systems originally for fireproofing steel. Three different kinds of firms may be distinguished in the early years. There were some firms who were essentially in the fireproof flooring business and who developed a form of reinforced concrete as an alternative to their other products. Homan & Rogers is an obvious example who, while having a patent bar system for floor slabs, showed no interest in the design of beams and columns. Specialist reinforced concrete companies restricted themselves to floors and had patented bar designs especially for that purpose, including those firms specializing in the production of mesh or fabric reinforcement. There were also firms whose interest was in the complete reinforced concrete frame.

Indeed, in some cases, their systems seemed ill-adapted to floor construction. Thus, to some extent, floor-construction systems have to be seen as a separate development from that of the reinforced concrete frame. It was certainly seen in this way at the time because *Specification* placed a number of reinforced concrete systems in the category 'Fireproof Constructor' rather than 'Concretor'. As a result, in spite of the comments made above about the importance of reinforced concrete floors in the history of this form of construction, it is convenient to discuss the systems which were developed by those firms which only made reinforcing for floors quite separately from the beam-and-column systems, although the two cannot be completely disentangled.

The evolution of the steel frame appears, in hindsight, as a fairly natural progression. The cast-iron beam replaced timber beams to create the fireproof mill at the turn of the nineteenth century, wrought iron was seen to be more reliable than cast iron, leading to the use of rollings and fabricated girders in the second half of the century, with steel a natural successor to wrought iron. Moreover, the frame evolved alongside this development in material technology so that the steel frame appears as an accumulation of simple improvements which were generally understood and widely adopted. Steel is little more than a framing material while the property of concrete, so often commented on for its architectural possibilities, means that it can take many different forms and be used in many different ways. Architectural historians have been less concerned to recognize the variety of basic forms suited to reinforced concrete than they have the architectural shapes possible. Its importance has been that it could be used for floors, foundations and retaining walls which have all had an influence on building form. How, for example, would we have deep basement buildings if it were not for the reinforced-concrete wall?

As there were far more uses for reinforced concrete than the building frame, the firms involved in its use were carrying out a much wider range of work. Advertising brochures and books produced by various contractors show not only factory floors and foundation work in buildings which were otherwise of steel frame or masonry construction but also the wide range of civil engineering works which they carried out where reinforced concrete had become a substitute for masonry. Not only was the structure of the firms producing concrete buildings different from those producing steelwork, but also the development of many reinforcing systems, particularly the production of steel mesh, was designed as much for the civil engineering market as it was for frame buildings.

Another difference between steel and concrete which results from their different pattern of development is the way in which they were marketed. The essence of the iron and steel frame was simply the components from which it was assembled and the behaviour of these components was well understood by building designers. In contrast, reinforced concrete depended upon bringing together a number of different materials which could be formed in different ways. It involved much more complex on-site operations and in the early days of its use the behaviour of reinforced concrete was not as well understood as steel, particularly as it depended far more upon the particular form of the individual components and on the way in which they were put together.

In these circumstances there were a number of different ways in which the patentees of reinforced concrete systems might operate. One approach was to produce manufactured components, for example, floor systems, but of the *in situ* reinforced concrete systems there were also different approaches to their promotion. Either they were offered as complete systems, designed and constructed under the control of the patentee, or the building designer was offered a patented type of reinforcing bar with which he could design his own structure. The method favoured by Hennebique and used very successfully by Mouchel, his agent in Britain, was an example of the former. Contractors were licensed to use this system and, on winning jobs, would be technically responsible for the structural design, although this would in fact be carried out by Mouchel's engineers. This followed the system used in France where contractors had combined to form the Chambre Syndicale des Constructeurs en Ciment Armé de France (Hamilton, 1956, p. 7). There has been some suggestion that this was a way of ensuring a degree of secrecy over the method. Perhaps so — after all, there was hardly anything very special about the system of reinforcement. It would seem that once one knew how it was designed it would not be very difficult to design something very similar. The operating method was also a way of restricting rival companies because licensees were prohibited from using any other system of reinforced concrete. However, it had advantages for clients since they only had to deal with the contractors. Through this approach, the Hennebique system became one of the most successful in Britain and in providing this design service for contractors Mouchel built up a successful engineering design firm that has survived to this day.

The alternative approach used by another successful firm, the Trussed Concrete Steel Company, later to become Truscon, worked in a quite different way. Their product was the American Kahn trussed bar and, although they operated as a contracting firm using this system of reinforcement, profits were to be made by selling the bar to others as well as using it themselves and it was marketed for floor and beam construction. There was no secrecy behind this system: it was clearly in the interests of the firm to demonstrate to building designers how the bars were to be used and they therefore published a handbook on its use. It is worth noting that, although the basis for the company was a patent bar system for floors and beams, they became one of the more important reinforced concrete companies in the inter-war period.

Professional concerns

Manufacturers and contractors did not have the field entirely to themselves and it was not long before the architectural profession began to take notice of this form of construction. The British Fire Prevention Committee (BFPC) was concerned with the fire resistance of concrete and appointed a special committee on concrete aggregates in 1906. In the same year RIBA set up the Reinforced Concrete Committee which produced its first report in 1907.[1] Cusack (1986) has presented a good case for the motivation behind the establishment of this committee being the desire on the part of the profession to break the monopoly then enjoyed by the specialist contractors. One concern was the strategic implications of the foreign origins of construction methods, which encouraged the War Office to participate in this committee. The report of the committee encouraged by-laws to be altered to recognize reinforced concrete as a method of construction, but there was no immediate response to this request. In 1908, the Concrete Institute was formed on the basis that it was undesirable for reinforced concrete design to be limited to a variety of patent systems. The founding of this new professional body (later to become the Institution of Structural Engineers) was based on the need to understand and develop this form of construction which, unlike RIBA's committee, admitted contractors and patent holders to its membership. The Institution of Civil Engineers had stood aside from these concerns and did not establish its own committee until 1910.

Representatives of a number of other institutions — the District Surveyors' Institution, the Institute of Builders, the Municipal and County Engineers Association, the War Office, the Admiralty, London County Council, and the Concrete Institute.— were invited to collaborate with RIBA and the real importance of this Joint Committee, chaired by Sir Henry Tanner, was its second report in 1911. This was to become the basis for the standard guide to reinforced concrete design in Britain. When the 1909 London Building Act established the rules for steel design it had been felt that there was insufficient knowledge about the behaviour of reinforced concrete for rules to be laid down at that time. Provisions were therefore made in the Act for the LCC to establish regulations to govern construction in reinforced concrete and, in 1915, these were eventually published, largely based on the second report of the committee and they were then adopted by many other local authorities.

By this time there were a number of books available on reinforced concrete, Marsh (1904) and Twelvetrees (1907) being two of the earliest British authors. The latter published two companion books, one concentrating on the theory of reinforced concrete providing examples of calculations, while the other described a large number of buildings, both in Britain and abroad giving a detailed account of the construction process of many of them. Naturally, many of the books came from the US and although the material had been developed in Europe, with France being the origin of some of the systems marketed in Britain, the common language made American books on reinforced concrete the more popular. More important perhaps was the publication of *Concrete and Constructional Engineering (Concrete)*, under the editorship of E. O. Sachs, which provided a monthly forum for presenting developments in reinforced concrete technology and which produced practical articles on the design and detailing of reinforced concrete, E. S. Andrews, C. F. Marsh and Oscar Faber being the most frequent contributors.

The change from load-bearing to frame buildings naturally brought with it changes in working relationships, either between the architect and the contractors or between architects and consulting engineers. We have already seen how this affected steel design but, if anything, reinforced concrete created greater problems. It was not simply a question of responsibility for the design of the structure; reinforced concrete required a greater degree of supervision than a steel frame, so that the consulting engineer was to become more important in the design process. This was quickly recognized by Tanner (see below) but was to become significant in the inter-war period. Ideas for structural forms dependent upon the use of reinforced concrete were to be developed by engineers, a development that became of serious concern for the architectural profession when it seemed as if engineers might be taking over work which architects considered as theirs (see Cottam, 1986).

Reinforcing types

The different origins and the method by which the companies operated have already been discussed by Cusack (1986, 1987) particularly in relation to the development of the Hennebique company although the complete history of reinforced concrete has still to be written, involving as it does both the development of professionals' understanding of the technique and the struggle for survival by the different systems of construction that were offered. If any aspect of technological development resembles a Darwinian process, it is surely that of the early development of reinforcing systems. In the first years of the century there were very many systems with new ones being regularly invented. Marsh (1904), who wrote the first

English text on reinforced concrete, claimed that there were over 50 different systems by the time he was writing. But in 1907, *Concrete* described little more than a dozen as the principal systems being used and many of these do not seem to have enjoyed a particularly long life. All were to either die out or to be modified until the standard method which we use today — the construction of frames as cages of loose bars — became the universal method. Those that we know about are naturally those which were used for larger and therefore well-reported projects. Tracing this process of struggle for survival among the various competing companies lies outside our concerns here and it will be sufficient briefly to summarize the principal forms of reinforcement that were available. Reviews of the early experimental work in reinforced concrete have been provided by Hamilton (1956) and Collins (1959).

While there was no hindrance in the regulations to the construction of reinforced concrete floors, the LCC regulations governing the thickness of walls, which had inhibited the development of the steel frame, naturally inhibited the development of the reinforced concrete frame in the same way. It is quite understandable therefore that while flooring systems were developed in Britain, the first concrete-frame systems were to be imported into this country from abroad where there were no such regulations to restrict their use and there had been more freedom for this development to take place. Thus, the earliest reinforced concrete frame building in Britain were the product of French companies.

Weaver's Mill, Swansea was the first reinforced concrete building to be put up in Britain, and this used the French Hennebique system: beams were simply reinforced with round bars in the bottom of beams and with steel in the top of beams at supports, but there was no top steel towards the mid-span, unless the beam was to be designed as a doubly reinforced section. This meant that there was no steel to fix the top of the shear reinforcement, which simply comprised U-shaped pieces of hoop iron with their ends turned out slightly. The company claimed that as this reinforcement was vertical it was unlikely to be displaced during the ramming of the concrete that was necessary to ensure proper compaction. This may have been so, but these strips of steel were modified with a kink

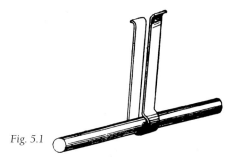

Fig. 5.1

formed in them (Fig. 5.1) to grip the main steel so that they were held in place better. It also meant a complex sequence of placing operations (see below). Where top steel was needed over the supports, the same arrangement of bars and steel strips was used but simply turned upside down with the flat shear steel suspended from the main bars. Column steel comprised simple round bars and links but the bars were much larger (up to 2 in. in diameter) than those commonly used today.

The Coignet system, another French patent introduced into Britain, had a quite different reinforcement arrangement not unlike today's arrangement of loose bars. Pairs of bars laid in the bottom of the beam were connected together by steel 'stirrups'. These bottom bars were wired to short horizontal pieces of steel to keep them apart. Coignet later (about 1907) modified this steel so that the bottom bars were bent up to form shear reinforcement. In this arrangement there was a concentration of main steel at the centre of the beam where bending moments were greatest. Each of the bars, having been carried to the top of the beam, was then simply hooked over a single top bar (Fig.5.2). Coignet's earliest buildings in Britain were tobacco warehouses near Bristol (1904) and warehouses at Rainham, Essex (1905).

Compression steel of various diameters was provided with the Considère system, with the intention of ensuring that the beams could be of uniform depth throughout. Some other systems accepted that, in order to reduce the amount of top steel, it was necessary to have haunches near the supports. Structures in the Hennebique system often

had the beams formed as shallow arches to provide this additional depth. Presumably the intention of the Considère system was to reduce shuttering costs. This system featured the use of spiral binders in columns, regarded with disdain by Hennebique, but which Considère had developed on the basis of considerable experimental work and had patented in Britain in 1902, though the system was not used here until 1907 (see Hamilton, 1956, p. 11). To accommodate these binders, columns in his system were either circular or octagonal in section. Spiral binders were also used by the British Reinforced Concrete Company (BRC) who claimed that the main feature of their reinforcement was that it was machine-made in their works, reducing the amount of site labour and improving accuracy.[2]

All of these systems used round bars but other shapes were also used. The most important of these was produced by the Indented Steel Bar Company, a square bar rolled with indentations as its name suggests and patented in 1904. It was claimed to be capable of higher working stresses than mild steel with the indentations providing additional bond. Another successful special rolling was produced by Wells whose reinforcement was formed as double bars joined by short cross-pieces to give a dumb-bell-like section.

One of the problems to be overcome by the designers of the various systems was to ensure that the bars were kept in place during the placing of the concrete, and for some it could not have been easy to ensure that shear reinforcement was held correctly in position. The Paragon bar was rolled with a projecting perforated rib intended to accept a wide variety of shear reinforcement shapes and a form of Paragon bar was at one time used by BRC. BRC also illustrated construction using stirrups with loops at the end through which the main bars were threaded, suggesting that they may have used more than one type of bar. The Keydon system (also British) was, as its name implies, designed so that the stirrups which were looped round the main steel were also held in place by metal keys which wedged them in place on the main bars (Fig. 5.3). As the advertisement shows, this was intended for use with fabric reinforcement, unlike the Kahn and Moss systems where the same kind of bars were used in beams and slabs.

Fig. 5.2

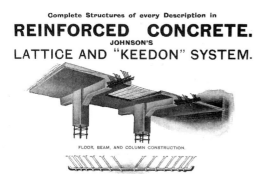

Fig. 5.3   THE "KEEDON" BAR.

Fig. 5.5

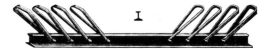

Fig. 5.6

The 'Kahn Trussed Bar' used a rather more ingenious way of keeping the main and shear reinforcing in the correct relationship by having them formed together as a single bar. This was shaped as a square section with the sides of the square at 45° and a pair of wing-like flat sections projecting from the horizontal axis. Lengths of these 'wings' were then bent up at 45° to form the shear reinforcement with the larger rollings used in beams and columns and smaller ones for slabs (Fig. 5.4). Although there was a standard pattern for the bar it could be varied to suit particular circumstances if necessary. At first these bars were also used in columns but they could not have been very convenient there. They had to be placed so that the bent-up bars were at 45° to each column face, that is, diagonally across the column, and because of the difficulty of ensuring proper compaction round this inward projecting steel, it was recommended that the column concrete be placed and compacted in 12-in. lifts. When drawings of Harrod's depository at Barnes were published,[3] they showed round bars

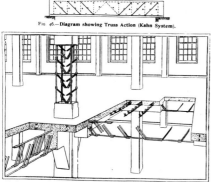

Fig. 5.4

and binders in the columns, suggesting that the clumsy pretence that the bar had universal application was quickly abandoned.

The Kahn trussed bar was by no means the only type that combined main and shear reinforcement into a single product that could be placed as manufactured. The Sidéolith bar seems to have been very similar in shape except that it included top as well as shear reinforcement, these two being pressed out of a flat sheet (Fig. 5.5). William Moss who claimed (de Colleville, n.d.) to have carried out contracts 'under most of the leading systems' nevertheless had their own patent form of reinforcing which comprised a light asymmetrical I-section to the web of which was attached stirrups of flat bars to provide shear reinforcement (Fig. 5.6). Among other advantages, one of the claims for this was the certainty of the steel remaining in the proper position. There were sizes suitable for both beams and slabs and these sections might be used upside-down to provide top steel. The Williams system also used an I-shaped rolling but it seems to have been restricted for use in beams.

Relative success

The Hennebique/Mouchel and Truscon organizations make an interesting contrast. Each was based on a patent system of reinforcing but each developed in ways that enabled them to survive the obsolescence of their particular system. While the former centred its operation on Mouchel who was Hennebique's agent in Britain acting as a consulting engineer and providing the designs for the contractors licenced to use the system (Cusak, 1986 & 1987), Truscon was principally a firm of manufacturers and contractors, less concerned with the design of structures. The firm was founded in the United States and a British subsidiary was established here in 1907. Unlike many others that relied upon a patent system of reinforcement, Truscon survived because of the variety of products which it produced and because the firm operated in a variety of ways. At first their bars were imported but they soon had them rolled in Britain at the Round Oak steelworks. Initially, they simply supplied reinforcement but were prepared to tender for jobs if no contractor was willing to do so; in this way they developed their own contracting capabilities. In 1909, Hy-Rib expanded metal was developed by the parent American company and imported into Britain in the following year. J. Sankey first manufactured Hy-Rib in Britain until Truscon set up its own works. This material must have been more successful than anticipated because capacity was not enough to meet demand and supplies had to be imported. Hy-rib was used as a metal lath for suspended ceilings and walls, and also as permanent shuttering in two patent flooring systems, 'Floordome' and 'Floortyle'. In addition to these *in situ* systems the company also marketed precast concrete flooring (discussed in Chapter 3). By means of these wide interests in construction, the contracting firm outlived its original patented bar — by 1930, the Kahn trussed bar was little used. It survived for the Truscon *in situ* floor but Weeks (1957) noted that it was eventually only sold for the manufacture of lintels, specified by architects who had become accustomed to using it: its production eventually ceased in 1936.

Both of these firms were concerned to keep themselves in the public eye through publicity but again they differed in their approaches. Operating in the way in which it did, it was clearly in Truscon's interests to keep architects and engineers well informed about the product: 'From its beginning the company produced a continuous stream of publications . . . detailed specifications, illustrations of work done and full technical data. All served to keep our name in front of architects and to ensure that the work was well carried out by the contractors' (Weeks, 1957, p. 13).

Truscon published a manual, *Reinforced Concrete and some facts about the Kahn Trussed Bar*, which was in its second edition in 1908, and later the *Hy-Rib manual* which illustrated how to use this metal lathing. In 1914 they launched *Kahncrete Engineering* which not only publicized jobs carried out using the system but, unlike its obvious rival *FerroConcrete*, the organ of the Mouchel organization, it also contained some technical information. As a source of technical information, *FerroConcrete* is disappointing. Since Mouchel carried out the design, there was no need for their method of design to be explained and the journal remained largely one for propaganda, illustrating structures built with their system, explaining its advantages and occasionally indulging in a little criticism of their rivals.

The abandonment of the Kahn trussed bar in preference to round bars, first as column reinforcement and eventually for beams and floors, while the company survived as a contracting business, raises questions about the survival of other patent bar systems which may have been favoured by the contractors who developed them. While William Moss had their own bar system they were prepared to use other methods of reinforcement, although under what circumstances is not clear. Such patent systems were often devised with particular applications in mind, to reinforce a beam or a slab, and many could not be used outside these limited applications. Some that were used for a variety of applications seem to have been ill-suited, so that the Kahn bar seems a poor idea for columns and the Moss system seems a curious device to use in slabs, while neither could have been used in wall structures or for the construction of arches. Such systems may have offered the advantage of speed in the placing of steel in those locations for which they were designed, but the round bar's advantage was its greater flexibility, or perhaps one should say its adaptability, and the fact that it lent itself to the application of standard formulae in design.

Concrete materials and their use

Cement

Portland cement has always been the basic material of concrete even though other cementitious materials were available.[4] Portland cement is a mixture of calcerious and agrillaceous materials which are burnt at clinkering temperature and the resultant clinker then ground to produce the cement. In Britain, the raw materials are chalk and clay with the cement's quality depending both upon its chemical composition and upon the degree of fineness to which it is finally ground. The former depends upon the selection of the raw materials and the degree of control which can be exercised over the 'burning', in particular, controlling the amount of free lime present in the product. The raw materials are first ground and mixed with water to produce a slurry. Originally burning was carried out in chamber kilns in which alternate layers of dried slurry and coke were placed in the kiln and then fired. This gave poor control over the process and quality was variable.

Much greater control was made possible by the introduction of rotary kilns which comprise a long rotating tube into which the slurry is fed at the top while the fuel, originally ground coal, is fed in at the other end. In the nineteenth century, there were no rotary kilns in Britain but the first were established here in 1900 which enabled buyers to obtain cements of better quality than those being imported. The importance of good-quality cement to the building industry can be seen from the early date of the British Standard for the material which was first published in 1904, but the cements actually used at that time were still of questionable quality and remained so in spite of the standard. The problem was that, even though the RIBA committee recommended that only cements complying with the British Standard should be used, cements imported from abroad were not subject to the same standards as those produced in Britain and were often marketed under misleading brand names which caused confusion among buyers. This was of considerable concern to the industry at the time: with articles appearing in *Concrete* referring to 'fictitious portland cement' and attempting to draw attention to the differences in quality. There was also a brochure published by the Portland Cement Manufacturers' Association under the same title.

Aggregates

A variety of materials was considered suitable as aggregates for concrete although a distinction must be made between the materials used for reinforced concrete and those concretes used in conjunction with rolled-steel sections, that is, either in steel-joist floor construction or as protection for steel frames. There are references to coke breeze, clinker, broken brick, ballast, broken sandstone, limestone or flints shingle, crushed granite and even slag.[5] If the concrete was principally to act as a filler in a floor then a lightweight aggregate was preferred. Thus, for filler-joist floors, *Specification* recommended the use of coke breeze or broken brick to 'combine as far as possible the qualities of lightness, strength and resistance to fire'.[6] If coke breeze was used as an aggregate, the resulting concrete was capable of taking nailing which was clearly an advantage where timber floors were to be fixed down to the concrete slab.

As this specification makes clear, the other desirable property to be considered in the design of concrete mixes was resistance to fire. There was some early prejudice against the use of limestone aggregate because it was assumed that it would be converted into quicklime in a fire and lead to failure of the structure; it was some time before it was realized that limestone aggregates behaved better that silaceous aggregates in fire. The second report of the RIBA joint committee of 1911 stated that concretes made with coke-breeze aggregates resisted fire better than limestone or sandstone, based on a test carried out by the BFPC in 1905 which compared the effect of a three-hour fire on seven similar slabs using different aggregates and placed side-by-side in the furnace (see Mitchell, 1888, 3rd ed. 1925, p. 44). But although coke breeze showed the best fire resistance, attitudes towards this material were gradually to change and as early as 1919 an article condemned its use (Perkins, 1919). These first warnings against the use of the material concerned its expansion which, when used in floors, was said to be sufficient to result in the walls being pushed out of plumb. In the late 1920s a number of papers were produced by BRS dealing with the use of coke breeze and pointing out the dangers it presented to possible corrosion of embedded steel because of its high sulphur content (Lee & Brady, 1927). This could happen even when it was used internally because of its tendency to absorb atmospheric moisture. Nevertheless, its use persisted — although to what degree is difficult to tell — this being one of those cases where, once a practice had become established, it took some time for the industry to change, even in the face of growing concern.

Mix specifications

How then were these materials to be mixed together? A good picture of the state of the art at the time is given by the report of the committee of the Institution of Civil Engineers (1910). For a while they had stayed rather aloof from the interest taken in reinforced concrete by other professional bodies, but in 1910 they examined the various systems then in use and drew comparisons between them. The report divided systems of reinforced concrete into two kinds: those 'using a special arrangement of the reinforcement' — which included Hennebique, Considère and Coignet, and those using 'material of special form' — which included BRC, Truscon and the Indented Bar Co. This second group also included expanded metal and other types of reinforcement used for flooring systems.

The degree of control exercised by these various companies over all aspects of construction varied considerably — from the standard of cement, its testing and method of storage, to the placing of the concrete and the testing of the final product. The way in which the mix was specified also varied, some were defined by weight and some by part (see Table 5.1) and they differed in the specification for the amount of water to be used. Hennebique required a 'plastic' mixture capable of being rammed, but the terms used by the different companies varied and none could be described as precise descriptions of the consistency of the mix. BRC for example described their mix as 'slightly wet'. The Expanded Metal Company had no requirement for wetness of mixture but Truscon specified a wet mix, reflecting American practice where engineers were accustomed to wetter mixes than in Europe. Apparently there was experimental evidence to show that dry mixes gave poor adhesion between the steel and the concrete. There was certainly no understanding at that time of the effect of the water:cement ratio on concrete strength, and although buildings by the Hennebique system used fairly stiff mixes, this may not have been common.

Table 5.1 Mix specifications

Company	cement	sand	aggregate
BRC	6.5 cwt	13.5 ft^3	27. ft^3
Truscon	1 part	1.5 parts	2.5 parts
Hennebique	1bag (224)lbs	4.5 ft	9 ft
Considere	5.5–7cwt	11.5 ft^3	23 ft^3
British Steel	1 part	5 part	
Coignet	3 parts	5 parts	10 parts
Expanded Metal-from	1 part	1.25 parts	2.75 parts
to	1 part	1.75 parts	3.25 parts

for floors and walls depending on thickness -otherwise

	1 part	2 parts	4 parts

Note that the mixes for British Steel and Coignet are essentially the same.

Source: Institute of Civil Engineers (1910), Preliminary and Interim report of the Committee on Reinforced Concrete, London.

It is difficult to know how actual practice might have related to these specifications or how attitudes might have changed with time: although the specifications recorded by the Institution of Civil Engineer's report suggests otherwise, Hamilton (1956) reported that wet mixes were in common use by 1910, though he does not identify the source of this information. Without any means of mechanically vibrating the concrete there was naturally an incentive to use rather wet mixes for easier placing and the belief also developed that better concrete was obtained in this way. The RIBA committee also noted that wet mixes were better than dry for fire resistance.

Fire resistance dominated thinking and at that time the cover to the steel was also regarded as ensuring adequate fire resistance rather than its effect in preventing possible corrosion. Not all companies specified the cover for the steel. BRC suggested 1.5 or 2 in. in columns and ¾-in. in slabs, while Truscon specified that the cover never be less than 1 in.

Fig. 5.7

Mixing, placing and construction

Apart from the materials used, the quality of the concrete would be dependent upon the proportions of the mix and upon the thoroughness of the mixing. Volume batching was most commonly used for making up concrete, but Johnson (1915) questioned the accuracy of batching, claiming that contractors were skimping on the quantities of cement used. Mouchel disapproved of volume batching, even though this was the basis of the mixes recommended by the RIBA committee, because cements might have different densities. Here he was reflecting French practice: weight-batching had been recommended by the French Commission du Ciment Armé. Specifications required the quantity of the cement in the mix to be increased for hand mixing but concrete mixing naturally improved with the growing availability of mechanical mixers. Both batch and continuous mixers were available in the early years of the century and in a wide variety of sizes. These were both British manufactured and imported (Fig. 5.7). Some mixers worked on rather curious if ingenious principles, but the simple drum mixer was clearly the most popular and portable varieties which could be used on quite modest sites were also available.

Without mechanical vibration, placing the concrete was more difficult than it is today. Concrete had to be tamped and rammed into place by hand, a laborious process but one which had to be carried out properly if there were not to be voids in the concrete; quite early there were attempts to improve this process. As early as 1911 Ransom showed their

'vibrant consolidator' at the Building Trades Exhibition. This was a hand-powered compacting machine with the operating head activated by turning a handle. Ingenious it may have been but it does not look as if it would have been a popular device. Much more likely to have been used were pneumatic rammers being advertised by the Ingersol Rand Co. in the same year.[7] It was not until 1917 that Freyssinet discovered the value of vibration on poured concrete but there were practical problems to be overcome before it could come into general use.

In the Hennebique method, concrete was placed in beam shutters in several stages so that it could be properly consolidated and the steel placed correctly. Column formwork comprised a three-sided box with the fourth side closed as the concrete was placed and consolidated in lifts. The reinforcement of a Hennebique floor and its method of construction was quite complex and described in detail by Twelvetrees (1907). In casting beams or slabs, a layer of concrete was placed first, sufficient to provide the required cover to the steel. The beam stirrups were then placed, their length being sufficient to project 3 in. into the floor slab, and the bottom steel laid inside them. If there was to be more than one layer of steel, then the placing of concrete and steel had to alternate. The floor slab sequence was, if anything, more complex as the concrete was placed in a sequence of ridges and hollows to follow the profile of the steel that went from the bottom to the top of the slab.

Quality

With little or no independent evidence, it is difficult to know how the methods of design and construction used in the early years of reinforced concrete may have worked in practice or how effective they may have been in ensuring standards of construction. Witnesses to the Institution of Civil Engineers' committee who had experience of working with reinforced concrete gave some account of the practice of the day but also showed some confusion of understanding. One commented that while dry concrete appeared to adhere badly, an excess of water was dangerous, but failed to say how to define the happy medium. One who had experience of Hennebique and Coignet systems commented on how difficult it was to get the steel in the correct position.

Hunter, who was doing work for Manchester Ship Canal, considered himself responsible for the design even though he was using the Hennebique system where they prepared the calculations and detailed drawings. He claimed that he went over these but presumably not all building designers were as conscientious.

The quality of the final concrete was naturally dependent upon the standards of workmanship and if this was to be ensured it required a far greater degree of supervision than structural steel. This was recognized in a report of the Concrete Institute in 1919, which suggested that it might even be necessary for more than one clerk of works to be employed on some sites. The best evidence that we have for the quality of structures produced during this early period of reinforced-concrete construction is a study made when Weaver's Mill was demolished and the opportunity was taken to examine the condition of the structure with tests carried out on the concrete (Malinson and Davies, 1987). The concrete was fairly porous which was attributed both to the poor grading of the aggregate and poor compaction. It was found that the grain size of the cement was large and hydration still not complete. The cement content was high and it was suggested that Hennebique would have designed it that way to ensure a good-quality product as a way of encouraging confidence in the use of this new material. Thus, we cannot assume that all structures would have had a similarly high cement content.

Testing at the time might be based as much on load tests of actual structures as on samples of the concrete. Only BRC required that test cubes be taken specifying a 4-in. cube and a 28-day crushing strength of 3000 psi. Coignet suggested a crushing strength of 2225 psi and a factor of safety of 3.5 — 4. While some firms required test loads and others described them in case they should be thought necessary in particular circumstances, practices again varied. Truscon, for example, required the test load to be twice the design load with deflection limited to span/360. Hennebique had a smaller limit on deflection, limiting it to span/600, but with a test load of only one-and-a-half times the design load. While tests on floors might be relatively simple to undertake they could be quite elaborate for more complex structures, as when the arch-shaped roof of Hammersmith Baths was tested.[8]

Buildings erected

Many of the early buildings noted by Cusack (1986 & 1987) as being built by the Mouchel/Hennebique organization were of quite modest scale, but by 1907, Twelvetrees was able to give a number of examples of very substantial reinforced concrete buildings in Britain including a major warehouse at the docks in Manchester, one at Bristol for the Great Western Railway as well as Weaver's Mill which was itself a large building. Naturally, most of these reinforced concrete frames were industrial or warehouse buildings. It was simpler for frame buildings to be built outside London, where the building regulations were more relaxed, or in situations where the regulations did not apply such as on railway or dock company land.

Warehouses were large buildings whose scale alone must have demonstrated the value of reinforced concrete but they hardly presented a case for its architectural value. Their form can only be called basic. But the more visible, early examples of reinforced concrete frames, those built in London streets rather than on remote railway and dockland sites, were also poor advertisements for the architectural use of the material as their frames were disguised behind brick or stone fronts. Saint (1991) has noted that the first examples of the Kahn system in London — Friars House, New Broad St, and Portland House, Lloyds Avenue, which was the headquarters of the Associated Portland Cement Manufacturers — were both stone-clad on their street fronts and he cites other buildings which adopted the same conservative approach. The Benbow works at Hayes, Middlesex was built using the Wells system but was brick-clad even though Saint notes that its architect, Cave, being 'on the edge of the arts and crafts movement' might have been expected to show an interest in the expression of the structural material. Only the Clays Printing Works, Southwark, another example of the Kahn system which was built at much the same time, is a clear expression of its construction.

What then encouraged these designers to use concrete? In the early years, simple novelty must have attracted some but for others it must have held out the possibility of improved fire protection, improved efficiency in construction or even extended structural possibilities, and there are some firms and some professional figures that can be identified with concrete because of this. While the LCC regulations inhibited the development of reinforced concrete as much as steel frames, Sir Henry Tanner, who was chief architect of the Office of Works (and chairman of the RIBA Joint Committee), used the exemption from the regulations enjoyed by the Post Office to put up a number of sorting offices, both in London and elsewhere, which were built using the Hennebique system (Fig. 5.8). These were important demonstrations of the method because both Twelvetrees and the early editions of *Concrete and Constructional Engineering* reported their construction. *Concrete* reported the building of a number of these post offices in 1907 and 1908 all but one using Hennebique's system.[9] In 1913, Tanner presented a paper to RIBA on their construction and discussed the co-operation needed between the engineer and the architect in the design of this type of building, a question which was to surface again in the inter-war years.

Few of these could be called prestige buildings. The Liver Building, Liverpool (1909),[10] was the first

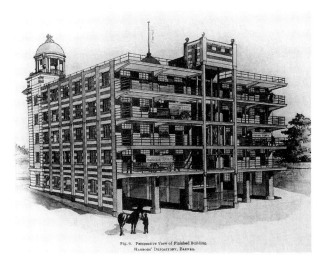

Fig. 5.9

example of a major office building in reinforced concrete, trumpeted as 'the first Ferroconcrete skyscraper' and built using the Hennebique system. This system was also used for the YMCA building in London two years later while at the same time the YMCA building in Manchester was built using the Kahn system. Again, there was hardly any exploration of the architectural possibilities of the material, clad as the Manchester example was in glazed terracotta. However, architectural expression in the surface treatment is not the only possibility. Concrete as a material offers certain structural possibilities over the steel frame; for example, the use of deep cantilevers as seen in Weaver's Mill and in the transit sheds at Manchester Docks, where cantilevered towers were used for the hoists. On a much smaller scale, deep cantilevers were used for Harrod's depository at Barnes, although in a more imaginative way. At each floor there was a cantilevered gallery, all served by a wide central lift tower so that delivery vans could be brought up to the floors for loading (Fig. 5.9). But surely this was an architectural conceit. Could there have been any necessity for a cantilever?

Another kind of structure possible in reinforced concrete is the use of a wall to act as a beam. This can be done with steel framing and it is even possible in reinforced brickwork to form deep beams: Twelvetrees described a concrete tramway depot in Paris which had a reinforced masonry wall

Fig. 5.8

Fig. 5.10

over the open ground-floor space which 'entirely avoids the use of the massive steel beam which would otherwise have been necessary'. The rest of the structure was reinforced concrete (Twelvetrees, 1907, pp. 138—54). However, it was perhaps simpler to achieve this effect in reinforced concrete, especially for the construction of internal walls where openings are required and where structures like this are wanted above large spaces on floors below. This occurred in the Manchester YMCA where deep, reinforced concrete walls were used over the swimming pool. The construction of this was illustrated in some detail in *Concrete*[11] which in 1913 also described a modest office building in Birmingham, with a wall used in a similar way and built using the Wells system.[12] However, it seems as if the potential for this kind of structure was not commonly recognized by architects, possibly because of a tendency to plan in terms of frames.

Understanding

The First World War can be seen to mark a change in the development of reinforced concrete, with the publication of the regulations in 1915 and then interest in the use of reinforced concrete as a substitute building material in the years immediately following the ending of the war. There was considerable interest in concrete housing in the 1919 volume of *Concrete*; the housing shortage and rebuilding needs after the war, were to dominate the building industry in the immediate post-war period and so they equally dominated the pages of this journal in both 1919 and 1920. In 1920, there was a housing exhibition at Olympia where a number of ingenious forms of construction appeared, some concrete-based and described in detail by Weaver (1926). Although many were based on blockwork, some used precast reinforced concrete. But in spite of this interest in non-traditional methods for housing, there was no wide-scale adoption of reinforced concrete by the industry in the years following, and modern movement architects, who in the late 1920s and 1930s took an interest in the use of reinforced concrete to achieve their 'white-box' effects, often had to resort to rendered brickwork. As late as 1929, the housing built for Critall at Silver End, which had originally been designed for concrete construction, was changed to rendered brick because of the difficulty of finding a local contractor with the appropriate skills.

The early development of reinforced concrete, through the invention of many and varied forms of reinforcement by sometimes rather secretive patent holders, was hardly conducive to a parallel development in understanding the fundamental properties and behaviour of this form of construction. While considerable experimental work had been carried out by the patentees, this was naturally directed towards proving the performance of their own particular method. What was needed was the intervention of professional and academic research which would be able to examine more general aspects of performance. The pattern of reinforcing which was in the control of the designer clearly affected the behaviour of the structure, but how was not certain. Performance also depended upon site workmanship but again it was not clear how the behaviour of the completed structure was related to this. As reinforced concrete became more frequently designed by consulting engineers rather than by the system owners, the professions became interested in developing a greater understanding of its behaviour. The design and construction of buildings in reinforced concrete clearly needed more understanding and involvement by the engineer than did steel construction. In addition, while steel was limited to simple beams and columns, the plasticity of reinforced concrete offered the possibility of building forms which had not been at first envisaged and these needed to be understood.

The practical issues to be tackled concerned the understanding of complex structural behaviour, methods for the appropriate design of reinforcement and the design of the concrete mix and the supervision of its placing. Some of these issues were obvious to professional designers at the outset but for others it was to be some time before there was any serious concern. Calculation of stresses within the structure and the corresponding design or reinforcement was an obvious issue. Methods had to be devised for the design of continuous frames, where moments were transferred from beams to columns, and for continuous floor slabs and floor slabs spanning in two directions. The steel frame designer was able to control the properties of materials in the form of a manufacturing specification but the reinforced concrete designer could only do this for the quality of cement; the performance of the mixed concrete being dependent upon control of site processes.

Reinforcing

In the design of beams, the reinforced concrete designer must decide upon their proportions and the placing of steel to resist both shear and bending forces. Unlike the task of the steel designer it was not simply a matter of calculating the forces and selecting an appropriate section. There were different approaches to design and opinions about which was best naturally differed, especially as understanding was rather limited. The obvious example is in the design of shear reinforcement where strong opinions did not seem to be supported by sound evidence. If a reinforced concrete beam is thought of as being like a truss with the bottom chord formed by the reinforcing bars, the role of the top chord is taken by the concrete in compression while the diagonal members, which carry the shear forces, are formed partly of concrete in compression and partly of

steel bars in tension. This was the accepted model but the question for the early designers was how to arrange the bars which were to help to carry the shear forces. Bars could be bent up from the bottom of the beam near the supports, where they were no longer needed to carry bending stresses but where shear forces were higher. Alternatively separate shear reinforcement could be provided in the form of vertical links.

Some of the early patent systems relied upon bent-up bars for shear resistance, and it was perhaps as a continuation of the ideas embodied in these early systems that shear reinforcement continued to be provided in this way. Marsh (1914) for example published a method of calculating shear reinforcement which assumed the use of bent up bars but this was not necessarily the most efficient way of providing shear resistance. Oscar Faber produced a series of articles in 1916 that discussed the shear strength of beams and suggested that links could be used instead, there seems to have been some prejudice against their use (see Godfrey, 1923). It was not until Evans's work in 1935 showed that vertical stirrups were more efficient that engineers had a clear guidance on which was better, but the effect was that stirrups did not become the principal means of resisting shear forces until after the Second World War.

Concrete engineers also had to face the fact that reinforced concrete beams could not be treated as if they were simply supported. They were manifestly not and so the bending moments in continuous beams had to be calculated and reinforcement provided to accommodate these moments. Moment distribution (Cross, 1932) was developed as a method for analysing indeterminate structures and was quickly reported in Britain in the pages of *Concrete* (Coleman, 1932). Of course the moments used in the design of continuous beams and slabs need not be the elastic moments given by this method of analysis and it was realized that the actual moments could to some extent be controlled by the designer by modifying the amount of reinforcement used at the supports. There was considerable incentive to do this as it reduced the congestion of bars at the junction of beams and columns. In this respect, the practice of some engineers seems to have been ahead of the regulations. In commenting on the new code of practice which appeared in 1932 (see below), *Concrete* offered an interesting comment on the approach to the design of beams in noting that:

> For many years it has been the practice of some engineers to 'make the bending moment diagram fit the steel instead of the steel fitting the bending moment', in other words to draw a closing line across the bending moment diagram which would give decreased negative moments and increased positive moments in continuous beams.[13]

Concrete regarded this as an acceptable practice and was happy to see it incorporated into the new code.

Haunches were commonly added to beams to increase the depth at the point where there were high negative-bending moments and high shear. In the Hennebique system, this increased depth was often achieved by forming the beams as shallow arches (as in Fig. 5.8) but Twelvetrees (1907), describing some goods station and warehouse buildings in which this form of beam was used, was careful to point out that they were reinforced in such a way that these 'arches' did not transmit any horizontal thrust to the supports. It is not clear whether the increased depth at that time was used to reduce the area of top steel required or to cope with shear forces, but articles in the journals later showed that the intention then was to reduce the steel required to carry hogging moments and reduce congestion of the bars, a practice which continued into the 1930s. Then, instead of an arch shape, simple haunches were used at the ends of beams which otherwise had horizontal soffits. Normally no account was taken in design of the effect that the haunches had on the stiffness of the beam, and hence on the distribution of bending moments, but Ashdown (1932) did eventually consider this and showed that some advantage could be taken of the increased stiffness.

Bending moments in slabs also presented a problem. While a simple slab was simply a broad shallow beam, it was realized that slabs could span in two directions but the theoretical treatment of this was not simple. Andrews (1914) discussed the alternative approaches to their design but what was wanted was a simple set of tables. Formulae were provided in the 1915 LCC regulations for two-way spanning slabs but only for simply supported slabs

with the longer span no more than twice that of the shorter. The moments in flat slabs were even more problematic and were to become the subject of a long period of conflict between designers and the regulations (see below).

Materials and mix design

The 1915 regulations recognized that the strength of a mix varied with the mix proportions. The basic mix used was 1:2:4 (cement:fine aggregate:coarse aggregate) but there was some concern among professionals about the way in which the standards of workmanship in mixing might also affect the strength. Johnson's concerns about the accuracy of batching have already been referred to; shortly afterwards the *Report of the Special Committee of the Concrete Institute on the relations between architects and specialist engineers* noted the greater degree of supervision required for reinforced concrete work and suggested that it might be sensible to employ more than one clerk of works on some contracts.[14] It is not certain how much notice was taken of these comments because nearly 20 years later Manning (1934a) was expressing some concern about the strength of concrete in practice, having examined defects in a number of structures. The way round this was for the standard of workmanship to be incorporated into the design strength of mixes recognized by regulation, but here there was to be a long lag between the appearance of theoretical ideas about mix design and their incorporation into general practice.

It had been recognized quite early that the strength of concrete was dependent upon the density of the mix and so upon the correct proportioning of the aggregates, and text-books soon referred to this. Marsh (1905) had drawn largely on French experimental work while Taylor & Thopmson (1909) naturally referred to US work in which Thompson had participated. By 1920 Twelvetrees was also largely reporting American work. While this relationship may have been intuitively understood there was not necessarily the will to carry out a sieve analysis and the fineness modulus method of proportioning the ingredients of the mix (described well by Childe, 1927) and an understanding of the importance of controlling the water content of mixes was slow to develop: an example of the resistance to the adoption of scientific principles that can sometimes be found.

Duff Abrams's work on the effect of water:cement ratio was carried out in the US but the results of his work were soon published in Britain through articles in *Concrete*[15] which included sets of design tables putting the results on a practical footing. If this were not enough, an article in the following year included graphs of the relationships between strength and both fineness modulus and water:cement ratio which showed the effects quite clearly.[16] Naturally, if these ideas were to be used in practice, a greater degree of control needed to be exercised over the mixing. Moreover, they involved a change in attitude because this was at a time when the use of wet mixes was common; although it might have been recognized that wet mixes were initially weaker than dry ones, there seems to have been the general belief that the difference was short-lived (see, for example Hool, 1912). Following the first articles on this subject, *Concrete* also published a clear description of the slump test:[17] the means were available to exercise control should there be the will to do so, but the industry was slow to change.

In 1926, Wynn published both a series of articles in *Concrete* and a textbook (Wynn, 1926 a & b) on controlling the strength of concrete showing that by now the relationship was well understood and that it was possible to make use of this in practice. He followed these in 1930 with articles which included reference to the US standard specification. Of course, at that time the use of dryer mixes would still have made the placing of the concrete more difficult and in spite of all these publications practice did not seem to improve. Wynn (1926, p. 595) had been realistic enough to point out that 'thirty years' experience of "1:2:4" wheelbarrow measurements, and "water as you like it" cannot be thrown over in a day or a year.' In 1932 an editorial note in *Concrete* (commenting on a new concrete code that had appeared in Germany) could still note that: 'The theory of proportioning has made little progress in this country. In this country it is generally agreed that if a definite strength is required at 28 days, it is immaterial how it is produced so long as the concrete is satisfactory in other respects, and it would be a mistake to *complicate concrete making* [author's italics] by the introduction of water-cement-ratio, fineness

modulus etc...'[18]

It appears, however, that things were no better in Germany because their new code also made no use of these ideas.

This begs the question, how were they achieving adequate strengths? Presumably if mixes were still wet, contractors must have obtained an adequate water:cement ratio by using a correspondingly high cement content. This is the implication of remarks made by Singleton-Green (1928) and was certainly the case in 1930 when Scott defined two kinds of mix, a 'damp mix' and a 'floating mix'. He then recommended that: 'If the floating mix is used for highly stressed concrete, the engineer may require up to 10% increased quantity of cement over the specified amount (E. A. Scott, 1930, p. 151).'

The treatment of the slump test by Scott and his corresponding table of strengths suggests that the concern was more to control the workability, and hence the ease of placing the concrete, than to control strength. Of course, the use of volume batching hindered correct proportioning and just before the war the Road Research laboratory was advocating the use of weight batching (Glanville et al., 1938).

The important innovation was the development of techniques for the vibration of concrete. An article entitled 'Vibration as applied in the laying of concrete with special reference to Canadian practice'[19] showed vibrators attached to shutters but a year later, in 1935, an article described the use of what we would today call poker vibrator for the construction of the Bay Bridge, San Francisco.[20] There were four articles on vibration in *Concrete* in the following year and two further articles in 1938 as well as a number of advertisements for vibration equipment. Poker vibrators appear to have become available in Britain by 1933 when the Consolidated Pneumatic Tool Company, which made these, first began advertising in *Concrete*. A committee was set up by the Institution of Structural Engineers in 1935 to look at vibration and test available equipment and their work was reported in 1937[21] while Glanville (1939) discussed the position of vibrators just before the Second World. This technique had obviously arrived, and what was of course noticed was that it allowed much dryer mixes to be placed without difficulty.[22]

Cements

While mix proportions was dependent upon controlling work on site, the manufacturers of the basic material, cement, were making continuing improvements in the quality of their product. Since the first publication of BS 12 in 1904, the standards were raised at frequent intervals. In the mid-1920s, Davis (1926) noted the improvement that had taken place in the fineness of cement. Early cements would only pass meshes of 50 — 70 wires/in. while at the time he was writing, the norm was 180 wires/in. The obvious effect is a more rapidly hardening product and a more complete hydration. The increase in strength was such that by the early 1930s Owen Williams (1932) was able to note that the increase in concrete stresses had allowed concrete columns to be as small as steel columns.

A more important change occurred with the introduction of rapid-hardening aluminous cement which was first produced in the early 1920s, originally produced for its sulphate resisting properties. This had a greater calcium oxide content than Portland cement and required better quality control in its manufacture. An editorial comment in *Concrete* in 1923 gave this material a cautious welcome. The rapid-hardening properties were clearly advantageous to precast concrete manufacturers and in the same year tests were carried out on Siegwart floor beams made with rapid-hardening cement.[23] The advantages of rapid hardening were not only in precast work and in 1926, it was reported that the construction of the Wrigley Factory had been hastened by the use of rapid-hardening cement.[24] However, in this case it was rapid-hardening Portland cement which the Portland cement industry had produced as an answer to aluminous cement. In 1925, an article 'Rapid Hardening Portland Cement' noted that this was the latest development of the cement industry and reported tests carried out on full-scale beams by 'Ferrocrete', one of the cement manufacturers.[25]

There may have been a reluctance on the part of some local authorities to accept such new materials because Oscar Faber, who had carried out tests on both types of rapid-hardening cements, noted (1925) that the use of the rapid-hardening Portland cement depended upon its acceptance by local authorities. There was a comment on restrictive regulations two years later and two years after that

Owen Williams (1930) reported that a manufacturer had asked him to comment on the use of the material, seemingly as a means of obtaining some endorsement for its use from a respected professional. Of course, innovations in building require a degree of caution because ignorance may result in misuse and the aluminous cements may not have been used properly by all contractors: in 1933, *Concrete* published an article which made clear the harmful effects of mixing aluminous cement with ordinary Portland cement.

There was some use of both calcium chloride and sodium chloride as admixtures to concrete. The intention was to protect the concrete against frost during construction and an early BRS publication considered its use (Thomas, 1929). It gradually became apparent that the former affected the corrosion of steel but it was not until the war that this led to a recommended maximum of 2 per cent admixture (Newman, 1943). Nevertheless, calcium chloride continued to be used as a common admixture to concrete in post-war years (see Chapter 3).

Development of the regulations

The LCC regulations which were drawn up in 1915 followed the recommendations of the Joint Committee; at the time representing professional thinking on the subject. However, as these regulations remained in force into the inter-war years, it was soon realized that they did not continue to represent the current state of knowledge. Reinforced concrete was a comparatively new material, more complex than structural steel and there were continuing developments in its understanding and use. When the Steel Structures Research Committee was formed the LCC approached the Building Research Board with a view to setting up a similar committee to consider that state of the reinforced concrete regulations. The Reinforced Concrete Structures Committee was thus appointed by the Building Research Board and an editorial in *A&BN* commented with apparent unconscious irony that 'The editor is pleased that the design of reinforced concrete will now become as scientific as that of steel.'[26] Unfortunately, this committee did not have the funds that were available to the SSRC and so was not able to carry out a similar series of experiments to investigate the behaviour of reinforced concrete structures. As a result, perhaps, it carried out its work much faster. It reported in 1933 and its recommended code of practice for design was published the following year.[27] The LCC then revised its 1915 regulations in draft form but these were to go through two revisions before they finally appeared in 1938. In the interim period, the LCC used its powers of waiver, accepting designs prepared in accordance with the new code. Presumably authorities in other parts of the country also accepted this new code as a suitable basis for design.

This, then, was the official position during the 1930s but it does not represent the complete picture. If, as is clear from only a casual perusal of the articles being published in *Concrete*, reinforced concrete was attracting considerable development work as a method of construction, this was affecting practice independent of the development of the codes and regulation. Understanding of the material was improving, ideas of design and detailing were changing as a consequence and while there may have been small firms of consulting engineers who worked within the limits of the published regulations, there were large firms carrying out major projects whose concern to produce efficient designs drove them to develop their understanding and use of the material beyond the limits of the official regulations. The obvious example is Oscar Faber who had taken part in the work of the SSRC and who made several major contributions to the development of reinforced concrete design and published basic books on its use. Another firm was Sir William Arrol and Company who produced a comprehensive manual on reinforced concrete design (Scott, 1930).

The Arrol company was a well-established firm that had a long-standing reputation for steelwork design before its reinforced concrete department was set up. Within a decade, this department had designed a large number of structures, many bridge and dock works but also a number of commercial and industrial buildings. Their handbook has to be seen partly as an advertisement for the firm but also a useful guide to the design of concrete structures, preceding the first (1932) edition of Charles Reynolds's handbook by a couple of years. Indeed, it took the form which has been adopted by so many handbooks since. There was a section dealing with basic structural mechanics, which included formulae

for finding the moments on statically indeterminate structures. There was then a section dealing with the principles used in the design of reinforced concrete elements and with the specification of materials and the control of workmanship, while the book concluded with useful tables and graphs.

The foreword to the discussion of the principles of design is informative. It notes that in Britain 'the only authoritative publications for regulating the use of reinforced concrete are apparently limited to: The recommendations of the Royal Institute of British Architects (1911), The London County Council Regulations (1915), The Reports of the Institution of Structural Engineers, "Loads and Stresses" (1927) and "Materials and Workmanship" (1928)' (Scott, 1930, p. 110). It also noted some recent British Standard Specifications for materials and implied that only these and the reports of the Institution of Structural Engineers were sufficiently up to date to be of use. They were therefore 'compelled' (their word) to consult the standards being used in other countries and cited those of several countries on which they had drawn. For example, they preferred the Canadian code for flat slabs and this approach also allowed them to produce design recommendations for composite steel and concrete floors 35 years before the publication of the BS code of practice for this form of construction. The implication is clear: firms with the resources and/or the experience to do so were operating well outside the confines of the LCC regulations and designing buildings using up-to-date knowledge and foreign codes of practice.

Eventually, when the new regulations were published, Grundy (1939) summarized the differences between the old and new LCC regulations and the code of practice and produced worked examples to show their effect on typical structural sections. The following is a brief review of these differences.

1) The strength of concrete in the early regulations had varied with the mix proportions but it had been recognized that workmanship was also a factor and the new regulations made allowances for this by allowing a higher strength to be used for each mix design where there was a greater degree of supervision. It recognized two grades of concrete: 'Ordinary' and 'Quality A'. The code of practice had

gone a step further and given working stresses for three classes of concrete which it called 'Ordinary', 'High Strength' and 'Special', allowing stresses for the third category which were 25 per cent higher than those subsequently recognized by the regulations.

2) There were changes which affected the design of columns. In the early regulations the area of concrete considered to be carrying the compressive load was the area within the binders while, in both the new regulations and the code, the full area of concrete could be used. The reduction in load for slender columns was now less and columns of greater slenderness were allowed but there were differences here between the code and the regulations because the former allowed slightly longer columns. A table by Grundy summarizes this (see Table 5.2). These figures are given for comparison. The new regulations used the radius

of gyration as the basis for calculations rather than the dimension of the column while the code provided both.

3) The design of columns was also affected by the reduction in live load allowed for multiple floors. The 1915 regulations had assumed a reduction of 5 per cent/floor up to a maximum of 50 per cent . This had been criticized at the time and the new regulations allowed a reduction at the rate of 10 per cent/floor, essentially following the changes that had been made in the steel design rules.

4) There were other changes in the approach to the determination of live loads. Apart from the general reduction in the live loads for all classes of building there was also a reduction in the assumed wind loads. At the same time, it was now recognized that higher loads should be used for small spans or small areas. This was catered for in the new regulations by requiring higher design loads for concrete slabs than for the beams which supported them.

5) In the design of beams there were modest changes in the bending moments. It had always been recognized that some redistribution of moments in continuous beams was possible (see above) and the new regulations reduced the bending moments assumed over interior supports from $WL/10$ to $WL/12$, all other moments remaining the same.

6) The new regulations also altered the effective width that was to be assumed for the flanges to T- or L-beams.

7) The regulations continued to assume that the modular ratio between steel and concrete was 15 in all circumstances while the code allowed different ratios depending upon the mix design. Presumably designers would have favoured the simpler approach adopted by the regulations.

8) The 1915 regulations had provided a means of calculating the bending moments on two-way spanning slabs but had only allowed differences in span up to 2:1. The new regulations recognized slabs with ratios of spans as high as 3:1 as two-way spanning. This included an understanding of the effect of edge restraint and the publication of means of designing for point loads.

The regulations might have caught up with

Table 5.2 Column slenderness ratios		
1/b	Old regulations	Code
15 (12)	1	1
18 (15)	0.8	0.9
21 (18)	0.6	0.8
24 (21)	0.4	0.7
27 (24)	0.2	0.6
30 (27)	0	0.5
33		0.4
36		0.3
39		0.2 but 0 for the new regulations
42		0.1
45		0

The figures in brackets are for round columns in the first regulations. The code made no distinction between round and square columns except to note that for spiral reinforcement the governing dimension should be the core and not the overall diameter

Source: Knight's Annotated Model Byelaws of the Local Government Board, London: Local Government Publishers, 6th ed., 1899.

professional practice but already they were well behind the scientific understanding of the material. Design had naturally assumed that concrete was an elastic material. This was after all the basis for design in other materials and, although it was more complex to calculate the combined behaviour of two materials, all that had to be done was to take account of their different moduli of elasticity: this was the basis of all design calculations for concrete. However, Oscar Faber (1927) had already demonstrated that concrete did not behave as an elastic material in a paper that examined its plastic behaviour and shrinkage and considered the implications of this. Work by Glanville at the BRS soon followed and it was clear that if design calculations were to represent more closely the true behaviour of reinforced concrete then some new approach had to be adopted. This was not to be officially recognized until the 1957 edition of CP 114.

Flat-slab construction

One example of the conflict between professional ideas and the limitations of regulations which needs to be considered is the development of flat-slab construction. In this form of construction columns support slabs with no down-stand beams. Instead there is only an enlarged mushroom head on the columns to spread the area over which the shear forces are carried. This technique was developed independently in both the US and on the Continent but can be counted among a number of innovations in reinforced concrete design that came to Britain from the US rather than Europe. The early developments of flat-slab design which occurred abroad lie outside our concerns here, but some background is useful to establish how well the ideas were developed in each continent. Following early experimental designs by Norcross and Turner (who were in dispute over patent rights), theoretical work was done by H.T. Eddy (1913) who also carried out a full-scale test on a structure of this kind. Turner, his collaborator in the writing of a textbook on reinforced concrete, was involved in the design of a number of buildings using this method. Gideon (1962, pp. 446—54) reports a publication by Turner on the subject in 1909, suggesting that his first building was the Bovey Building, Minneapolis in

1908. However, the first report in a British journal predates this (see below) and Wynn (1921) gave a date of 1903 for Turner's first essay in this form of construction, possibly taking Turner's own (1912) book on the subject as his source. At much the same time, Taylor and Thompson (1912) described the design and construction of flat slabs in their textbook.

Meanwhile, in Europe, Maillart was experimenting with mushroom construction and putting up a number of buildings (Bill, 1949). Having carried out some loading tests on slabs supported on columns at the corner, Maillart's first practical application of the idea was a warehouse in Zurich built by this method in 1910. There then followed a handful of buildings in Switzerland before the First World War and a number of factories in other countries, including France. Nevertheless, the earliest reports in Britain of the use of the method in *Concrete* all described American examples. The first appeared in 1907 which described the construction of an office block[28] but a more detailed accounts of the system including some details of the design method and methods of reinforcing were given by Brayton (1911) and Thompson (1913). The obvious advantage offered by the flat slab is the simplification of the shuttering consequent upon the removal of the beams. But how should designers imagine the flat slab to be working? Whatever the results of a theoretical treatment of an idealized slab of homogeneous material, the concrete designer needs a model of behaviour that will guide the placing of the steel reinforcing bars, which will to an extent determine the way that the slab is working. Different models of behaviour were possible and reflected in different reinforcing patterns. It is possible to imagine the slab being divided into broad beam strips between the columns. These beam strips will then be heavily reinforced while the rest of the slab acts as simple two-way spanning slabs on to them. This is the model used today and it is clear from the reinforcing pattern that he used that this was also the model adopted by Maillart, and would in any case seem to follow naturally from the way that he conducted his experiments with simply supported slabs on four corner columns. The alternative is to imagine the slab cantilevered from the heads of the columns.

Given this image, there are four directions in which a slab which is continuous over a number of columns needs to cantilever along the 'grid lines' joining the columns and along the diagonals across each structural bay. This model requires four-way reinforcing and was used in the US; Hirschthal (1933) describes three methods of analysis which he called the cantilever, the continuous-beam and the fixed-beam methods.

It was only after the First World War that there was an attempt to design a building in this country using flat slabs. When new premises for the Ford Motor Company were built in 1918, a note in *Concrete* reported that the original design had been in flat-slab construction but that this had not been accepted by the LCC building regulations so it had been re-designed using beams.[29] An explanation was not to be published until later, but it seems that the difficulty lay in regarding flat slabs as a series of cantilevers (see below). But in spite of objections to its use by the LCC, *Concrete* continued to show an interest in the flat slab, publishing a number of articles on its use, including editorial comment in its favour. The most useful of these was that by the American engineer Wynn which provided a detailed account of design methods. In this he commented that 'While on a visit to England last winter the writer was struck with the absence of reinforced concrete buildings built on the Flat Slab system, and was particularly surprised to learn that this type of construction was prohibited by the LCC Building Code' (Wynn, 1921, p. 95). He attributed the success of reinforced concrete in the US to the use of flat-slab construction and estimated that over 80 per cent of all buildings designed for a floor loading of more than 100 lbs/sq. ft. used this technique. He pointed out that not only did it have the advantages of simplicity in construction, but that the absence of beams improved light levels in the building and greatly facilitated the running of services, advantages which were to be cited in subsequent articles published in other journals in this country.

Wynn illustrated some systems of construction and gave details of the two principal methods then in use in the US. He pointed out that although a theoretical derivation of the behaviour of the slab was possible, the solution was complex and the formulae used in design were instead derived from experimental measurements which determined the position of the points of contraflexure in the slabs. Disturbingly, he also pointed out that the authorities in different cities in the US specified different bending moments to be used in design, regrettably giving no explanation for this curious situation, only noting that the Chicago regulations were those normally used. At that time, it was quite common to place columns in the external wall of the building and the moments in the slab naturally induced bending moments in these. Wynn gave advice on the design of these edge columns and made a number of practical points about construction. Here, if regulations had allowed, was sound practical guidance for designers in Britain.

Wynn's use of the word 'prohibited' needs a little examination for, as the system of construction was hardly well-known here when the reinforced concrete regulations were drafted, they could hardly have forbidden its use directly. Instead, what occurred was the inability of the building control officers to fit designs for this form of construction within the wording of the act because 'the clauses dealing with cantilevers among others are so worded that they cannot be stretched to cover mushroom construction; for it is the cantilever on which this interesting form of construction is based.'[30]

In the same year that Wynn's article appeared, a warehouse for Selfridge's was completed in Paddington to the designs by Bylander and reported in the *AJ* with plans and detailed sections showing the reinforcement.[31] The *AJ* looked forward to by-laws covering this form of construction in the near future — a vain hope. *Concrete* reported a test load carried out on a flat-slab floor in a building for the Garston match factory, near Liverpool, also by Bylander and based on a 20-ft. column grid.[32] While the design load was 3 cwt./sq. ft. the test load was 4 cwt./sq. ft. (Although the report does not say so the test was presumably carried out at the request of the local authority but the Bylander archives contain no correspondence to confirm this.) The designs for the two are curiously different; the *AJ* article shows two-way reinforcement while the drawings for the match factory that survive in Bylander's archives show four-way reinforcement. A feature of the column reinforcement was that it was not carried through the floor slab to form starters for the columns above but instead, the bars were turned down to form diagonal reinforcement across the drop in the slab to increase the shear resistance. It has been suggested that Bylander managed to build the flat-slab building in London because it was on canal property and possibly exempt from LCC scrutiny (Saint, personal correspondence). These were the only flat-slab buildings, and possibly the only reinforced concrete buildings that Bylander designed and it seems certain that they were simply intended as an experiment. He later commented that he had been introduced to flat-slab construction by Eddy when he visited the US (see Bylander, 1938).

Not all local authorities took the same view as the LCC, as the Garston factory shows, and in 1925 Concrete reported the construction of a factory in Norwich where the use of flat-slab construction 'was made possible because the local authority had interpreted the regulations in a generous way'.[33] This was designed by E. W. B. Scott, for Fred Sexton Ltd. and the incentive for the use of the system had come from the architect, another example of the use of the system depending upon the personal experience of the designer. Scott had earlier visited the US and Canada, had met Mauritz Kahn and was impressed by the advantages of flat-slab construction (Scott, personal communication). The system used may not have been the simplest to build. Although the beams were eliminated, placing the steel for the slab must have been difficult because not only did the contractor have to cope with diagonal reinforcement, implying four layers of bars over column heads, but they were 'arranged to hang in a catenary between the column heads'.[34] Wynn had suggested that the four-way system of reinforcing was more economical than the two-way system because less steel was used and, because the diameter of the bars was smaller, they did not need to be bent but could be allowed to hang under their own weight between the column heads. This explains the description given but one wonders how the bars were kept in the correct position during construction.

If Ford's had been frustrated in 1918 by the building regulations in London, two other American companies were not so hindered a few years later and did manage to use flat-slab construction. These were the Shredded Wheat and Wrigley companies

who in 1926—7 built factories both using the Trussed Concrete Steel Co. as contractors. Of the latter Concrete noted that as an American company '[The owners] knew that the cheapest and quickest method for such a building was the mushroom type of construction' but was still complaining that 'it is a little disturbing to realize that this method of designing is almost prohibited in those districts in England where reinforced concrete regulations are in force.'[35] In 1929, Manning reported on the use of flat-slab construction in a warehouse for the Michelin Company at Stoke on Trent, with Peter Lind as contractors. This was a six-storey, brick-clad building of no architectural merit but is an interesting example: the report states that, because of the need for holes for chutes and a limit on the deflection of the floor, 'Standard flat slab construction could not cope with all these adverse conditions' and that 'To suit this type of construction a two way system of reinforcement was adopted' (author's italics). The building has column centres at 18 ft. 8 in. by 20 ft. 6 in. and the intention was to do away with a drop panel. Manning's reference to 'standard' flat-slab construction shows that the use of this method was not uncommon but was reported simply because of the unusual absence of drops in the slab. This type of building, with its exposed concrete frame on the outside, brick infill panels and standard window frames, would hardly have attracted the interest of architects, and hence the architectural press but a number of buildings were soon to be put up which did.

Architectural possibilities

Although not the only essay in flat-slab construction which was designed by an architect, it was the Wrigley factory by Wallis Gilbert and Partners that seems to have received the most attention in architectural circles in this country. It was reported in Building (Watson, 1926), when it was still at the design stage, noting the use of Ferrocrete and in the AJ in 1928.[36] Architect & Building News, commenting on the completed building, said that the design showed that a plain building could still be beautiful.[37] The advantage which Wallis (1933) claimed for flat-slab construction used in this and other factory buildings was the ease with which services could be run and its suitability for use with heavy floor loads.

Wallis's steps toward an architectural expression of the flat slab had been tentative. The drawings of the Wrigley factory show the long strips of windows divided by three pairs of mullions, possibly a gesture to a felt need for visible supports but which were also to prove useful for running rainwater pipes down. The complete expression of the column-less elevation needed internal drainage of the roof. The architects' later essay in flat slabs was the Shipping Building at Hayes for the Gramaphone Company in 1930 where the Trussed Concrete Steel Co. were again the contractors. It was the removal of columns from the elevation there that impressed the correspondent of *Architect and Building News*[38] when it reported its construction and noted that 'Until the invention of mushroom construction . . . we believed that an essential to architecture was apparent firmness, the articulation and emphasis of supports upon facades.' Louis de Soissons and Arthur Kenzon achieved this column-less elevation in a factory building at Welwyn Garden City that was built at the same time as the Hayes building but which received little attention.[39] Later, F.A. Broadhead's Viyella factory also made use of set-back columns to give uninterrupted strips of glazing but this was rather eclipsed by Owen Williams's nearby Boots factory.

The possibility that the flat slab provided for dispensing with the wall was demonstrated by the Van Nelle factory, Rotterdam which attracted attention as far away as the US where *Architectural Record* was impressed by its striking use of curtain walling.[40] Owen Williams achieved a similar effect in his 'Wets' factory for Boots at Beeston, near Nottingham; the building that must have awakened architects in this country to the possibilities of the glazed facade. It was not a conventional flat-slab structure and neither did it provide quite the same uninterrupted glazing of the Rotterdam building. The mushrooms were broad inverted pyramids looking more like a thickening of the slab than a widening of the columns. By this means, Williams achieved structural bays of 30 ft. 8 in. by 23 ft. compared with the smaller bay sizes of earlier flat-slab buildings. (Similar large bays were used for his warehouse at Blackfriars.) The glazing was also interrupted by the edge of the floor.

It was about this time that *Architect's Journal*

became interested in the possibilities of flat-slab construction, referring to it in an article on factory design and in the same year reporting the construction of a warehouse for the Co-operative Society in Salford, built to the designs of their own architect, J.A. Johnson. In the following year, an information supplement in the same journal dealt in more detail with flat slabs explaining the principles behind the method. Clearly the momentum was growing and if flat-slab buildings could be put up successfully in other cities then London could hardly resist them for long. In 1934, *Concrete* reported what it claimed was the first building in London to be built using the flat-slab principle, designed using the Chicago building regulations, although modified to suit the LCC, and using four-way reinforcement. This may be an indication of the time between design and construction because the Institution of Structural Engineers' draft code for flat slabs was published in 1932 and had it been available it would surely have been used. It was also in 1934 that the flat slab eventually received official recognition in London with the publication of amendments to the regulations, and by 1937 *Architects' Journal* could report a number of factories using the system.

The reasons for the use of flat-slab construction appear to have been entirely functional, the absence of beams facilitating the running of services in industrial buildings. Although today it is normally used with set-back columns, early examples had columns in the face of the building and, perhaps surprisingly, it took a long time for the expressive possibilities of the method to be recognized even though set-back columns were a feature of the modern style of architecture. The earliest examples reported in the journals were of buildings either designed by engineers or were examples where the client or architect were familiar with the method of construction. In all these cases the source was the US rather than the Continent.

Use of concrete

In spite of improvements in the design of reinforced concrete, and a recognition that it was cheaper than steel, it did not enjoy the same success as a material for the construction of building frames. Bowley (1966) points to a number of reasons for this. In part, it was the effect of simple prejudice against the material which, in projects funded by local authorities, resulted in building loans only being made for a 15-year period for reinforced concrete structures compared with 30 years for steel buildings. (This discrimination continued until the Second World War.) Bowley also suggests lack of promotion. The raw material came from the cement industry for whom reinforced concrete structures was only a part of their market and, as no more cement was used in concrete frames than was used in the fire protection of steel frames, there was little incentive to promote the former. One might equally ask whether reinforced concrete contractors were particularly interested in the construction of building frames. They might have been useful as prestige jobs which could be used as a means of advertising their services but it is hardly likely that they saw themselves in direct competition with steel erectors. Surely plenty of concrete was going into foundations and floor slabs, grain silos and water tanks; all the kind of work that suggests a greater return for less effort than a building frame.

This suggests another reason for Bowley's observation. Steel was far simpler to design and most engineers would have seen no advantage, and certainly little profit, in undertaking a more complex design process, especially when the understanding of the behaviour of the materials was still in a state of flux. Not only was the design a more complex process, it presumably involved more supervision of construction. One other attraction of the steel frame, noted in Chapter 4, was that it was quickly erected and provided a working platform for the crane so simplifying other building operations. Given such disincentives, the use of reinforced concrete must have depended upon special circumstances and it is worth briefly reviewing these.

One use for reinforced concrete might be for the construction of building forms for which steel was ill-suited and concrete had an obvious advantage. Saint (1991) has suggested the arch roof form as an example, used with such dramatic effect in Oscar Faber's structure for the Horticultural Hall, London. Here the combination of the arch with a series of flat roofs provided a high level of lighting through 'clerestory' windows. The dramatic effect was heightened by raising the base of the arches from the floor of the hall and containing their outward thrust by turning the roofs of the aisles into horizontal beams spanning between the ends of the building. The form of arch and windows used in this way was not original and Saint has described other similar structures. What is significant in this context is that the form was then used in a number of municipal swimming pools during the 1930s and even found its way into the roofs of other types of building where a high level of lighting was required.

Personal interest on the part of the designer, whether architect or engineer is another clear possibility. This has been demonstrated in the case of flat-slab construction to which Owen Williams made a contribution. His early years had been spent as an engineer with Truscon and the knowledge which he gained through his work with them was put to use in his subsequent career as an engineer/architect, a career that has been traced by Cottam (1986). But Williams was not the only engineer to come from a contracting background and make a name in building design. Ove Arup's early career involved the construction of grain silos and he began his highly successful business as a consulting engineer with his designs for Highpoint flats in association with Tecton. This, and the successful competition winning entry for the 'Workingmen's Flats Competition' with the same firm of architects, used a structure that was clearly drawn from his previous contracting experience (Yeomans & Cottam, 1989) and based on the use of structural concrete walls rather than a frame. This design approach offered both planning advantages and the possibility of savings through the method of construction used and Arup was to continue the partnership with this firm (among others) in subsequent flat designs which used other novel structural forms.

At a more prosaic level we may look to the possible involvement of the client in the selection of reinforced concrete. Examples of flat-slab construction have been cited here, in particular the aborted Ford building design and the Wrigley factory, and it was in multi-storey factory design that the clients were more likely to be aware of the cost advantages of the concrete frame. The design of factories in the early years of the century was influenced by a developing interest in efficient factory management and a concern for the welfare of the workers (Loader & Skinner, 1991) Both of these developments were given an impetus by the need for munitions and other war products during the First World War which focused attention on factory design. Loader and Skinner suggest that in the early years of this century the multi-storey form was adopted because factories were located in urban areas, while the development of the suburbs in the inter-war period led to a greater use of the shed form. However, at the time Kahn (1917) argued that single-storey buildings were 15 per cent more expensive per unit area and cost more to heat. He also claimed that vibration was not the problem in multi-storey buildings which people might suppose, particularly if reinforced concrete was used which he claimed provided a building at 87 per cent of the cost of a steel frame.

An article in the first volume of *Kahncrete Engineering* began what can only be called a campaign for improved factory design and illustrated the HMV factory.[41] Given the difficulty of introducing reinforced concrete for the construction of other building types what better than to try to emphasize the advantages of reinforced concrete in a developing area. This was especially so since the idea of the 'daylight factory' which the company was promoting depended upon the use of frame construction. To this end the company illustrated in their journal a number of reinforced concrete factories built in various parts of the world. Naturally many of these, although by no means all, were in the US. The second volume of *Kahncrete* pointed out the cheapness of reinforced concrete construction (Black 1915—16), introducing the term 'daylight factory', while two years later there was an article demonstrating the speed with which this form of construction could be built (Perkins, 1917). In 1927, *Concrete* was describing the construction of the huge Carreras factory in London which was a reinforced concrete frame and *Arrol's Reinforced Concrete Reference Book* (Scott, 1930) illustrated a wide range of industrial premises. Although unsupported by any definite statistics, there is the strong impression that it was in this type of construction that concrete predominated, rather than in offices, shops or hotels. The exploitation of the greater flexibility in design which reinforced

concrete offered, in particular the development of its use in modern movement architecture still needs to be explored.

Notes

1 'Report of the joint committee on reinforced concrete', *RIBAJ*, 14 (1907), p. 513—41.
2 *BRC Structures*, Manchester, 1923
3 'Harrod's depository, Barnes', *Concrete*, 6 (1911), p. 225.
4 For example, *Specification* 1898 makes reference to slag cement: BS 146: 1923 Portland Blast Furnace Cement.
5 'Aggregates for concrete', *AJ*, 27. (1910), p. 435.
6 *Specification*, 6 (1903), p. 259.
7 *FerroConcrete*, 5
8 'Tests on reinforced concrete conducted in Great Britain', *Concrete*, 5 (1910), pp. 36—44.
9 'GPO in reinforced concrete', *Concrete*,.2 (1907), pp. 321—3. Built in London but the location is only identified as 'opposite the General Post Office North'. 'Reinforced Concrete for post office buildings', *Concrete*, 3 (1908), pp. 11—19, describes post offices in Manchester and Birmingham. 'Reinforced Concrete for post office buildings', *Concrete*, 3 (1908), pp. 203—7, (Western District, Post Office, London) & 437—44 (St. Martin's le Grand, London). The Western District Post Office used the Coignet system.
10 'Royal Liver Building, Liverpool, the first Ferro concrete skyscraper', *FerroConcrete*, 1 (1909), pp. 91—4, 150—3, 172—7, 210—14.
11 *Concrete*, 6 (1911), pp. 368—77.
12 'Office Premises, Birmingham', *Concrete*, 8 (1913), pp. 525—9.
13 *Concrete*, 29 (1934), pp. 115—20.
14 *Concrete*, 14 (1919), p. 17.
15 'Standardisation in proportioning concrete', *Concrete*, 17 (1922), pp 665—9 and 745—8. The work was published in the US as Duff Abrams & Stanton Walker, Bulletin No. 9 of the Lewis Institute, Chicago.
16 'Proportioning concrete mixtures', *Concrete* , 18 (1923), pp. 253—60 and 350—9.
17 *Concrete*, 16 (1921), p. 791.
18 *Concrete*, 27 (1932), pp. 261—2.
19 *Concrete* , 29 (1934), pp. 393—400.
20 'Internal vibration of concrete', *Concrete* , 30

(1935), pp. 576—8.

21 'Joint research on the vibration of concrete',
    Structural Engineer, 15 (1937), pp. 133—43.

22 See, for example, 'Grading of aggregate:
    experiments on the relation of grading to
    vibration', an editorial comment in *Concrete*, 31
    (1936), p. 263 and 'The use of vibrators:
    recommendations of the American Concrete
    Institute' *Concrete*, 31 (1936), pp. 348—52.

23 'Rapid hardening Portland cement and precast
    beams', *Concrete*, 20 (1925), p. 351.

24 'Rapid concrete construction', *Concrete*, 21
    (1926), p. 727.

25 'Rapid-hardening Portland cement' *Concrete*, 20
    (1925), p. 85.

26 *A&BN*, 130 (1932), p. 2.

27 Building Research Board, 1934, *Report of the
    Reinforced Concrete Structures committee of the
    Building Research Board with recommended
    code of practice for the use of concrete.*

28 'New buildings in the United States on the
    "Mushroom" reinforced concrete system',
    Concrete, 2 (1907), pp. 407—11.

29 *Concrete*, 13 (1918), p.70, 161.

30 *A&BN*, 120 (1928), p. 567.

31 'Construction 17, "Girderless" floors', *AJ*, 51
    (1921), pp. 329 —30.

32 'A floor test', *Concrete*, 16 (1921), p. 128.

33 'Flat slab system at Norwich: new reinforced
    concrete building embodies latest American
    methods' *Concrete*, 20 (1925), pp. 601—7.

34 *Concrete*, 20 (1925), p. 607.

35 'Rapid concrete construction', *Concrete*, 21
    (1926), p. 727.

36 'Wrigley's New Factory', *AJ*, 67 (1928), p. 354.

37 'Mushroom construction — the problems and
    advantages of a new method', *A&BN*, 120
    (1928), pp. 567—8.

38 'Mushroom Construction Again', *A&BN*, 124
    (Aug, 1930), pp. 232—7.

39 It was reported in *Architecture Illustrated*,
    Dec. 1930.

40 *Architectural Record*, 66 (Oct 1929), p. 362.

41 'A model factory', *Kahncrete*, 1 (1914—15), p. 9.

6 Timber engineering

Carpentry at the turn of the century

In earlier centuries, carpentry was one of the most important building trades, and the timber of buildings an important part of their structure. Even the brick-built Georgian house relies on its timber floors and internal partitions for the stability of its walls, but the relative importance of the trade declined with the introduction of iron and there was little development of structural carpentry in Britain during the latter part of the nineteenth century. Increasing spans of roof trusses had been achieved by the gradual substitution of iron in trusses (see Yeomans, 1992, Ch. 10), while iron also became more common in long-span floors, particularly as a response to concerns about fire protection. Some roof and bridge structures were built using laminated timber, drawing on scientific work carried out in France, but the largest timber structures built in England were those for the Navy's ship-building slips which, in spite of their size, still used fairly conventional carpentry methods. These long-span structures are not without interest but they were all built in unusual circumstances while the general use of timber structures declined. The development of a scientific understanding of the timber, which had begun with the work of Barlow in the early nineteenth century and was then disseminated through Nicholson and Tredgold, was effectively curtailed as engineers turned their attention to the new materials, iron and steel, so that a full treatment of timber as an engineering material had to wait until this century.

The state of carpentry at the turn of this century is best illustrated by George Ellis (1927) who described the roof structures and trussed partitions which had been in use throughout the nineteenth century and which had changed very little during that period except for some modest improvements with the introduction of metal connectors, used at the junctions of members. Ellis showed a design of standard king-post roof trusses produced by Messrs Cubbitt which was designed round simple cast-iron shoes but he also illustrated the comparatively new Belfast truss (see below) which used small section timbers and so presaged the kind of developments which were to occur much later.

Changes in the supply of timber had occurred in the nineteenth century as different species and larger sections became available through the exploitation of both North American and colonial sources and the importance of timber in general construction is reflected in the large number of different species that continued to be available. General building softwoods were being imported from both the Baltic countries and North America under a variety of names which still often reflected their port of origin as much as the actual species: the result was confusing. Table 6.1 provides a list of some of the common species used together with some of the names being used by the trade at the time. In addition to these species, wainscot oak was imported from the Baltic and continued to be quoted in price lists into the inter-war years.

Much of the development of timber construction in this century may be attributed to the two world wars, both to design efforts during the wars and to the post-war shortages, partly because ways had to

Table 6.1 Common names of timbers

Species	Common name
Pinus sylvestris	Baltic fir (sometimes Memel fir), Baltic pine, Northern pine, Red deal, Scotch fir, Yellow deal
Abies excelsa	Spruce, Norway fir, White deal
Pinus resinosa	Canadian pine, Red pine, American deal
Pinus strobus	Yellow pine, Weymouth pine, White pine

be found to economize on the timber used and partly because timber was seen as an alternative to other materials which were also in short supply. There is a paradox: timber becomes scarce in time of war because war consumes timber, but while in Britain most timber has to be imported, it is still seen as a substitute for other materials and developed as such. This is partly because it offers a light-weight building material for temporary prefabricated construction but also because there may be shortages of other building materials or building skills. After the First World War timber was looked to as a possible material for house-building because of the shortages of men in the traditional building trades, while it was developed during the Second World War as a substitute for steel and aluminium in the form of plywood for boat and aircraft building: developments which have eventually benefited building have not always originated in the building trade.

Stress grading

There could be no development of timber as an engineering material without its structural properties being fully understood. The sizes of structural timbers to be used in different situations had been largely established by custom and by rules of thumb which, as they were known to be adequate for the sizing of floor joists and roof timbers, were eventually incorporated into building by-laws and then into the Building Regulations. There were some attempts to regard timber as a possible engineering material in the early nineteenth century when the first tables comparing the properties of different species were published by Barlow (1817) and Tredgold (1820), but they made little attempt to understand how the variability of the material affected its properties apart from distinguishing between different species. The kind of calculation methods which were by then being used to determine the sizes of structural members of other materials could not be routinely used for determining timber sizes until there were accepted methods of grading timbers for structural use, but these did not appear until this century. The need for stress grading and for determining the structural strength of timbers first came with the development of aircraft production rather than from any need of the building industry. Because

airframes were built of timber, their designers needed to establish testing methods to determine the structural properties of the material and it was this need rather than construction which led to an improved understanding of timber. A British Standard for testing was first issued in 1929 [1] but it was to be some years before a knowledge of timber properties could be used as a basis for engineered building structures.

Builders and architects continued to rely upon the commercial grades available from the turn of the century and throughout the inter-war period. Grades for Baltic timbers had been established with the publication of the Hernosand rules in 1880. Timber was imported in unsorted lots described in such terms as 'not lower than 4ths' (or sometimes even 5ths) but there was no definite specification for these grades and it was still common practice to specify the country of origin of building timbers, with the preference for certain areas of supply persisting, just as in the nineteenth century (see Yeomans, 1989). There was no established data on the strengths of Baltic timbers as late as 1936 when Chaplin published figures showing that the modulus of rupture might vary from 4680 to 10,000 lbs/sq. in. The effect of this on structural sizes in use is seen from tables then published in *Wood* giving structural design data for joists.[2] Although these tables distinguished two timber groups — redwood or yellow deal and white fir or spruce — seldom were the recommended sizes for the two groups any different.

The position was better in Canada and the United States. The first American grading rules based on standard tests had appeared in Forest Services Bulletin No. 108 in 1912. The US Department of Agriculture published further rules in its Circular 295 of 1925 which then led to the American Society for Testing Materials (ASTM) standard. This meant that timber graded for strength could be imported from North America, and Douglas fir, which was readily available, was normally specified for structural work in Britain (Barnes, 1941). Although Grundy (1930) had earlier published a table of timber strengths (Table 6.2), the first incorporation of allowable stresses in design regulations was in London in 1937 when the LCC timber by-laws regulated for the use of Douglas fir and pitch-pine based on the use of timbers graded to the ASTM standard (Table 6.3). Two grades of timber were introduced by the by-laws, 800 and 1200 psi timber, thus allowing a more rational design, although only for stress-graded North American timbers. Chaplin (1937) summarized the position that had existed previously, pointing out that only joists, rafters and purlins were controlled by the rules of thumb which had been incorporated into current by-laws. As the by-laws assumed only traditional roof construction, they made no recommendations for purlins to support roofs sheeted with corrugated steel or asbestos and Chaplin noted that such rules as there were for trimmers in floors were inadequate and could lead to unsafe structures.

The lack of adequate structural data for timber construction had meant that alternative materials enjoyed an advantage. A British Standard committee was working on the development of timber grades for Britain but, that it was attempting to 'make the grading conform with the present understanding and trade usage relating to the ordinary commercial

Table 6.3 LCC Timber Bylaws issued 30 Nov. 1937–1 Jan. 1938.

'Graded timber known as "Grade 1200 1b.f." shall be Douglas Fir or pitch-pine of the long-leaved variety. Columbian or Oregon Pinewould come within the description'

Table of loadings

Stresses	Non–graded	Graded
Bending	800	1200
Shear–par.	90	100
Shear–perp.	165	325
Compression s.r> 10	800	1000
Tension	800	1200
E	1,200,000	1,600,000

Source: Grundy, F.R.B (1930), Builders Materials (London: Longman), p.14

Table 6.2 Timber strengths – All figures in lbs/sq.in.

	Tension parallel	Compression	Shear perpendicular
Baltic Deal	4500	500	3500
Pitch pine	6000	6500	4500
English oak	7500	7500	4500

Modulus of elasticity, E=1,500,000 lbs./sq. in.

Source: Grundy, F.R.B (1903), Builders Materials (London: Longman), p.14

grades of redwood and whitewood' (Chaplin, 1936, p. 238) may not have helped to improve the status of timber as an engineering material. The position for an importing country is quite different from countries growing their own timber. Not only do the latter have a plentiful supply but they also have a limited number of species which simplifies grading. An importing country like Britain must be prepared to buy from number of countries to ensure supplies and so needs a method of grading which

accommodates a correspondingly wide range of species. BS 940 published in 1942 had 18 grading schedules. Writing a decade later, Reece (1951) opined that it was necessary to reduce this number and compared the situation in Finland with that in Britain. The former had just three grades of redwood and whitewood, while Britain had 27 grades and 23 species. The remedy for this was to group species together and at that time Reece proposed just two classes of softwoods and a simple method of grading which relied upon limiting the size of knots and shakes depending upon the size of the piece of timber.

Timber grading must accomplish several tasks which are not easily achieved at the same time. It has to simplify the process of design while at the same time minimizing the rejection rate, so making maximum use of the timber available. To some extent, these requirements conflict with the design of most efficient structures since the resulting compromise may result in some timbers being used below their actual structural capacity. The principal developments which were to lead eventually to the introduction of engineering grades came first in the immediate post-war period with the experimental work of Chaplin on the behaviour of timber, and the effect of knots on strength, and then with the subsequent publications of the Forest Products

Research Laboratory (FPRL).

The possibilities of using stress-graded timber for structures and the advantages that could be gained were clearly demonstrated in 1948 when Silvester reported the construction of a jetty in which savings had been made in the sizes of timbers used by grading the material. He carried out the grading himself as a demonstration in front of a number of invited members of the timber trade and showed not only how rapidly timbers could be stress graded by visual inspection but also that the normal criteria of assessment could not be relied upon because it was the position of knots and not their number that was critical. Two years later, a major framed structure using stress-graded Douglas fir was designed by Phillip Reece at the Timber Development Association (TDA). The timber for this was stress graded in Britain to 1200 and 1400 lbs./sq. in. from 'Selects Merchantable'.[3] These were both demonstrations by specialists, and timber could not be considered as a material for general structural use until the publication of CP 112 in 1952. At first, this contained its own grading rules based simply on the size and position of knots visible on the surface of the timber but a change came in 1973 with the adoption of a quite different approach. This used the 'knot area ratio' method, previously used in North America but published as BS 4978, which uses the position of the pith within each piece and so recognizes the shape of knots within the timber and not simply their surface effect. This is the method of visual stress grading in use today. However, the older grading rules are still valuable for timbers in standing buildings which have to be graded in place. The knot-area-ratio method depends upon knowing the position of the pith which is not possible if the end of the timber cannot be seen.

Initially all grading, whether carried out in this country or in the country of origin, was done visually and the rules were not unnaturally conservative. However, it was known that the modulus of rupture of a piece of timber was closely related to its modulus of elasticity and if a machine could be devised to measure the deflection of timber under a constant load the modulus of elasticity could be calculated and the strength deduced from that. It was thus theoretically possible to grade timbers mechanically and as that would be more accurate than visual grading, there would be a consequent improvement in the yield of higher-grade timber. Work began along these lines at FPRL in 1959 (see Fewell, 1982), and by 1962 a prototype machine had been developed. However, funding difficulties prevented the continuation of this work and it was not until the late 1960s that machines were bought from Australia with the 'Computermatic' developed to grade timber in this way. The pressure to adopt these machines came from the trussed rafter industry (see below), for whom the improved yield had a commercial advantage, although there was some initial suspicion from building sites of the timbers thus graded. Just as Silvester's 1948 demonstration — that timber which superficially appeared to be of low quality was structurally adequate had surprised members of the trade — timber with more knots than would be accepted by visual grading was now also being shown to be adequate and was finding its way into the completed roof structures.

A disadvantage with CP 112 as a design tool was that it required designers to specify the species, or at least the species group, as well as the grade of timber to be used. This placed them in a difficult position since they might not be aware of the availability of the various grades and species while it was clear that a range of alternatives might perform equally well. The situation was drastically simplified in 1984 with the issue of BS 5268 which grouped timber species and grades into strength classes. Since then engineers have been able simply to specify the strength class needed and leave it to the suppliers to provide whatever grade and species happen to be available in stock to meet their requirements. This may not make the maximum structural use of the timber available but it has had the effect of making timber design more generally accessible.

Mechanical fasteners

The second requirement for the development of timber engineering was the design and understanding of the performance of timber fasteners. This includes an understanding of those well-established devices, the nail, the screw and the bolt, but the more modern timber fasteners were vital to the construction of many large structures. As Antoine Mole (1949) pointed out in his *Histoire des Charpentiers*, properly triangulated frames cannot be built easily without metal connectors of some kind because the bending stresses which occur with so-called 'traditional' methods must limit the scale of possible structures. Mole himself had developed his own form of connector which was used with great success in the construction of a number of large trussed-timber structures in France. One might have expected the development of mechanical fasteners to have occurred first in the US, the country that had come to rely so heavily on the material for its early development and where large timber structures had already been built in the nineteenth century. However, the supply of timber was so abundant there that there was little incentive to look for ways to improve its economy of use and although a simple bulldog connector was patented in the US in 1889, it was not widely adopted. It was the First World War in Europe, and the timber shortages that resulted, which stimulated progress in these devices with various timber connectors invented in both Scandinavia and Germany. The important years were 1916—1922 during which time 60 European patents taken out. The bulldog connector was invented by Theodorsen in Norway and the advantages of the split-ring connector were separately discovered by Samuel Voss of Germany and Kreuger of Sweden, the rights of the Voss patent of 1919 being taken up by Carl Tuchscher of Breslau.

Fig. 6.1

Britain, with its poor native timber supplies did not share as much in these developments. Theodorsen's bulldog connector was marketed here by the Palnut Co. in the early 1920s and then by McAndrews Forbes. These were available in a number of sizes up to 5 in. square, the larger sizes taking the form of a hollow square of steel plate pressed to form projecting teeth both round its outer edge and round the inside square hole (Fig. 6.1). Smaller plates were circular with a square hole in the centre. The timbers were held together with bolts, but the type of connector in which the bolt was a close fit in the plate were not to be developed until later. While early brochures produced by the Palnut Co. noted the advantage of these connectors and illustrated structures in several countries which had been built using them, there were no recommended safe loads for designers to adopt until McAndrews Forbes published a guide to the use of connectors after the war (Walters, 1951).

The US began to use timber connectors in 1933 when the National Committee on Wood Utilization of the US Department of Commerce in conjunction with the Forest Products Laboratory at Wisconsin carried out tests and published their results in *The Structural Application of Modern Connectors*. The National Lumber Manufacturers Association formed the Timber Engineering Company (TECO) to hold the US patents on these connectors and by the late 1930s, there were several manuals on their use available. Perhaps more usefully for practising designers, TECO published design sheets showing a number of simple structures fully detailed,[4] but the most dramatic demonstration of the possibilities of timber structures came with the construction of airship hangars built on the west coast of the US during the war. Timber was used for these because of the shortage of steel at the time and although (again because of the war) the design stresses used in these was higher than normal, they have survived in good condition to this day.

In Britain it was the immediate post-war shortages of steel that provided an opportunity for a British design for a triangulated timber-frame structure using such connectors. Experimental work to establish acceptable loads for bulldog connectors had begun in Britain in 1947 and Reece (1948) was able to report the interim findings of this research. However, his earlier design for a large shed had already relied upon the use of such connectors (see below).

Glues, cements and composites

Other developments in structural timber rely upon the availability of glues and cements. Glues are made from animal products of various kinds and depend upon drying action for the bond which they give. They suffer the disadvantage that they will be affected by wetting and may also suffer fungal attack. Nevertheless, these were the first adhesives available and were used to great effect. Cements, which commercially are a largely post-war development, rely upon setting through an irreversible chemical reaction and are more durable.

The earliest adhesives used were based on casein, a substance occurring in milk, and this type has a very long history. Casein is produced as a powder and mixed with other materials, such as lime, sodium silicate or borax, to produce adhesives with an irreversible set and which are suitable for the particular conditions of use. Some variation in properties is possible depending upon the admixtures used but they tend to be mutually exclusive. Thus, addition of lime increases the water resistance at the expense of working life while sodium hydroxide increases working life at the expense of water resistance. They are attacked by mould growth. Soyabean has been used as the basis for casein glues, and used in the production of some plywoods since 1923, while blood albumen has also been used as a base. Interest in casein and vegetable protein cements developed during the First World War when water-resistant glues were wanted for aircraft production. Although there is a loss of strength with increased water content, it is regained on drying so that these glues were important for the production of water-resisting plywood before the introduction of synthetic resins. (A full account of the early production of plywood is given by Wood and Linn, 1950)

Synthetic resins were developed for the manufacture of plywoods to be used in aircraft and boat production and became available for this purpose in 1930. At that time it was produced in the form of a film or paper impregnated with the resin. Further development, which made the resins available as emulsions, solutions or in powder form, together with a fall in prices, led to these glues becoming common in the production of plywood by 1939. A range of synthetic resins — phenol-formaldehyde (PF), urea formaldehyde (UF), etc., —became available in the 1950s and resorcinol cements also became available after the Second World War which had the great advantage of being gap-filling and water- and boil-proof.

The great advantage of synthetic resin cements is that although they are permeable to water, their strength is not affected while the choice between the different types is dependent upon both the production methods and the conditions of use. Some of the cements require heat and pressure to form an effective joint while others may be cold-setting. For internal use, where the moisture content remains low, resins might be extended with flour-and-water paste without impairing strength: they might also be foamed. Gap-filling qualities are also important in timber engineering, and the plywood used in building the Mosquito aircraft was based on urea-resin gap-filling cements. Unfortunately, many of the cements are not resistant to prolonged exposure to high moisture content and are not suitable for external use. In the absence of any better test, boiling in water has been used as an indication of the weather-resisting properties of adhesives and it is the so-called WBP (water- and boil-proof) resorcinol adhesives which need to be used for external conditions. However, in the late 1950s, manufacturers were also reported (Weatherall, 1957) to be using resorcinol adhesives for laminated timber structures to be used internally because of the likely exposure during transport and site storage.

Apart from the improved qualities of plywoods possible with improved adhesives, and the development of laminated timber structures (see below), their availability produced a minor revolution in the wallboard industry. When Brookes discussed the development of wood adhesives in 1949, he looked forward to the bonding of wood waste and by the mid-1950s, a wide range of particle boards was available. The development of these went beyond their use as wallboards. They have become important in general construction, particularly for flooring and roofing, although it does not always seem to have been apparent to users that care has to be taken in their use and selection. Products in which the adhesive was not water-resistant have sometimes been used either in unsuitable situations or have not received sufficient care in their treatment before being within the protection of a water-tight building.

The more recently developed technique dependent upon glues has been finger jointing. This was first used in Germany during the Second World

War for timber bridges built to replace those lost through Allied bombing. Finger joints were used in joining beams in these bridges and their durability was later demonstrated when a bridge made in this way was eventually demolished after ten years' service. Research at the Otto Graff Institute led to the publication of DIN 68140 in 1960, but experimental work was still being carried out at FPRL in 1963 (Sunley & Dawe, 1963). Although a British Standard for finger joints did not appear until 1984 they were being used well before that and, in spite of some early suspicion of the technique in the UK, Rainham Timber had a machine in operation in the early 1960s. Because demand was then greater than the capacity of the small number of machines in Britain, finger-jointed material was even being imported.

The great advantage of finger jointing is the speed with which it can be carried out. Finger-jointing machines were available from the US but German machines were commonly used here. The machine cuts the fingers in the two ends of the pieces to be joined, applies the glue and presses them together. The joint is then strong enough for handling so that the timber can be immediately removed from the machine and used in production. The efficiency of the joint makes it eminently suitable for use in laminated timber structures where it superceded earlier and less efficient scarf jointing. In such structures, it was essential to be able to join timbers in their length simply because the structures were longer than the lengths of timber available, but even where only short lengths of timber are needed the facilty to join pieces in this way avoids a great deal of waste. Finger joints have therefore been used in the manufacture of trussed rafters and joinery. The early joints were 55 mm. long but much shorter joints with consequent improved economy in timber began to be used during the 1970s.

Sheet materials

While the development of plywood owes much to the aircraft industries of both world wars, it became a source for other designers in the inter-war period, for both decorative interiors and furniture making and for standard products like veneered block-board and flush doors. Its development depends upon two separate

technologies, the cutting of veneers and their glueing. The oldest method of producing veneers was by sawing and although this is an inherently wasteful method, its use persisted into the inter-war period. Decorative veneers have been produced since the 1830s by slicing across the log, rather than by sawing, so producing the matching patterns of grain used in furniture and panelling, while today veneers for general construction are obtained by rotary cutters in which the log is rotated against a long knife, thus producing long lengths of veneer.

The simplest form of glueing, adopted for early plywoods, was a wet process using animal-based glues. In this method, the veneers were glued and pressed together without any preliminary drying, and the result was a poor-quality ply with inbuilt stresses as a result of the pressing and subsequent drying process. However, it is a simpler and more rapid process than the dry-glued process in which the veneers are first kiln-dried before being assembled into plywood and, because demand was high relative to supply, wet-glued boards were extensively imported and used in the inter-war period. However, Wood and Linn (1950) reported that no wet-glued plys had been imported after the Second World War.

There was some technical development of plywood during the war again with the aircraft industry in mind. BS 4V3, which had governed aircraft plywood since the early 1930s, was replaced by BS 5V3 in 1939; BS 6V3 was produced in 1943 as a response to the need for economy in what was an imported material. But aircraft was a rather special need and, writing in 1964, Curry pointed out that at that time there was little information on the strength of plywood for building purposes. American and Scandinavian plywoods tended to be single species while there was considerable variety of species in those imported from other countries. Commercial grades simply distinguished between interior and exterior plys dependent upon the species of timber and the adhesives used. Nevertheless, the structural possibilities of a sheet material was clearly recognized and manufacturers of proprietary structures were already making use of plywood: in 1965 a standard for British-made plywoods was produced.[5] By 1970, a speaker at the conference on wood-based sheet materials referred to 'deemed to satisfy' clauses within regulations which enabled the use of structural plywood. Fibreboard has also been gradually adopted as a structural material, principally as an alternative to sheathing ply in timber-frame houses, a development made possible since experimental work on the racking resistance of such panels.

Timber floors

Timber, the basic material of floor construction, does not provide adequate fire separation in many circumstances, but nevertheless has often remained the preferred flooring and provided the most convenient structure unless fire protection was needed. At the beginning of the century double floors were still being used in construction, particularly for commercial premises. This form of floor dates from the eighteenth century, when it comprised binding joists spanning either between walls or large timber beams, with bridging joists over these to carry the flooring (Fig. 6.2). The bridgings were normally notched over the bindings which in turn were jointed to the main beams with tusk tenons. As iron and steel were introduced into construction the detailing changed: in 1898, *Specification* could recommend that 'Binders to be framed with stub tusk tenons and oak treenails or *hung in cast iron stirrups* ' (author's italics). Ellis (1927) showed iron stirrups used for connecting binders to timber girders, so avoiding the labour-intensive tusk tenon that had been common until then. But by now the main beams might also be of iron with binders commonly carried on plates on the lower flange, although *Specification* recommended joists to be supported on hoop iron from the upper flange in preference to being built on to a wood plate. We are left to guess the reason.

Sizes of timbers for domestic construction were still determined largely by rules of thumb. The inclusion of timber-floor sizes in regulations has already been discussed in Chapter 1. Ellis included an appendix in his book which showed how the sizes of large members could be calculated from basic principles using experimental results for the strength of individual species but, with no stress grading of timber, large factors of safety were suggested. *Specification* recommended that binders should not be more than 6 ft. nor girders more than 10 ft. apart. The safe limit for bridging joists was said to be 16 ft. with joists 10 in. deep. It gave the common rule of thumb for sizing joists (half the span in inches plus two inches) and

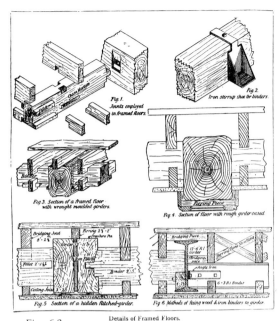

Fig. 6.2 Details of Framed Floors.

recommended herringbone strutting every 4 ft. Pugging in timber floors might still be used, requiring pugging boards to be laid between the joists with slag wool and silicate cotton used as the pugging material.

Timber-frame housing

The simplest form of all-timber construction is the small framed building of which the timber house is the most important. There were several scattered examples of timber house construction in the inter-war period but these early essays in what was a radically new method of building made little general impact. Some local authorities used timber construction because of the shortage of traditional building-trade skills and there was some interest in the material for private housing. However, there was little similarity between many of these construction systems and it was not until after the Second World War that timber-frame housing emerged from the experimental stage. A factor affecting inter-war development, particularly in the private sector, was that timber still had the image of the army hut and the chicken run and, although Boulton, technical director of the TDA, was to complain about this image (1938), the products of Boulton and Paul, who actively marketed timber buildings could hardly have encouraged a feeling for the timber house as a high-quality product as many of their products were cheap village halls and sports pavilions.

Construction of timber houses in the inter-war period can be usefully divided into three groups. There was an early phase in which timber was seen as a possible solution to the housing shortage which it was anticipated would follow the war, and this period is characterized by the use of army huts. It was realized that the traditional building industry would be incapable of meeting the demand for housing when the war was over and schemes were put in hand to convert and auction off these now redundant buildings. There was some opposition from *The Builder* to this move,[6] but it could be described as a period of emergency action. Later, local authorities who were building semi-detached and small groups of houses within the framework of the 1924 Housing Act experimented with a number of different systems of prefabricated housing, including timber. However, the use of timber frame failed to become well established even though some substantial groups of houses were built, and it was not until the post-Second World War period that there was a much more successful use of timber framing in both public and private sectors. Within the private sector, there were two kinds of timber housing: timber was used by a few architects for one-off houses, and there were also off-the-peg houses offered for a wide range of pockets.

The private sector

The timber-hut image may have hindered the development of timber houses in the middle-income market, but there were companies who saw a demand for timber at either end of the range. Small, inexpensive, prefabricated cottages and bungalows were advertised for the lower end of the market, and Westholme Bungalows of Houslow offered a complete range of timber buildings from a privy to a £400 bungalow.[7] They produced a range of cottages at under £100, but their cheapest sensible dwellings sold for about £180. For this, the customer could have four habitable rooms contained within a little less than 800 sq. ft. They all had tongue-and-groove weather-boarded finish below sill level and a kind of half-timbered appearance above, which resulted from using asbestos sheets between studs. The better-known Boulton and Paul Company were much more up-market, as were their prices. In 1927, their bungalows and cottages

could be bought for as little as £300, for buyers to put up themselves, but were in the £500 range if erected by the company.[8] For this, one appeared to recieve rather less space than in the Westholme product but perhaps a higher standard of construction. They had brick dwarf walls and timber floors while the softwood frames were assembled using mortice-and-tenon joints. Many were advertised with thatch roofs and there was some variety in the external claddings used. The interiors were either lath and plaster, or lined with asbestos cement sheeting; the latter to reduce costs rather than for fire protection. It was this company that also sought to exploit the upper end of the market and their catalogue illustrated a number of very large houses which they had erected before the war with prices between £2,000 and £4,000.

A number of architects, some of them well-known figures, used timber in the construction of private houses. There were both 'traditional' designs, like one by Lutyens, and others like Chermayeff, with distinctly modernist leanings, but, while interesting as examples, their impact on general building could only be the extent to which publication of these designs demonstrated timber to be a practical method of construction. This influence might have been reinforced by such details as those provided by *Wood* for a house by Gropius.[9] Jordan (1936) produced a little book extolling the virtues of timber houses and illustrating historic examples as well as modern designs, while Boulton's (1938) more extensive collection of entirely modern timber

Fig. 6.3

buildings drew heavily on foreign examples. There was also some commercial effort to promote timber framing. A timber house designed by W. Tatton Brown, in association with the recently formed TDA, was commissioned by the British Columbian Timber Commissioner for the 1936 Ideal Home Exhibition.[10] This was more than a simple box and so demonstrated the flexibility of timber framing (Fig. 6.3). By using a lattice beam under the wall plate to carry the roof, the design incorporated a forward projection of the ground-floor wall (although this is not very clear in the photograph). It also had a balcony and projecting roof on the front carried on timber columns. The TDA also organized a competition for the design of timber houses as a way of encouraging interest in this material.

Local authority projects

Timber-frame housing schemes by local authorities did not draw on this home-based industry but tended to look abroad for their product. The first scheme of this kind was a small group of houses built in Newton near Swansea which used building methods brought over from the US. Sir Charles Rutter (1919) in an article entitled 'British House-building Methods' gave an account of American timber-frame methods applied to British conditions. He looked first at the statistics of demand and the capacity of the industry, the mismatch between which suggested a need for new methods of construction. Based on this analysis he suggested timber as a solution and then described the construction of these houses. They were balloon framed with 4 x 2-in. studs at 16-in. centres. Three types of house were built, one stucco-finished, one of brick veneer and the third of brick to the first floor with 'half-timbering' above. Rutter was aware of the problem of the temporary appearance of timber cladding to the British eye and this may have suggested some of the finishes used. One of the advantages he noted for timber was the avoidance of the drying-out problem that occurs with the use of wet bricks, mortar and plaster.

This was not only a very early scheme, built before the 1924 Housing Act, and so unlikely to have had any immediate influence on local authority construction, it was also untypical in being of American origin. Local authorities later looked more towards Scandinavian

countries for their systems. Many of the inter-war local authority schemes using timber housing have been described in detail in Sjorstrom's 1943 study, also in an article *Post-War Building Studies*[11] and in a small booklet first produced by the TDA (1944) in the same year (see also Corkhill, 1938). *Post-War Building Studies* noted the numbers of houses of various types built by different authorities, which included the Scottish Special Housing Association, Newcastle Corporation and the LCC. However, these were by no means the only schemes and reports of others can be found.[12] The earliest and largest schemes appear to be the LCC estates at Watling and Becontree, totalling 689 houses.

The studies show that the methods of construction fell into three broad types. So-called English construction which used 4 x 2-in. timber studs and horizontal boarding, Norwegian construction which had 3-in. square studs with vertical boarding externally, and Swedish construction which was based on a solid wall of 3-in. tongue-and-groove planks with a vertical board-and-batten cladding. The houses of English construction were entirely site-built while the others were prefabricated with two-storey height panels. Of all the local authorities, the LCC built the largest number of timber houses between the wars and may have built more had they not had labour disputes when the bricklayers saw their jobs threatened by this method of construction.

War-time developments

The Second World War encouraged the development of prefabricated construction. Timber was used during the war for temporary military accommodation and for emergency hospitals and the publication of the two commercially sponsored studies (Sjorstrom, 1943; TDA, 1944) before its end suggests that there was some anticipation that timber could contribute to post-war housing. The TDA held another house design competition in 1945 with this object in mind. At the time, there seemed to be several possible lines of development: one based on the production of temporary huts, the adoption of American methods, the revival of the pre-war techniques, and a new building technology based on stressed skin construction. For a while, it seemed as if design and production in this country might draw on American experience as there was some importing of American prefabs (at this time

British timber prefabs were based on army huts) and reports of American construction methods in the journals as well as a Government report on American house construction. There were also some experimental systems which, like the use of aluminium for construction, were developed out of manufacturing capacity that had been needed for the war effort and which was now seeking alternative uses. These are more interesting as technical curiosities rather than for having made any permanent influence on construction methods. The best known was the Weybridge house developed by the British Power Boat Company[13] but this and the Scottwood house (TDA, 1944, pp 22, 24—6), systems relying upon plywood and stressed-skin construction, remained curiosities. It was not to be a fruitful line of development as much simpler forms of construction based on studs and plywood sheathing were to prove more successful, presumably because they were much simpler to manufacture. To this extent, the Spooner house (Fig 6.4) described by the TDA booklet as partly prefabricated, pointed the way forward.

Regrettably, the post-war restrictions on the importing of timber frustrated any immediate exploitation of timber techniques. It has been suggested that one of the motives for this restriction was to facilitate the development of the aluminium prefab to absorb what had suddenly become the surplus capacity of the government-owned aluminium plants (Finnimore, 1985). At the time, the timber trade

lobbied for the lifting of restrictions to allow more timber to be imported from Canada, but the statistics of timber imports in the pre-war period suggest that this would have had little effect. The fall in the quantity of imported softwoods can be largely accounted for by the drop in the Russian trade and it remains debatable whether North American supplies could have quickly made up the shortfall. Unable to build for the home market, because of the restrictions, some timber-building manufacturers in this country built for export. Restrictions did not apply to softwoods which were to be re-exported and some single-storey prefabricated housing was produced for export to Australia and Canada.[14] Riley Newsum were associated with two such schemes. It is also necessary to point out that the restrictions did not apply to imported hardwoods which came from our own colonies and there were suggestions at the time that hardwoods should be used for floor joists in houses.[15]

There was limited use of timber frame for local authority housing but a report of a development of prefabricated houses in Scotland calls into question the level of thermal insulation that may have been included in all of the timber-frame house construction up to this time. Its construction used 2 x 3-in. studs at 18-in. centres, which clearly used less timber than normal for frame construction, and a similar scheme was reportedly built in Hull. The Scottish scheme had $\frac{1}{2}$-in. x $\frac{3}{4}$-in. fillets to carry plasterboard between the studs with an outer cladding of vertical tongue-and-groove boarding backed by a layer of bituminous felt. All this was factory-fixed with an inner plasterboard lining site-fixed after erection, but there was no other insulation provided. (Some examples of timber frame had blockwork set between the studs which would have improved the thermal performance a little.) Panels were bolted together rather than nailed and external corners were formed with steel angle cleats screwed to the studs. Clearly, timber frame was not yet an established vernacular.

The most successful development of the pre-war methods was the solid wall Swedish system which began to be imported almost immediately after the war. Houses were put up to designs by the Ministry of Works and they produced an instruction manual for their erection[16] but it was still to be some time before frame methods became established. Official recognition of timber frame as a method of construction suitable for

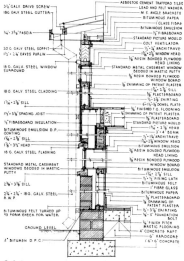

Fig. 6.4   22. *Vertical Section showing construction of Spooner House*

local authority housing came in 1963 when Simms CDA built some houses at West Bromwich. This was the first example of timber-framed housing sanctioned by the Ministry of Housing for the 60-year loan period.[17] A number of other systems then followed. The Yorkshire Development Group (YDG) was formed to build timber-frame houses in Hull based on the earlier Spooner house[18] and in 1965 the Wier Group, which had earlier been associated with a steel-based method of house construction, developed its Multicom system which used timber framing clad with aluminium.[19]

Construction systems developed at this time were not part of a general development of timber framing. They might be designed round particular construction methods or plant, or perhaps for particular contracts. There was even an example of volumetric construction when Calder Homes built houses at Washington, County Durham in this way.[20] Volumetric construction is based upon the factory fabrication of complete 'boxes' which usually form part of one floor of a building, often with interior linings and finishes and possibly with exterior finishes as well. This is essentially the technique for building mobile homes and although it is a construction method that has been used occasionally, it has never become an established method for ordinary housing as it has in Sweden. The Calder system was in production in the 1960s (see below) and in the 1980s, Potton Timber Engineering built a number of local authority houses in this way which had a factory-applied rendered wall-finish; TRADA have been involved in the development of this type of construction which has achieved some popularity for hotel or motel developments, but it remains a rather specialized method.

To complete the picture of timber walling in housing during the 1950s and 1960s requires a brief discussion of cross-wall construction. At this time brick chimneys were still needed even in timber-frame houses, so some form of mixed construction was almost inevitable. In 1957, the LCC built some housing at Farnham Royal the design of which was reportedly based on a study of Canadian methods.[21] This had solid masonry party walls carrying the floors while timber front and rear walls carried the roof. The roof structure used TDA trusses (see below). The party walls, that is the cross-walls, projected beyond the timber walls, a feature that was almost to become a signature of cross-wall construction, but curiously the chimneys in this scheme were freestanding within each dwelling. Many cross-wall schemes followed, and within a very short time, so that this became a well-established method of construction. Moreover, with the introduction of trussed purlin and other roofs that spanned between the cross-walls, the timber walls could be completely non-load-bearing.

Post-war technical development

The development of timber-frame housing as it is presently used in Britain was encouraged by two organizations, TRADA, with the interests of the Timber Trade Federation in mind, and what is now the marketing organization the Council of Forest Industries of British Columbia (COFI) which represents Canadian interests. Advocating platform frame construction, the Canadians built demonstration houses at the Ideal Home Exhibition, first in 1957 and then in 1960. They had earlier produced an album of houses built in British Columbia to illustrate the possibilities of timber frame[22] and in 1962, they invited a fact-finding commission to visit Canada to see timber house construction there. This resulted in a Government White Paper with recommendations for the development of this method of construction in Britain. In 1964, they built a number of demonstration homes at Abbotts Langley.[23]

TRADA, with its full-time technical staff, was in a better position to develop the techniques for this country and to do more building. Their early schemes were balloon framed, but this technique is less convenient for prefabricated construction than platform frame, unless a crane is used for erection, because the height of wall units make the panels difficult to handle. They built experimental schemes at Penkridge with load-bearing timber-framed external wall panels where different forms of construction were used for party walls, including timber-framed units with 1-in. fibreglass blanket suspended in a 6-in. cavity. This was done so that site measurements could be made to compare the sound-reduction performance of the different structures. TRADA was also interested in the possibility of higher-rise schemes for local authorities, and in 1966, completed some four-storey maisonettes at Glory Hill[24] for High Wycombe RDC, also using balloon frame but this time with masonry party walls.

This was also the year in which it published its design guide for timber-frame housing.[25] Four years later, it was to built more four-storey maisonettes at Watery Lane but now using platform frame and timber party walls. An article describing this provided some construction details, probably bringing this type of construction to many architects' attention for the first time.[26]

Although this was a period when there was considerable interest in prefabricated housing, timber frame did not enjoy a large share of the market, perhaps because the simplicity of platform frame was unknown to many designers. Powell (1967) reported that only 11 per cent of low rise housing completions in 1965 and '66 were timber frame compared with about 70 per cent in *in situ* concrete. As part of a special *AJ* issue on industrialized housing systems the only complete timber system described was the Calder system based on box units.[27]

Once the platform frame had been developed, the basic structure remained little changed and technical development was directed towards improving some of the details. The importance of providing adequate moisture barrier on the inner face of the wall was recognized but this might be achieved through the use of either polythene sheet or foil-backed plasterboard, depending upon the particular manufacturer. The function of the sheathing is to give in-plane stiffness to the panels and so provide the stud frame with some resistance to wind loading. Before the war, the sheathing of timber frames had been by diagonal boarding, and there were some houses still constructed like this after the war, but by the 1960s the availability of plywood for sheathing made the production of timber frames much easier. Panels could also be stiffened with other sheet materials once the relationship between sheet thickness, nailing pattern and the racking resistance provided had been established. In 1968, TRADA carried out tests which provided the data for fibreboard to be used as a sheathing material.

The common use of brick veneers in Britain and the associated cavity between this cladding and the timber frame presents concern for the fire protection of timber frames because of the possibility of fire spread within the cavity. It also means that an effective connection has had to be provided between the frame and the brick veneer and developments in both of these areas have gradually improved the performance of this type of construction. Initially, cavity barriers were formed from timber but recognition of the difficulty of ensuring a good seal against brickwork cladding encouraged a move to fibreglass stops. There was also a period when a variety of cavity ties of uncertain efficacy were available. Even flammable plastic ties were marketed at one time but there has now been a general move to stainless-steel ties.

The disadvantage of timber-frame housing has been that material costs have been greater than for masonry construction but the rise in interest rates in the 1970s gave it an economic advantage simply because of the speed of construction. Released from the pace of bricklaying, it also allowed builders to plan their operations with more certainty. The effect of this was to produce a major shift towards timber-frame construction by a number of large speculative house-builders. This was possible because frame assembly is a relatively simple operation so that the change in construction method involved little training. Although capable of a high degree of factory mechanization, the manufacture of timber frames is equally possible with very small capital investment. Here it is useful to point out that there is a considerable difference between small open-panel construction and large closed panels which are common in Scandinavia. The latter require a much greater degree of mechanization both in the factory and on site. Another factor which favoured timber frame has been the relative ease with which the demand for increasing standards of thermal insulation could be accommodated and the popularity of this form of construction in the late 1970s and early 1980s also encouraged the importing of large-panel systems from Scandinavia which already had higher thermal standards.

This was a period when timber-frame construction was increasingly used for local authority housing, especially in new town developments, and was taken up in the speculative housing market by major builders who were able to let contracts for the fabrication of frames to manufacturing joiners. Then, suddenly the market collapsed; its decline can be dated to a single night in July 1983 when Granada TV screened a programme which 'exposed' poor site control being exercised by one of the major users of timber frames. The result was an immediate rejection of this type of house by the general public. Timber-frame houses became difficult to sell and builders of masonry houses began to advertise their products as 'traditionally built,' as if by that time such a thing as traditional construction still existed. The principal concern was that the possible high moisture content of timbers might lead to decay of the structural frames, although there was no evidence that this was occurring. One official response to this that is worth noting was a change requiring all the timber of wall frames to be preservative-treated; previously this requirement had only applied to sole plates.

The development of timber-frame housing in the post-war rebuilding programme and beyond has to be seen in two different ways. Closed systems of construction for local authority housing, developed by contractors or manufacturers may have been built in large numbers but where their developers made no attempt to enter the general construction market they have had no lasting influence. Such systems may have lasted only as long as the organizations, as long as their interest in this particular method of construction, or possibly only as long as a single contract. At the other extreme, timber frame has been treated as a general building method which can be used in competition with other methods of construction. Since the 1980s at least one firm specializing in timber-frame construction has tendered for work in competition with other builders using masonry, employing 'design' staff to draw up framing layouts as a preliminary step in estimating. It is a method that is still attacting technical development both to improve its thermal performance and to increase the number of floors over which it can be used.

Other timber-framed building

Just as Boulton and Paul offered a number of standard timber buildings during the inter-war period, in post-war years there were a number of systems devised for other low-rise buildings. There was a clear market for the rapid construction of classrooms, motels or small offices and these generally require a completely different form and method of construction from timber-frame housing because the functional requirements are different. With daylighting requirements governing the design of classrooms and offices, large windows dictate the form of construction. The wall usually comprises windows between posts so that the construction becomes a series of frames filled with window frames in

their upper part and with a solid panel of sheet material below. This results in an appearance quite different from other forms of construction with a definite temporary feel about it. There seems to be no rational basis for this response since such buildings have stood the test of time and many schools still have such classrooms which have given many years service. These systems appeared in the mid-1950s with Derwent[28] and Medway[29] schools, although some schools in Derbyshire were built in a similar way to designs by the county architect. Timber buildings of this type were also developed for a wider market.[30]

Post-war roof construction

Until the Second World War, the common method of framing roofs, whether gabled or hipped, was to assist the rafters with heavy purlins at mid-slope and to strut these purlins from internal walls. While post-war restrictions limited the quantities of timber that could be used, it was a restriction on softwood rather than on all timbers, and hardwoods could be obtained from British colonies. The irony was that even though steel was also in short supply, it was used for some domestic roof structures in preference to timber and steel window frames were still popular. The use of the latter, together with solid floors, may have enabled builders to keep within the limits imposed on the use of softwood without needing to save timber within the roof structure. Nevertheless, with an extensive rebuilding programme, timber savings in domestic construction were clearly advantageous and one place where this could be made was in roofs. Savings could be achieved if structures could be developed which did not need the large-section purlins and there were two possible approaches here. One was the use of trussed purlins, or some similar form which used less timber, while the other was the development of light-trussed rafters. Another saving was possible by using interlocking tiles which were both lighter than plain tiles and allowed lower pitches (Langley London Ltd, 1951).

The first development of trussed rafters came with the TDA roof, a structure relying upon the assembly of trusses from small scantling timbers with the aid of toothed-plate connectors. This was not a true trussed-rafter roof since the trusses occurred every fourth rafter to carry light-section purlins which supported the common rafters, but the advantages to be gained from

Fig. 6.5

this type of structure was that it overcame the need for large-section purlin. It could also be constructed using short lengths of timber and did not depend on support from internal walls below, so that there was improved flexibility of planning. It was also possible to prefabricate either individual trusses or even have complete roofs framed on the ground and craned into place (Fig. 6.5). Their design, which was launched at the Building Exhibition of 1947, had been developed from designs originally produced for a housing scheme for Leyland Urban District in that same year,[31] although we can perhaps see the beginnings of the idea in wartime designs for national camps.[32] Standard design sheets, which are still available, were produced for a range of pitches and spans and the type was later extended to shallow-pitch roofs and longer spans suitable for buildings like schools and industrial sheds.[33]

The introduction of such an engineered design into traditional construction presents some problems of quality control, particularly because the designer of the engineered components could not exercise control over the way in which his designs might be used. There are two concerns here. An engineered design assumes correct assembly of the trusses but subsequent inspection of these roofs shows that some assemblers (carpenters seems hardly the word) were not aware of the need for the teeth of the connectors to be fully embedded: either that or they did not have the means to achieve this. Assembly is relatively simple and may be carried out on site (Fig. 6.6) but it does need special equipment and at least a little training. The other problem has been that, in spite of the cheapness of the design sheets, variations on the basic TDA trusses have been found, some of which seem to have been made without any structural appreciation of the original design.

The TDA roof was designed on the assumption that the front and rear walls of the house would be load-bearing but, as noted above, the use of cross-wall construction was facilitated if the purlins carried the roof load. Moreover, it was advantageous if the purlins were positioned so that they would carry all the load from the rafters and not just a proportion. What was required was some form of purlin which would occupy the depth between the rafters and the ceiling joists, enabling both to be fixed to it. TRADA showed some designs which could achieve this at the 1959 Building Exhibition,[34] which included both a trussed purlin and a plywood girder, the latter comprising plywood web with timber flanges attached, and both to be used in conjunction with common rafters. They also showed scissor trusses and a design which combined a form of TDA truss with trussed purlins, although the relative complication of these would hardly have recommended them to the average builder. Trussed purlins used much the same approach as TDA trusses in their detailed design, that is, they were fabricated from small scantling timbers using timber connectors. No standard sheets were available for these so they needed to be designed for the particular job. On the other hand, plyweb beams, that is, I-section beams with timber flanges and plywood webs, could be bought off the shelf. A number of companies manufactured these so that they were convenient both for the designer and contractor, and because they involved no assembly, they were more popular.

All of these roofs were to be largely superseded by the trussed rafter roof which became common in the 1970s and 1980s. This type of structure had been in

Fig. 6.6

use in the US from where the technique was imported into Britain, first being demonstrated at the Building Exhibition of 1963. The principle is that light-trussed rafters of small-section timber may be constructed by joining the members together with gusset plates. These gussets could be of plywood or fibreboard, and in the 1964 Canadian demonstration houses, the rafters were trussed using nailed plywood gussets. However, more rapid production of trusses is possible using the pressed-metal truss-plate connectors that were part of the American development. These are galvanized plates from which projecting teeth are punched. Satisfactory performance of the trusses depends upon the design of the plate, its accurate positioning at the junctions of the timbers and proper embedding of the teeth. Although the plates' longevity was ensured by galvanizing there have been problems where plates were used in association with some timber treatments, particularly flame retardants.

Following its first appearance in Britain, several types of plate were introduced and their use rapidly spread, but its apparent simplicity was deceptive. Performance of the roof depends upon more than the performance of the individual trusses, it also depends upon the satisfactory design of the complete roof; unfortunately, failure to understand this led to failures of these roofs in the 1970s. Although they had proved satisfactory in the US the common form of roof covering there was asphalt shingles which have to be laid over a sheathing, normally of plywood. This sheathing stiffens individual rafters against buckling and ensures overall stability of the roof. Tiling battens could not provide the same stiffening effect (although in Scotland the use of sarking boards had the same effect as the sheathing used in the US). This meant that in England and Wales some form of bracing needed to be added to the trusses to ensure roof stability. This became particularly important in masonry houses as construction became lighter and the stability of the walls was dependent upon the roof for transmitting wind loads to return walls. It was thus essential for the roof structure to be adequately fixed to these walls although it seems that many designers were unaware of this.

One reason why these structural issues were not fully recognized was that the use of trusses shifted the design of the roof from the architect or structural engineer to the supplier of the trusses. Truss-plate

manufacturers provided the manufacturers of the trusses, often timber merchants or manufacturing joiners, with computer programmes to design trusses using their plates. Given such an apparently simple procedure, building designers, or even just builders, could order trusses by providing the manufacturer with no more information than the span, pitch and load, and not infrequently this was insufficient for their proper design. However, it should be noted that the advertising material produced in the early promotion of such trusses hardly suggested any caution was necessary in their use, even suggesting the easy trimming of chimney or loft access openings.

Although originally designed for domestic roofs, like the TDA roof, its potential for much larger spans was quickly realized and manufacturers were quite happy to meet customers' requirements for other than domestic roofs. It was increasing spans that eventually led to a realization that all was not well when a roof collapsed during construction. This roof had a long span over a school sports hall and was shown in the subsequent report to have been inadequately braced (Menzies & Granger, 1976; Yeomans, 1988a). Once attention was directed towards these roofs, it was realized that they were not always treated as the engineered structures which they were. The result was that the International Truss Plate Association (ITPA) began to issue information sheets on the proper handling of trusses and construction of this type of roof and TRADA set up a quality assurance scheme covering manufacturing standards. Subsequently, the code of practice was modified to ensure that the clear responsibility for the roof design was placed with the building designer.

Timber engineering

By the 1960s, quite modest buildings, even domestic buildings, were having to be treated as engineered structures. In contrast, large-scale timber structures in Britain have not been used on a regular basis although some examples have been very dramatic. The largest structure known from pre-war years was a warehouse roof constructed at Greenford in 1938. There were only two types of large-scale timber structures in use before the Second World War — the Belfast truss and the lamella — and there seem to have been very few examples of the latter. Both were possible because, as they only used timber in simple compression and tension and relied on very simple fasteners, they needed only limited knowledge of timber behaviour. The Belfast truss was a bowstring arch with a web of small timbers between the arch and the bottom chord. An article on cheap roofs in *Specification* in 1903 called these 'Irish roofs' (Mitchell, 1903); sometimes called the 'Anderson truss', they were advertised by a Belfast firm of that name well into the 1920s. However, there were other suppliers of this type of structure and also some variations in the arrangement of the diagonal timbers forming the web (see Gould et al., 1992), but all had the characteristic that under uniform loading there should be no forces in these diagonals, the load being taken by arch action in the upper chord with simple tension in the tie. The spanning capacity of this simply constructed structure made it ideal for First World War aircraft hangars and in the inter-war years, it became a standard structural device for warehouse sheds and workshops because it could offer savings over a steel roof. One report suggested that it was two-thirds the price of an equivalent steel structure,[35] and they continued to be used into the post-war years.

Timber was used extensively in exhibition structures if only because it is a material admirably suited to temporary structures enabling rapid construction, in which even quite large structures are light enough to be handled relatively easily and this occasionally led to structural developments. In 1915, Henry Dewell, who was the chief structural engineer for the Panama Pacific Exhibition in the US carried out research on the strength of lag screws and washers in conjunction with Douglas fir. In Britain, large timber structures were used in the 1938 Empire Exhibition in Glasgow. The Canadian pavilion, for example, had large Howe and lattice trusses. The TDA also put up a pavilion designed by Furneaux Jordan (Fig. 6.7), but when Bethams-Williams reported on the structures for this exhibition he noted 'Advances in building techniques attributable to the exhibition were not seen in the skeletons but in the coverings especially in the development of moulded asbestos and the fixing of both curved and flat sheets' (1938, p. 461). This was achieved because the sheet claddings were fixed to large subsidiary frames of timber studwork with mastic jointing between them. This separation of frame from the cladding enabled work on the structure to continue without waiting for decisions on the latter. It was a demonstration that the advantages of timber construction were not to lie in any direct economies in the cost of the structure but rather in the complete system.

Trussing timber

In 1949, the first large trusses were put up in Britain which depended upon an understanding of the behaviour of mechanical fasteners. These formed the roof and columns of a timber storage shed at Shoreham designed by Philip Reece to replace a building of 1900 which had a wrought-iron roof on timber columns.[36] The original applications for a licence to build a steel shed had been refused while a timber scheme had been accepted. Because of the licensing restrictions the form of the shed was designed to conform as closely as possible to the volume of storage required: the result was a portal frame with overhangs and a span of 87 ft. 6 in. Reece's specialist knowledge has already been noted but there was clearly much information already available for engineers to learn about timber use. For example, when describing the structure, Reece pointed out the ability of timber to carry higher loads for short periods and the consequent effect on design for wind loads, a factor which he said was not fully realized at that time. However, some development was still needed. In designing the purlins, there was a problem with the shear failure of end 'notches' which they had to overcome and the detailed design was also evolved as a result of tests at FPRL (though a structures laboratory was only officially established in 1956).

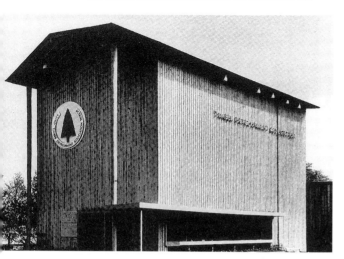

Fig. 6.7

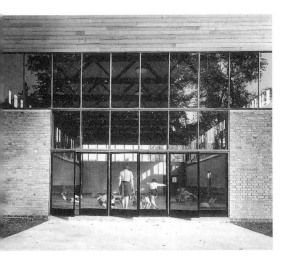

Fig. 6.8

The ability to stress-grade timber in this country and the availability of timber fasteners of known capacity might have enabled timber to be used with some structural efficiency, but there is more to the acceptance of a new structural material than the ability of engineers to design with it and in this context the observations by the builder are instructive. He noted the difficulty of pricing, especially in assessing the work involved in making the joints. Moreover, reports of two later sheds of a similar scale, and built in the same area, showed that it was difficult for engineers in Britain to balance the complexity of design, and hence the number of joints, with the savings in the quantity of timber.[37] It seemed likely that the design of timber frames of this type would remain a specialist task and a much more valuable role for timber fasteners has been their use in association with laminated timber or with composite steel and timber structures rather than complex all-timber trusses.

Because timber engineering in the early 1950s was a specialist activity, many early designs of both bolted and connected timber structures and laminated structures were produced by the TDA. But for this organization timber design would not have established itself in the way in which it was able to in the 1950s and 1960s, although credit cannot be given to the TDA alone. Some firms of consulting engineers had the ability to design timber structures and to develop interesting combinations of timber and other materials. In 1956, Ove Arup & Partners engineered deep timber trusses for the gymnasium at Mayfield School, Putney

(Fig. 6.8) but, although this attracted some attention at the time, it was not the most satisfactory form of truss, relying as it did upon timber for all the members. Because the sizes of members in a timber truss tends to be dictated by the fasteners needed, actual member stresses may be low and much more efficient structures can be achieved using steel as tension members in combination with the timber for bending and compression. Felix Samuely demonstrated this in his 1957 structures at Hammersmith School and Christopher Wren School, trussing timber rafters with steel cable. Harris and Sutherland built what appears today to be a more conventional structure at the Furniture Industries Research Association building in Stevenage by combining steel tubes with timber to form triangular cross-section trusses. The tubes were simply flattened at their ends so that they could be connected to the timber with bolts and shear-plate connectors, an approach which has echoes of the nineteenth century when wrought iron began to be combined with timber; it is a method that has been successfully used since by other engineers.

Glulam

Laminating involves fastening several pieces of timber together to form a larger cross-section. The earliest examples used in Britain during the late seventeenth century were 'vertically' laminated while horizontally laminated timber was developed on the Continent and introduced into this country in the nineteenth century, referred to at the time as 'bent timber'. These two methods of laminating need to be distinguished. In a vertically laminated timber arch, flat boards are set on edge and nailed together side by side. It is thus the joints between the boards that are vertical. As they were most often needed for the ribs of vaults or domes, the boards might be cut to the required curve. Wren did this in some of his City Churches and the method was later used in the nineteenth century for buildings like the Crystal Palace. Horizontally laminated timber, which is the more common form today, has the boards bent to shape and fastened one above the other with the joints horizontal and early examples also used mechanical fasteners. The major nineteenth-century developments in this techniques were by Emy in France who carried out some experimental work and built a number of railway structures. It was also used in this country for railway stations and bridges (Booth, 1971) and other buildings, like drill halls and the attics of woollen mills, where long spans were needed. It is difficult to estimate the extent to which either of these techniques were used during the nineteenth century because they tended to be used for utilitarian structures which have since been demolished. Both, of course, are as equally suitable for glued construction as they are for mechanical fastening.

Glued laminated timber has a history both in Britain and Germany. Booth has recently identified late nineteenth-century buildings in England that had roofs based on glued laminated arches though the extent of the use of these structures has yet to be determined because a number were used in the roofs of nineteenth-century woolen mills in West Yorkshire (see Booth, 1994; Booth & Heywood, 1994). However, in 1905, Otto Hetzer took out a patent in Germany for a system of laminated timber using casein adhesive. This form of construction spread rapidly to countries adjoining Germany and is still known as the Hetzer system in parts of Europe today. It was introduced into Switzerland in about 1909, where it was used extensively in the construction of railway stations; it appeared in Denmark in 1913, in Norway in 1918, and in Sweden in 1919. Although originating in Germany, the industry did not prosper there and Hetzer went into liquidation in the 1920s, possibly because war conditions resulted in a shortage of casein. Meanwhile, the idea, while not being taken up in Britain, had spread to the US where experimental work was carried out on laminated timber arches in the 1930s. It is from the US that we have a good account of the state of the art in Europe at the time because Wilson (1939), as part of the American programme of research into the behaviour of laminated timber arches, visited and reported on the condition of many of the early laminated structures built over here. Although he noted some deterioration of structures under adverse conditions and the poor performance of but joints in laminations (scarf joints were not introduced until later), the structures that he saw were generally performing well and his prognosis for their continued life was good, certainly good enough to encourage their development in America.

Curiously, in the years immediately after the Second World War, Britain was the only country in Europe where there was an expertise in laminated timber. It had been stimulated by the needs of war, for the construction of airframes and boats, and had been supported in the following years by Admiralty contracts. When the Festival of Britain was built in 1951, there were several examples of timber structures, used for the architectural possibilities of the material. Entry to the exhibition was under a series of large laminated timber arches. Five parabolic arches with a span of 100 ft. and a rise of 62 ft. 6 in. were laminated from Douglas fir, using casein glue.[38] Laminated timber arches spanning 60 ft. were also used for building the Royal Reception Suite,[39] which was an octagonal pavilion clad with Douglas-fir plywood, while at the nearby Royal Festival Hall the orchestra canopy was made of plywood and supported from laminated timber and plywood box beams. This distinctive feature of the auditorium consists of a series of stressed skin plywood forms suspended from the box beams above, 37 ft. long, 3 ft. deep at the centre and tapered to each end. They were assembled from vertically laminated top and bottom chords of Douglas fir with internal struts and sides of 3/4-in. gaboon ply and made by Airscrew Co. & Jicwood Ltd., the same firm that built the entrance arches to the exhibition site. Here was an example of the transfer of a technology from the aircraft industry into building. There was also a very shallow lamella roof for the Lion and Unicorn building fashioned out of oak boards with a covering skin of gaboon plywood.[40] It was said that these timbers were used because softwood was unobtainable in this period — although this was not the case for the royal pavilion.

In 1954 the Organization of European Economic Co-operation (OEEC) sent a commission to the US to inspect the laminating industry there and to see what lessons could be learned from the techniques which it had developed. The subsequent report noted that production of laminated timber in the US had tripled between 1953 and 1955 and recommended that an industry be established in Europe to make use of the timber supplies this side of the Atlantic.[41] Naturally, this was directed more towards countries other than Britain, that is, those which had native supplies of timber, although reports of buildings show that at that time there were a number of firms in Britain producing laminated structures. A firm associated with laminated structures from the mid-1950s is Kingston Craftsmen of Kingston upon Hull whose capacity then is exemplified by a 101 ft. 6 in. span at Wigan built by them in 1955.[42] By the end of the 1950s, there was sufficient

Fig. 6.9

demand for laminated timber for Muirhead and Sons to arrange for De Coene Freres to supply them with the structure for a laminated-arch shed for the construction of a laminating shop at Grangemouth.[43] The Belgian firm who made these structures had been responsible for timber structures at the Brussels exhibition. The 95-ft. span of three hinged arches (Fig. 6.9) were built of laminated Baltic redwood and supported a three-ton travelling crane. Construction at the apex of this seems a little unusual because it was fixed with a hardwood dowel and the joint plated at the side with glued-on plywood cover plates. Today, designers are less inhibited about using exposed steel connectors in timber structures.

While there has been some development in the number of companies manufacturing laminated timber, the material has always had the disadvantage that the design is often seen to be more complex than other materials and few professional engineers have become competent in its use. Although TRADA engineers and some manufacturing companies have provided a design service in Britain, it is still often seen as a specialist material to be used for special circumstances, generally when the structure is to be exposed. Advantage has been taken of its low maintenance requirements for buildings like swimming pools, but today imported standard beams may be the largest use of laminated timber.

Surface-acting structures

Timber shared in the enthusiasm for shell structures in the late 1950s and early 1960s. In some ways, timber was ideally suited to this form of construction because the use of two or three layers of boarding formed a good surface structure. Its low density means that self-weight stresses are comparatively low; either nailing or glueing, sometimes both, can be used to fasten the boards together, and larger laminated sections can easily be incorporated to provide stiffening ribs. Moreover, unlike concrete, it does not require a heavy falsework for its construction. Sometimes shells have even been constructed on the ground and craned into place. The two obvious forms for timber are the conoid and the hyperbolic-paraboloid roof because both are generated by straight lines, ideal for boarding.

The first use of timber shells was in 1957 at the Wilton carpet factory[44] where four timber hyperbolic-paraboloid shapes were put together on four reinforced-concrete columns to provide an uninterrupted floor area 110 ft. square. The shells (Fig. 6.10) rose from 18 ft. at the columns to 30 ft. high at the apex and were made with three layers of ⅜ x 5 in. boards. A ¼-scale model was made and tested by TDA for this, but the calculation of forces in both the curved surface and the edge beams of such structures was relatively simple and it was not long before this was becoming a popular form of construction. It was used in a number of schools for roofing gymnasia or assembly halls[45] with a large number reported in *Wood* during the mid-1960s.

Conoid roofs began to be used at much the same time. The TDA used such a roof for their own laboratories at Tylers Green. British Rail had already used laminated timber structures for the structure of railway station canopies and, at Oxford Rd Station, Manchester laminated arches were combined with three large conoid roofs to cover the main station

Fig. 6.10

concourse.[46] This was an imaginative solution to the problem of a triangular space created by the track arrangement. The recently completed shells to cover the machinery on the Thames Barrage were prefabricated and surface acting structures. They were built in a workshop in Liverpool, using three layers of boarding over laminated timber ribs, constructed in sections and transported by barge to the site.

HB and other nailed structures

While it is often pointed out that the strength:weight ratio of timber is better than steel, this has seldom led to the construction of very large structures rivalling those in steel. The experience of the early post-war trussed shed roofs suggests that the problems lie in the need for mechanical fasteners in structures of this type. Design of the joints may be difficult for engineers unfamiliar with the material but the problem is as much one of unfamiliarity by contractors. To some extent, these problems are solved by using nailed joints which, while increasing the number of connectors, reduce the load that each must take and also reduce the assembly to a simpler repeated operation. Of course, the disadvantage is the labour content of making the nailed joints, particularly if pre-bored holes are required, although higher nail loads and thus fewer nails are possible with so-called 'improved' nails.

In the late 1950s Beeves introduced the Swedish HB system of construction to Britain, building a garage at Lewis with roof beams of 91 ft.[47] The method, which was developed by Hilding Brosenius (hence HB) in 1939, is based upon forming an I-section of timber in which the web comprises two or more layers of diagonal boarding with flanges of laminated timber. All this is assembled using closely spaced nails (normally improved nails). The possibilities of this method of construction were dramatically demonstrated in 1960 at Gatwick Airport when aircraft hangars were constructed using HB portal frames spanning 150 ft.[48] (Fig. 6.11). The concrete floor of these hangars was prestressed to provide the necessary tying force. A year later, HB portals were again used for roofing the wave basin building at the Hydraulics Research Station.[49]

In complete contrast, the availability of large-section timbers, either Douglas fir or tropical hardwoods, has facilitated the construction of

Fig. 6.11

utilitarian portal frames of more modest span. An early example of this kind of structure was developed by TDA using solid sections and a welded steel gusset plate to form the knee joint. At the time it was reported that solid sections were used because of the cost of laminated sections. More recently TRADAfarm, a subsidiary of TRADA specializing in the design of agricultural buildings, developed standard designs for timber barns using solid columns and rafters with nailed plywood gussets at the knees.

Proprietary roof and beam systems

In spite of there being no reliable structural grading of commercially available plywoods in Britain, a number of companies used plywood as the basis for proprietary systems of construction; in 1960, a letter to *Interbuild* claimed that, according to Canadian sources, there was a greater use of plywood for structural purposes in Britain than in Canada.[50] This letter accompanied an illustration of plywood-based portals frames being erected, and by the mid-1960s, there were several successful structural systems available based on plywood. Some of these were simple I- beams using plywood webs and solid-timber flanges with web stiffeners at intervals. These were ideal for roof purlins and have been discussed above. The most sophisticated of these was Rainham Timber's 'Corply' beam which avoided the need for stiffeners by forming the plywood web in a sinusoidal curve between the flanges. The other obvious form was the box beam which had the advantage that it could be used where it was visible. Most were simple boxes with interior web stiffeners but Walter Holmes' 'Bow-vee' box beams were a more complex design. The beam may be thought of as assembled from three components, two side pieces and a centre section. The centre section is a ladder comprising top and bottom chords with vertical web stiffeners at 4-ft. centres., but the chords were trapezoidal so forming a section wider at the top than the bottom. On either side of this, the side panels have solids at the top and bottom rebated to take the plywood sides while within the space formed is a bow of timber, reminiscent of the trussing of eighteenth-century trussed girders. They were made in sizes from 12—30 in. deep by 3-inch steps. Decking systems were also made using plywood, some relying upon single-spanning elements, but some two-way spanning.

Timber can never be a major part of construction in a country that has no native supplies: it is not the material that is normally used in Britain for housing or even for roof structures, in spite of advantages that it might appear to have in its lightness and the ease and speed of construction that it affords. Its other disadvantage *vis-à-vis* other materials was the lack of engineering data available, either of the material itself or the behaviour of mechanical fasteners. Nevertheless, once such data was available, considerable use was made of it and its advantages were capitalized upon both in housing, where speed of construction was important and in a number of major structures where lightness proved advantageous. The fairly rapid development of patented construction systems in the 1960s based on plywood and the corresponding appearance of a number of large-scale surface-acting structures may be a reflection of a rather more general spirit of the time. The immediate post-war years had seen a need for more sophisticated engineering solutions in other materials, simply as a means of overcoming material shortages and restrictions. This can be seen, for example, in the rapid development of prestressed concrete and concrete-shell structures at that time. The design of the TDA roof was one expression of this in timber and it does not seem unreasonable to see these other developments in the same light. In the long term, it has been those that have offered clear commercial advantages — timber-frame housing and trussed rafter roofs — that have been the significant changes in construction.

Notes

1   BS 373: 1929 *Methods of testing small clear specimens of timber*. See also BS 8810.

2   'Structural Design Data #1', *Wood*, 1 (1936), p. 253.

3   'A new timber building designed in stress graded Douglas fir', *Wood*, 14 (1949), pp. 296—304.

4   Supplementary sheets were produced in 1943 and a 1949 edition of the book was available in this country. Typical Designs of Timber Structures, a reference for use of architects and engineers, Washington, DC: Timber Engineering Company

5   Association of British Plywood and Veneer Manufacturers. BP 101: 1965 *British made plywood for structural purposes*.

6   See also 'The wooden house controversy', *AJ*, (1919), p. 407.

7   *The Westholme Bungalow* (n.d.), Houslow. Trade catalogue.

8   *Homes Built by Boulton & Paul* (c.1927). Trade catalogue.

9   'Wood House at Sevenoaks, designed by Professor Walter Gropius', *Wood*, 2 (1937), pp. 524—7.

10 'The Ideal Home in timber' *Wood*, 1 (1936), pp. 172—5.

11 *Post War Building Studies No. 1 House Construction* (1944), London: HMSO.

12 For example, Hull built timber frame houses: 'Two prefabricated timber houses at Hull', *Wood*, 3 (1938), p. 212. These are semis with concrete (Lignacrete) blockwork party walls, 3-in. solid timber wall plus a boarding of cedar. The article says that the two houses were erected in two days.

13 'The Weybridge House, Stressed skin construction', *Wood*, 9 (1944), p. 285; 'British laminated houses', *Wood*, 10 (1945), pp. 185—9.

14 'Cedar house, Canadian house built at Burton on Trent', *Wood*, 11 (1946), p. 198; 'Precut timber houses: manufactured in Britain for the Victorian railway Commission', *Wood*, 15 (1950), pp. 114—8; 'Prefabricated timber houses for the Australian government', *Wood*, 14 (1951), pp. 252—7.

15 *Houses that Save Softwood* (1953), London: HMSO.

16 A description of the various types was published in *Wood*, 11 (Nov. 1946), pp. 304—8.

17 *Interbuild*, 10 (1963, June), p. 36.

18 'Hull Prototypes', *Interbuild*, 10 (1963, March), pp. 32—5.

19 'Multicom prototypes opened,' *Interbuild*, 12 (1965, July), p. 34.

20 'System Building', *Interbuild*, 11 (1964, April), p. 24.

21 'Timber frame housing', *Wood*, 22 (1957, Nov.), pp. 440—42.

22 *Beautiful Homes of Wood* (n.d.). Apparently published by a consortium of British Columbian organizations, the back cover reproduced AJ Information Sheet 347 showing timber platform framing.

23 *Interbuild*, 11 (1964, Nov.), p. 33.

24 'Local authority tries timber framing', *AJ*, 144 (1966), pp. 80—1.

25 *TRADA Design guide for timber frame housing* (1966), TRADA.

26 Described in detail in a building study in *AJ*, 153 (1971), pp. 301—12. It was noted in an earlier report of this development (*AJ*, 152, p. 827.) that while this scheme was built within the Building Regulations which were introduced in 1965, the Glory Hill development was under local building by-laws.

27 *AJ*, 143 (1966), pp. 1149—56. Some other systems used timber in combination with either steel or concrete.

28 *Interbuild*, 4 (1956—7), pp. 108—10. Perwent system.

29 *Interbuild*, 3 (1955—6), pp. 55—8. Medway system.

30 See for example the A75 system by Farmer and Dark, *Interbuild* 5 (1958), pp. 103—07; the Terrapin system, *Interbuild*, 8 (1945, July) and the Kenkast system, *Interbuild*, 10 (1963, Oct.).

31 'The TDA roof', *Wood*, 12 (1947), pp. 321—3.

32 'National Camps', *Wood*, 4 (1939), pp. 413—9.

33 'A timber storage shed', *Wood*, 17 (1952), p. 418; 'A Thames boat house', *Wood*, 23 (1958), p. 126.

34 'Roofs for cross wall construction, TDA designs shown at the Building Exhibition',.*Wood*, 24 (1959), p. 482.

35 'Wood replaces steel', *Wood*, 2 (1937), p. 458.

36 The design and construction of this shed is described in 'A new timber building designed in stress graded Douglas fir', *Wood*, 14 (1949), pp. 296—304. Contributions to this article were made by the owner, P. O. Reece — the designer and the contractor.

37 *Wood*, 16 (1951), pp. 334—9, & 21 (1956), p. 342.

38 'Five laminated timber arches for an archway to the festival', *Wood*, 15 (1950), pp. 398—403.

39 'The Royal Reception Suite — South Bank Site', *Wood*, 16 (1951), p. 132.

40 *Wood*, 15 (1950), pp. 338—42. The architects for this were R. Y. Goodden and R. D. Russell.

41 'The technique of laminating',.*Wood*, 21 (1956), pp. 174—7.

42 *Interbuild*, 3 (1955—6), pp. 506—08.

43 *Interbuild*, 6 (1959, Dec.), 14—15; *Wood*, 25 (1960), p. 94.

44 'Timber shell construction', *Wood*, 22 (1957), p. 320.

45 For example 'Plywood HP roof at Auchentoshen School, Glasgow.— Double layer diagonal board HP at Ipswich school', *Interbuild*, 6 (1959, May), pp. 38—9.

46 *Interbuild*, 6 (1959, Jan.), p. 40.

47 *Interbuild*, 5 (1958), p. 608.

48 *Interbuild*, 7 (1960, Feb.), pp. 24—7.

49 *Wood*, 26 (1961), p. 366.

50 *Interbuild*, 7 (1960), p. 45.

Appendix 1 British Standards

The British Engineering Standards Association (Incorporated 1918) was formed initially in 1901 as the Engineering Standards Committee by the Institution of Civil Engineers, the Institution of Mechanical Engineers, the Institute of Naval Architects, the Iron and Steel Institute and the Institution of Electrical Engineers, eventually becoming the British Standards Institution. Over the years, representation on the drafting committees for building products' committees has included a number of government departments as well as the Office of Works and the DSIR, a number of trade and professional institutions, including RIBA, the LCC and representatives of the industry. The intention here is not to deal with the history of what is now the British Standards Institution , nor can it be a complete history of the development of standards for building. What is provided is a note of the development of some building standards simply in the form of a list of dates when changes in standards occurred. The information for this has been taken from the Institution's own 'History Book' which takes the form of a number of loose-leaf binders containing typed pages. The intention has been to provide a guide to the origins of the different standards and the frequency with which changes have occurred. At one time it was common for standards to include a brief review of their previous history but current standards no longer include sufficient historical information to take the reader back to its first issue. Moreover, a summary of the work of each division, including the building division, was once included in the BS handbooks, that is, the annual catalogue of standards then current, but this practice was discontinued after 1936.

Of the British Standards covering products used in building some choice has had to be made of those to be included in this list. Today the British Standards Institution publishes a summary of standards applicable to building which runs into four volumes and even a simple list of those would be quite extensive. However, it includes many items which are only peripherally relevant to building, literally so in the case of paving materials, and many items which may be regarded as almost ephemeral when compared with items of basic fabric. Items such as hot-water cylinders, cold-water tanks or electrical fittings are likely to have been replaced within the life of a building or be the very items which will be stripped out and replaced

in any present refurbishment. However, the importance of British Standards and the normal difficulty of discovering what standard may have been in force at any given time suggests a need for a little more than a simple list of those referred to in the text. Therefore, a more general summary has been provided here and some judgement has had to be adopted towards the selection of items to be included. Inevitably, comprehensiveness has had to be compromised for ease of use in both selection of standards to be noted and the layout of the information.

The first choice must be items of basic fabric: steel sections, bricks and the constituents of concrete, for example. Then there are items of historic interest, a very difficult category because it is impossible to know what will be of interest to an historian. However, I have attempted to include all items involving the basic fabric of buildings up to the Second World War. After then the proliferation of standards has made the selection much more difficult and the policy less clear. Items included are those which have been referred to in the text and those standards that have replaced earlier, pre-war standards. I have then eliminated the multiplicity of parts of many of the standards presently available as the titles and dates of issue of these can be obtained from the current BSI Catalogue. Thus the many parts of the standard for wall tiles or fire protection now available have not been listed although a summary is provided of dates considered significant.

It is also important to note that the scope of early standards may also have changed without any change in the number, even though the title may have changed.

The form of the list

As standards have become more comprehensive there have been changes in the numbering system to take account of this; a factor that hardly facilitates a simple presentation of the picture. What were once called Codes of Practice are now simply called British Standards, where standards were once divided into parts they may now be divided into sections. The picture was also confused when metrification was introduced into the building industry: while Part 2 of some standards was simply the metric version, Part 2 of others of a similar date might be a quite distinct part. For example, CP 112: Part 2: 1971 is the metric version of the code of practice for structural timber while CP 3: Chapter V: Part 2: 1970 is the section of the loading code for wind loads. The metric version of the part for floor and roof loads was called Part 1 when it was issued in 1967.

The list is in numerical order, which is not always the chronological order. The number is followed by the title (omitting the words 'British Standard Specification for'). The date of the first issue is then given. Numbers in brackets after the date are the number of amendments issued to that standard. Dates following are dates of the subsequent editions, again with numbers in brackets indicating the number of amendments issued to that edition. Numbers of parts of a standard are given before the number of the standard and are listed separately. The date when a standard was withdrawn is given where that information was available from the History Book although this is not always significant. A standard may remain current even when superseded by a more up-to-date standard simply because it is still referred to in regulations still in force. Where a standard has been superseded by another standard this is noted. The date of this may not be the date of first issue of the later standard into which the earlier one has been incorporated.

In compiling this list some errors have been found within the 'history book' which was used as a source. These have been corrected wherever possible but in some cases removing an error has meant leaving the information incomplete.

BS 1: 1903, Lists of rolled sections for structural purposes;
1904, 1916, 1920.
BS 4: 1903, Dimensions and properties of channels and beams
for structural purposes; 1921, 1932 (3), A/1934 (1), 1959 supplement to 1934; B/1959 (2).
pt. 1: 1962 (3), 1972 (1), 1980.
pt. 2: 1963 (1), 1965 (2), 1969 (1). Superseded by BS 4848: pt. 2 and B4 & 4: pt. 2 1969 Hot rolled hollow sections.
BS 6: 1924, Bulb angles and bulb plate; 1923, 1924. Superseded by BS 4: 1932.
BS 12: 1904, Portland cement; 1907, 1910, 1915, 1920, 1925, 1931 (1), 1940 (1), 1947 (5), 1958 (4), 1978 (2), pt 2 1971 (1), 1989.
The title of this was changed in 1940 to include rapid-hardening Portland cement.
BS 15: 1906, Mild steel for general structural purposes; 1912, 1930, 1936 (2), 1948 (1), 1961 (2). Superseded by BS 4361: 1968.
BS 28: 1906, Black bolts and nuts; 1908, 1912, 1932 (1). Superseded by BS 916: 1946.
BS 40: 1908, Cast iron spigot and socket low pressure heating pipes.
BS 41: 1908, Cast iron spigot and socket flue or smoke pipes and fittings; 1946, 1964, 1973.
BS 58: 1912, Cast iron spigot and socket soil pipes. Superseded by BS 416: 1931.
BS 59: 1912, Cast iron spigot and socket waste and

ventilating pipes.
BS 65: 1914 (2), Specification for vitrified clay pipes; 1934 (1), 1937. 1951, 1952 (2), 1963, 1981. Withdrawn 1988.
BS 73: 1915, Wall plugs and sockets; 1919,1927.
BS 78: 1917 (3), Cast iron spigot and socket pipes; 1938 (5),
pt. 1: 1961, Pipes. Withdrawn 1976, superseded by BS 4622.
pt. 2: 1965, Spigot and socket fittings. Partially superseded by BS 4772: 1980.
BS 144: 1921 (1), Coal tar creosote for the preservation of timber; 1936 (1), 1954 (1), 1973. Withdrawn 1990.
pt. 1: 1990, Specification for preservation.
pt. 2: 1990, Methods for timber treatment.
BS 146: 1923, Portland blast furnace cement; 1926 (1), 1932, 1941 (1), 1947 (5), 1958 (4),
pt. 1: 1958(4), superseded by BS 146: pt. 2, Metric units.
pt. 2: 1973, withdrawn and superseded by BS 146: 1991.
BS 165: 1929, Hard drawn steel wire for concrete reinforcement. Superseded 1938.
BS 187: 1923, Calcium silicate, sand lime and flint lime bricks; 1934 (1), 1942 (1), 1955 (1), 1967 (2). pt. 1: 1967 (2); pt. 2: 1970 (1), 1978.
BS 275: 1927, Dimensions of rivets.
BS 373: 1929, Methods of testing small clear specimens of timber; 1938, 1957.
BS 402: 1930, Clay plain roofing tiles and fittings; 1945 (1), 1979, pt. 2: 1970, withdrawn 1979,

pt. 1 : 1990, Specification for plain tiles and fittings.
BS 405: 1930, Expanded metal (steel) for general purposes; 1945, 1987.
BS 437: 1932, Cast iron spigot and socket drain pipes; 1933 (1), 1978, 1/1970 (1).
pt. 2/1969. Superseded by BS 437: 1978.
BS 449: 1932, The use of structural steel in buildings; 1935, 1937 (5), 1948 (2), 1959 (8).
The 1959 issue of this code represents an important change. A code of practice for structural steel CP 113 was issued in 1948 and the two codes contained much the same material. They were therefore amalgamated in the 1959 edition of the British Standard. At the same time the clauses dealing with loading were omitted because these were now covered by CP 3 Chapter V and the design clauses for welding reduced because this material was also covered elsewhere. In contrast the use of tubular members which had been dealt with in Addendum 1: PD 1953 were incorporated into the standard. From 1966 a number of amendments were issued concerning welded steel structures and although the metric version of the code was issued as Part 2 in 1969 (and revised in 1975) an imperial edition was subsequently issued (as Part 1) in 1970 to incorporate the amendments.
BS 459: pt. 1: Panelled and glazed wood doors; 1941 (1), 1942, 1944 (4), 1954 (5), 1982.
pt. 2: 1962 (3), Specification for wooden doors — flush wood doors.
pt. 3: 1946, Fire-check flush doors, 1951 (7).
pt. 4: 1951 (1), Specification for wooden doors, matchboarded; 1965 (1), 1988.
BS 460: 1932, Cast iron rain water goods; 1944, 1948 (2), 1960, 1964.
BS 473: 1932 (1), Concrete roofing tiles; 1944, 1956 (1), pt. 1: 1967 (1), pt. 2: 1971 (2).
BS 476: 1932 (2), Definitions of fire resistance, incombustibility and non-flammability of building materials and structures (including methods of test). From the mid-1950s this standard has been published in a number of separate parts covering a wide range of different tests and reflecting the growing understanding of the behaviour of fires.
BS 492: 1933 (1), Precast concrete partition slabs (solid); 1934 (1). In 1944 the standard was extended to cover all blocks — superseded by BS 2028: 1953.
BS 493: 1933, Air bricks; 1945, 1967 (1).
pt. 1: 1967, Imperial units. Withdrawn.
pt. 2: 1970, Airbricks and gratings for wall ventilation.
BS 504: 1933, Drawn lead traps; 1944 (1), 1961 (1).
BS 531: 1934, Grading of birch plywood. Withdrawn.
BS 538: 1934, Metal arc welding in mild steel as applied to general building construction. Replaced by BS 1856: 1952.
BS 548: 1934 (3), High tensile structural steel. Withdrawn.
BS 550: 1934 (1), Concrete interlocking roofing tiles; 1945 (1), 1956, 1967.
BS 565: 1934, Terms relating to timber and woodwork; 1938, 1949, 1963, 1972 (2). Replaced by sections of pt. 4 of BS 6100.
BS 567: 1934, Asbestos cement flue pipes and fittings, light quality; 1945 (1), 1948 (1), 1954 (2), 1963 (1), 1968, 1973 (1).
BS 569: 1934, Asbestos cement rain water goods; 1945, 1949 (1), 1956, 1967, 1973 (1).
BS 584: 1934, Wood trim; 1946, 1956, 1967. Superseded by BS 1186: pt. 3: 1990
BS 585: 1934, Wooden stairs; 1944, 1956, 1972.
pt. 1: 1984, Specification for straight stairs with closed risers for domestic use, including straight and winder flights and quarter or half landings. Superseded, 1989.
pt. 2: 1984, Performance requirements for domestic stairs constructed of wood-based materials. Superseded, 1985.
BS 588: 1935, Grading for plywood veneered with oak, mahogany, walnut, teak and other ornamental woods.
BS 589: 1935, Nomenclature of softwoods. Combined with BS 881: 1946
BS 644: 1935, Wood windows.
pt. 1: 1945, Wood casement windows; 1951, 1989 — withdrawn.

pt. 2: 1946, 1958, Double hung sash windows . Obsolete.
pt. 3: 1949, 1951, Double hung sash and case windows (Scottish type) . Obsolete.
BS 648: 1938, Weights of building materials; 1949, 1964.
BS 657: 1936, Clay facing and backing bricks; 1941, 1950 (1). Replaced by BS 3921: 1965.
BS 661: 1936 (2), Glossary of acoustical terms and definitions; 1955, 1969, replaced by BS 4727: pt. 3: 1985.
BS 680: 1936, Roofing slates; 1944, pt. 2: 1971, Metric units.
BS 690: 1936 (2), Asbestos cement slates and sheets; 1940, 1945, 1953, 1963.
pt. 1: 1963, Asbestos-cement slates, corrugated sheets and semi-compressed flat sheets. Imperial units.
pt. 2: 1971, Asbestos-cement and cellulose-asbestos-cement flat sheets.
pt. 3: 1973, Corrugated sheets.
pt. 4: 1974, Slates.
pt. 5: 1975, Lining sheets and panels. These were all withdrawn in 1981.
BS 743: 1937, Materials for damp proof courses; 1941, 1951 (2), 1966, 1970. See also BS 6398: 1983 & BS 6515: 1984, which partly replaces this.
BS 745: 1937 (1), Animal glue for wood; 1949 (1), 1969.
BS 747: 1937, Bituminous roofing felts; 1952, 1961 (2) (w. 1976), 1/1968 (2), 2/1970, 1977.
BS 774: 1938, Underfloor steel ducts for electrical services. Withdrawn 1965.
BS 776: 1938, Magnesium Oxychloride (magnesite) flooring.
pt. 1: 1963 (1), Imperial units.
pt. 2: 1972, Metric units. Both parts now withdrawn.
BS 785: 1938, Rolled steel bars and hard drawn steel wire for concrete reinforcement. pt. 1: 1967 (1); pt. 2: 1964. Both parts withdrawn in 1970, replaced by BS 4449: 1969 & BS 4482: 1969.
BS 798: 1938, Galvanized corrugated steel sheets. Superseded by BS 3038: 1956.
BS 812: 1938, Testing aggregates; 1943, 1951, 1960, 1967. Withdrawn in 1975 when the standard was then issued in four separate parts covering different properties.
BS 838: 1939, Tests for the toxicity of wood preservatives; 1961. Withdrawn, 1990.
BS 849: 1939, Code of practice for plain sheet zinc roofing. Partially replaced by BS 6561: 1985.
BS 877: 1939 (1), Foamed or expanded blast furnace slag lightweight aggregate for concrete; 1967. Withdrawn 1977, superseded by pt. 2: 1973, metric units, and replaced by BS 3797: 1990.
BS 881: 1939, Nomenclature of hardwoods.
BS 881 & 589:1946 (1), Nomenclature of commercial timbers, 1955, 1974.
BS 882: 1940, Aggregates; 1944 (1). The 1944 issue included British Standards 1198, 1199, 1200 and 1201 which dealt with sands and aggregates. It was reissued in 1954 (2) with BS 1201. Parts 1 and 2 covering imperial and metric units appeared in 1965 and 1973.
BS 890: 1940, Building limes; 1947, 1965, 1995.
BS 913: 1940, Wood preservation by pressure creosoting; 1954, 1973. Withdrawn in 1990 and superseded by BS 144:pts. 1 & 2.
BS 915: 1940, High alumina cement; pt. 1: 1947 (5), pt. 2: 1972, metric units.
BS 916: 1940 (1), Black bolts; 1946 (1), 1953. Obsolete.
BS 940: 1941, Grading rules for stress graded timber; pt. 1: 1944, pt. 2: 1942. Replaced by BS 1860: 1952.
BS 952: 1941, Glass for glazing including definitions and terminology of work on glass. 1953 (5), 1964 (1). Divided into pt. 1: 1978, Classification and pt. 2: 1980, Terminology for work on glass.
BS 968: 1941(1), High yield welding quality structural steel; 1962 (3). Withdrawn, 1968.
BS 973: 1941, Code of practice for glazing and fixing of glass in buildings; 1945. Superseded by CP 152: 1960.
BS 988: 1941 (3), Mastic asphalt for building (limestone aggregate); 1957 (1) combined with BS

1076, 1097, 1451. Further issues appeared in 1957, 1966 (2), 1973 (2). Superseded by BS 6925: 1988.
BS 990: 1941 (3), Steel windows, domestic, 1945 (8). Parts 1 and 2 in imperial and metric units were issued in 1962 and 1972. Both parts were withdrawn in 1984, the metric unit standard being superseded by BS 6510.
BS 1014: 1942, Pigments for colouring cement, magnesium oxychloride and concrete, 1961, 1975.
BS 1018: 1942, Timber in building construction. Replaced by CP 112: 1952.
BS 1043: 1942, Code of practice for the provision of engineering and utility services in buildings. Superseded by CP 3, Ch. 7: 1950.
BS 1047: 1942, Air cooled blast furnace slag, 1952, 1983. Withdrawn, 1987.
BS 1056: 1942, Painting buildings in wartime. Withdrawn, 1949.
BS 1057: 1942, Substitute paints for exterior finishing. Withdrawn, 1949.
BS 1067: 1942, Coal tar pitch felt damp proof courses for temporary war-time building. Withdrawn, 1959.
BS 1074: 1942, Fireclay bases . . . open coal fires. Withdrawn, 1945.
BS 1076: 1942, Mastic asphalt for flooring, 1956 (2), bound with BS 988: 1966.
BS 1091: 1942 (1), Pressed steel gutters, rainwater pipes, fittings and accessories; 1946, 1963.
BS 1092: 1943, Pitch mastic horizontal and vertical damp-proof courses, alternative to mastic asphalt. Withdrawn, 1945.
BS 1097: 1943 (2), Mastic asphalt for damp-proof courses and tanking; 1958 (1), bound with BS 988: 1966 (see also BS 1418).
BS 1105: 1943, Wood wool cement slabs; 1951, 1963, 1972, 1981.
BS 1108: 1943, Glazed tile fireplaces. Withdrawn, 1945.
BS 1125: 1943, WC cisterns; 1945 (4), 1956, 1959 (6), 1969, 1973, 1987.
BS 1142: 1943 (1), Fibre building boards, 1953 (2), 1961 (2).
pt. 1: 1971 (2), Methods of test.
pt. 2: 1971, Medium board and hardboard.
pt. 3: 1972, Insulating board (softboard).
These were all withdrawn in 1989.
BS 1144: 1943, Cold worked bars for reinforcement of concrete; 1967. Withdrawn in 1970 and replaced by BS 4461: 1969 & subsequently replaced by BS 4449: 1988.
BS 1145: 1943, Loadbearing concrete brickwork and masonry not reinforced. Withdrawn, 1949.
BS 1146: 1943, Reinforced brickwork. Replaced by CP 111: 1948.
BS 1161: 1944, Aluminium alloy sections structural; 1951 (1), 1977.
BS 1162:
BS 1165: 1944, Clinker and furnace bottom ash aggregates for concrete. 1947, 1957, 1966, 1985. Superseded by BS 3797: 1990.
BS 1175: 1944, Sizes of stress graded softwood timber. Replaced by BS 1860: 1952.
BS 1177: 1944, Pitch mastic flooring. Withdrawn, 1955.
BS 1178: 1944, Milled lead sheet for building purposes, 1969, 1982.
BS 1180: 1944 (2), Concrete bricks and facing bricks; 1972. Withdrawn in 1981 and superseded by BS 6073 pt. 1: 1981.
BS 1186: 1944 (1), Joinery timbers. Grading of softwood joinery,
pt. 1: 1952 (4), Specification for timber; 1971 (1), 1986, 1991.
pt. 2: 1955 (4), Specification for workmanship; 1971 (1), 1988.
pt. 3: 1990, Wood trim and its fixing.
BS 1187: 1944, Wood block for floors; 1959.
BS 1190: 1944, Hollow clay building blocks; 1951 (2). Replaced by BS 3921: 1965.
BS 1191: 1944 (2), Gypsum building plasters, 1955. Issues of 1967 and 1973 were divided into pt. 1, Excluding premixed lightweight plasters and pt. 2: 1967, Premixed lightweight plasters.
BS 1197: 1944, Concrete flooring tiles; 1955 (1). A metric standard was issued as pt. 2 in 1973. Now obsolete.
BS 1203: 1945 (3), Synthetic resin adhesives for plywood, 1954 (1), 1963, 1979.
BS 1204: 1956 (1), Cold setting resin adhesives, 1/1964 (2) (w. 1978), 2/1965 (1) (w. 1978).
pt. 1: 1964 (2), Gap-filling adhesives; 1979 (1).
pt. 2: 1965, Close-contact adhesives; 1979 (1).
Both parts withdrawn, 1993 and superseded by BSEN 301, 302.
BS 1205, pt. 1: 1945, Cast iron gutters; pt. 1: 1948. pt. 2: 1945, 1948. The 1948 issues of parts 1 and 2 were printed with that standard and then replaced by BS 460: 1964.
BS 1207: 1944 (1), Hollow glass blocks; 1953, 1961. Withdrawn, 1981.
BS 1209: 1945, Glass internal sills to wood and metal windows. Withdrawn, 1956.
BS 1217: 1945, Cast stone, 1975, 1986.
BS 1221: 1945 (1), Steel fabric for the reinforcement of concrete; 1964. Withdrawn 1970 and superseded by BS 4483.
BS 1230: 1955 (4), Gypsum plasterboard. Superseded by pt. 2; 1970.
pt. 1: 1985, Specification for plasterboard excluding materials submitted to secondary operations.
BS 1243: 1945, Metal ties cavity walls; 1954 (2), 1964 (4), 1972, 1978.
BS 1245: 1945 (2), Metal Door Frames, 1951 (2), 1975.
BS 1246: 1945, Metal skirtings, picture rails and angle beads, 1959 (2). Withdrawn, 1972.
BS 1248: 1945 (1), Wallpapers; 1954 (2). Withdrawn, 1979.
BS 1257: 1945 (1), Methods of testing clay building bricks. Superseded by BS 3921: 1965.
BS 1282: 1945, Classification of wood preservatives; 1959 (1), 1975.
BS 1285: 1945 (2), Wood surrounds for metal windows; 1955 (1), 1963 (3), 1980. Withdrawn.
BS 1286: 1945 (4), Clay tiles for flooring. Withdrawn 1974 and superseded by BS 6431: 1983.
BS 1297: 1946, Grading and sizing of softwood, tongued and grooved flooring; 1952, 1961 (2), 1970, 1987.
BS 1301: 1946, Clay engineering bricks. Withdrawn in 1956 and superseded by BS 3921: 1965.
BS 1310: 1946, Coal tar pitches for building purposes; 1950, 1965 (2), 1974, 1984.
BS 1324: 1946 (2), Asphalt tiles for paving and flooring, natural rock asphalt; 1962 (1). Withdrawn, 1974.
BS 1325: 1946 (3), Asphalt tiles for paving and flooring, mineral aggregate with no inherent bitumen. Withdrawn, 1962.
BS 1364: 1947, Aerated concrete blocks. See BS 2028: 1968.
BS 1410 — 3: 1947 (1) (w. 1960), Mastic asphalt flooring, see BS 1162.
BS 1418: 1947 (1), Mastic asphalt damp-proof courses and tanking; 1958 (1), see BS 1162: 1966.
BS 1444: 1948, Cold-setting casein glue for wood; 1970. Withdrawn, 1981.
BS 1450: 1948 (4), Pitch mastic flooring; 1963 (1). Superseded by BS 5902: 1980.
BS 1451: 1948 (1), Coloured mastic asphalt flooring; 1956 (1). Superseded by BS 988, BS 1096, BS 1097, BS 1451: 1966.
BS 1455: 1948 (1), British-made plywood for building and general purposes; 1956 (3), 1963, 1972 (1). Withdrawn in 1986 and superseded by BS 6566, pts. 1—8.
BS 1478: 1948, Bending dimensions of bars for concrete reinforcement;.1964, 1967 (2). Withdrawn in 1970 and superseded by BS 4466: 1969.
BS 1567: 1949, Wood door frames and linings; 1953. Obsolete
BS 1579: 1949 (2), Connectors for timber; 1953 (2), 1960.
BS 1860: 1952 (1), Structural timber: measurement of characteristics affecting strength; 1959. Superseded by BS 4978: 1973.
BS 2028: 1953 (2), Precast concrete blocks. Combined with BS 1364 in 1968 (2 amendments), withdrawn in 1981 and superseded by BS 6073 pt. 1.
BS 2760: 1956, Pitch fibre pipes.
BS 3139: 1959, High strength friction grip bolts for structural engineering.
BS 3797: 1990, Lightweight aggregates for masonry units and structural concrete.
BS 3921: 1965, Clay bricks; 1974, 1985, pt. 1: 1965 (3), superseded by BS 4729: 1971 (w. 1990), pt. 2: 1969. Superseded by BS 3921: 1974, 1985.
BS 4466: 1969, Specification for scheduling, dimensioning, bending and cutting of steel reinforcement for concrete; 1989.
BS 4449: 1969, Specification for carbon steel bars for the reinforcement of concrete; 1988.
BS 4482: 1969.(1985), Specification for cold reduced steel wire for the reinforcement of concrete.
BS 4483: 1970. (1985), Specification for steel fabric for the reinforcement of concrete.
BS 4729: 1971, Dimensions of bricks of special shapes and sizes. Withdrawn, 1990.
BS 4978: 1973 (5), Softwood grades for structural use; 1988. Withdrawn, 1989.
BS 5291: 1984, Manufacture of finger joints of structural softwood.
BS 5588 — Fire precautions in the design and construction of buildings.
The first part of this standard to be issued was pt. 4 in 1978 which dealt with smoke control in escape routes. This was followed in 1983 and 1984 by pt. 3 and pt. 1 which dealt with office and residential buildings. A number of other parts have since been issued.
BS 5628, Code of practice for use of masonry.
pt. 1: 1978, Structural use of unreinforced masonry; 1992.
pt. 2: 1985, Structural use of reinforced and prestressed masonry.
pt. 3: 1985, Materials and components, design and workmanship.
BS 5902: 1980, Specification for black and coloured pitch mastic flooring. Withdrawn, 1985.
BS 5950, Structural use of steelwork in buildings.
The first part of this to be issued was pt. 4: 1982, Code of practice for design of floors with profiled steel sheeting. This reflects the importance of this relatively new method of construction which was not covered by any earlier standards.
BS 5997: 1980, Guide to British Standard codes of practice for building services.
BS 6073 pt. 1: 1981, Precast concrete masonry units.
BS 6431, Ceramic floor and wall tiles.
Some 23 parts have been issued between 1983 and 1986.
BS 6510: 1984, Specification for steel windows, sills, window boards and doors.
BS 6515: 1984, Specification for polyethylene damp-proof courses for masonry.
BS 6561:1985, Specification for zinc alloy sheet and strip for building.
BS 6566, Plywood. Issued in 8 parts in 1985.
BS 6925: 1988, Specification for mastic asphalt for building and engineering (limestone aggregate).
BS 8110, Structural use of concrete. Issued in three parts in 1985.
CP 1: 1943, Protection of structures against lightning. Withdrawn.
CP 2: 1943, Heating and hot water service installations. Withdrawn.
CP 3, Code of basic data for the design of buildings.
Ch. I: 1949, Lighting.
Ch. I: pt. 1: 1964, Daylighting.
Ch. I (B): 1945 (w. 1983) — Sunlight (houses, flats and schools only). Withdrawn 1983.
Ch. I (C): 1945, Ventilation; 1950. Withdrawn and superseded by BS 5295: 1980 CP. 3
Ch. I: pt. 2: 1970, Artificial lighting; 1973. Withdrawn and superseded by BS 8206 Pt. 1.
Ch. II: 1970, Thermal insulation in relation to the control of environment. Withdrawn.
Ch. III: 1972 (1), Sound insulation and noise reduction. Withdrawn.
Ch. IV, 1948, Precautions against fire. Withdrawn.
Ch. IV: pt. 1: 1962, Flats and maisonettes (in blocks over two storeys); 1971 (4).
Ch. IV: pt. 2: 1968, Shops and departmental stores.
Ch. IV: pt. 3:1968, Office buildings.
The chapters of this code were superseded by various parts of BS 5588.
Ch. V: 1944, Loading; 1952 (3). This was CP 4 renumbered. For a summary of the history of this code see Appendix II.
Ch. VII: 1950 (3), Engineering and utility services. Withdrawn and superseded by CP 3, Ch. I: Pt. 2 and superseded by BS 5997: 1980.
Ch. VIII, 1949, Heating and thermal insulation. Withdrawn, 1983
Ch. IX, 1950, Durability. Withdrawn, 1982.
Ch . X, 1950, Precautions against vermin and dirt. Withdrawn, 1983.
CP 4: 1944, Renumbered as CP 3, Ch. 5.
CP 5: 1945, Renumbered as CP 3, Ch. 1B.
CP 6: 1945, Renumbered as CP 3, Ch. 1C.
CP 7: 1945, Renumbered as CP 3, Ch. VII F.
CP 101: 1948, Foundations and substructures for non-industrial buildings of not more than four storeys; 1963, 1972. Superseded by BS 8044 & 8103.
CP 102: 1963, Protection of buildings against water from the ground; 1973. See now BS 8102 & 8215.
CP 110: 1972, Code of practice for the structural use of concrete.
Issued in three parts, two parts of which were design charts, this code replaced CP 114, 115 & 116 (see below) and was noteworthy in introducing limit state design. It was withdrawn in 1985 and superseded by the various parts of BS 8110.
CP 111: 1948, Structural recommendations for loadbearing walls; 1964 (4), 1970. Superseded by BS 5628.
CP 112: 1952 (1), Code of practice for the structural use of timber; 1967 (1).
pt. 2: 1971, (5) Metric units.
pt. 3: 1973, Trussed rafters for roofs of dwellings. This code has now been superseded by BS 5268.
CP 113: 1948, Codes of Practice relating to the structural use of steel in buildings, including arc welded construction and use of steel tubes; 1951, 1953. Included in BS 449: 1959 (see above).
CP 114: 1948 (1), The structural use of reinforced concrete in buildings; 1957 (3), 1969 (5). The original 1948 code had sub-codes 114.101 to 114.104, 'Suspended concrete floors and roofs' which were merged into the 1957 revision. Superseded by CP 110 (see above).
CP 115: 1959, The structural use of prestressed concrete in buildings; 1964 (4), pt. 1: 1969, pt. 2: 1969 (4). Withdrawn.
CP 116: 1964 (3), The structural use of precast concrete; 1965, pt. 2: 1969 (4), 1970.
Addendum no. 1 (1970) to CP 116 : 1965 and CP 116: pt. 2: 1969, Large panel structures and structural connections in precast concrete.
CP 117, Composite construction in structural steel and concrete.
pt. 1: 1965, Simply supported beams in building. Withdrawn in 1990 and superseded by BS 5950.
pt. 2: 1967, Beams for bridges. Withdrawn in 1986 and superseded by BS 5400.
CP 144: 1968 (3), Roof coverings;
pt. 1: 1972, Built-up bitumen felt. Imperial units.
pt. 2: 1966, Mastic asphalt. Imperial units.
pt. 3: 1970 (2), Built-up bitumen felt. Metric units.
pt. 4: 1970 (1), Mastic asphalt. Metric units.
101: 1961, Bitumen felt roof coverings.
201: 1952, Mastic asphalt roofing.
All parts of this code have now been withdrawn.
CP 152: 1960, Glazing and fixing of glass for buildings; 1972. Withdrawn.
CP 204: 1951, In-situ floor finishes, pt. 1: 1965, Imperial units. pt. 2: 1970 (4), Metric units. Withdrawn
CP 211: 1949, Internal plastering; 1966. Withdrawn.

Appendix II Design loads

The safety of a structure depends upon its ability to carry a larger load than those imposed upon it, which means that as soon as methods were available to assess the capacity of the structure some estimate was needed of the loads that would be imposed in service. This needed to be accompanied by an acceptable safety factor. Eventually this became a matter for legislation but views about the loads to be used and the methods of assessing the safety of the structure have changed with time. During this century there has been a general reduction in the required design loads and an increasing precision in defining the uses of different spaces in buildings which affect the imposed loads. At the same time it must be remembered that there is a connection between the loads assumed and the methods of analysis employed with safety ensured through the mutual dependence of these two aspects of design.

At the turn of the century there were no generally accepted design loads; engineers used what seemed appropriate for the particular circumstances. This was simply because there had been little need to determine the loads in many cases, although one wonders how patent floor systems were designed. The design of domestic, public and institutional buildings with masonry walls and timber floors had evolved over time with sizes of joists and girders selected by experience to limit the deflections under load to acceptable limits. The properties of timber are such that deflection is normally more critical than the failure load, that is, if the deflections are acceptable, as judged by the floor not being too lively, then a floor is unlikely to collapse under normal working loads. This was convenient because, until the development of both theories of structural behaviour and the science of materials, there would have been no way to relate the imposed load to the internal stresses, nor to relate these to the behaviour of the material. Timber might 'fail' where large girders were used in warehouses and then some crushing may have occurred at supports. In these circumstances working stresses are well above those that would be acceptable today but this did not lead to collapse of the structure.

The need for some assessment of loading came with the introduction of iron as a structural material. Its brittle nature meant that failure would not be preceded by adequate warnings of danger and there were occasional catastrophic collapses. Design practice took the form of specified proof loads, the proof load taken to be a multiple of the assumed maximum working load in order to provide a factor of safety. Fairbairn (1854) gave a method for assessing the design loads for warehouses but,

although he provided some suggested figures, engineers must have had to make their own estimates of likely loads

With the development of structural theory during the nineteenth century and the introduction of rolled sections, first of wrought iron and then of steel, design practice changed. The working stresses could be calculated from the design loads and section properties and limits were placed upon these working stresses. At the same time increasing public control of building standards included control over design loads and working stresses and the regulation of steel and reinforced concrete structures required designers to submit proof of a building's structural adequacy before obtaining a permit to build — proof that took the form of demonstrating compliance with the regulations. But although design loads were determined by legislation, the requirements were no more logical than they had been until then. Such legislation appeared in the US before it did in Britain and, writing about the turn of the century, Freitag (1895) pointed out the quite different loads required by the New York and Chicago building codes. These differed from those applied in London, differences that were to be commented on in the report of the Steel Structures Research Committee in the inter-war years.

Of course, while the limits on working stress or the load to failure of a structural component may be determined with relative accuracy, the loads to which a building are subjected vary widely and there are two contradictory influences on the loads used in design. Structural safety requires that the design load be sufficiently large to ensure an acceptably low rate of failure. This can obviously be achieved with very high design loads compared with the working loads. In contrast, efficiency in structural design demands that they be set as low as possible commensurate with safety. The assumption is that the greater the precision in estimating the working loads and in predicting the behaviour of structures, then the more efficient the design will be. Of course this assumes that the designer has a correct model of behaviour of the structure as a whole which, as shown in Chapter 4, may not be true.

Using the minimum load commensurate with safety may produce an efficient design for the initial construction but, as those who are concerned with the rehabilitation will know, it is not necessarily the most sensible approach if the whole of the life of the building is considered. Changes of use, or changes to the construction of the building as part of its rehabilitation, may require higher loads than were originally envisaged so that an originally economical design may limit the changes that are possible later or require extensive structural alterations to ensure adequate structural performance for the new use. This aspect of design decisions may simply reflect the attitudes of the time. Today, when there is such a large amount of rehabilitation work being carried out, an engineer may regard any costs associated with 'over-design' as very modest compared with the increased flexibility in use that it will give to a building while it is equally understandable that a generation of engineers working within the climate of post-war restrictions and shortages of materials should have been striving for minimal design to do the job.

At the time Freitag was writing there were still no regulations governing design loads in Britain and, although some engineering textbooks made recommendations, it is often difficult, and frequently impossible, to know what the design loads were for any particular building . The first regulations for design loads came with the 1909 LCC regulations governing construction in steel and concrete. At that time the approach was to include the loading requirement as part of the regulations for design in each material so that the loads were defined separately in each code, although the 1915 concrete code in London followed the 1909 loads for steel-frame design. In the inter-war period, the design loads were revised when the design codes were revised. CP 4 Ch. V was the first standard for loading which was not related to the materials of construction and after it was replaced in 1952 by CP 3 Ch. V, the 1953 BS 449 referred to this code rather than including the loads within the design standard.

There was almost immediate criticism of the rules governing design loads in the Steel Frame Act when it was published, particularly the reductions allowed for live loads in multi-storey buildings. A reduction of 5 per cent per floor was regarded as too small and this was eventually corrected to 10 per cent per floor when the regulations were altered in the 1930s. The requirements of the various regulations and codes are given in Table A2.1 and two features of these should be noted. There has been a general tendency both to reduce design loads and to make more distinctions between different types of use. Designers today may wonder whether this second tendency might not reduce the flexibility of accommodation in present-day buildings. There have also been different approaches to design for concentrated loads and the fact that higher loads may occur over smaller areas than over a floor as a whole. At first some allowance was made for the possibility of large concentrated loads by making a distinction between the loads on beams and slabs. It was eventually realized that the same effect could be better achieved by making a distinction according to the area carried by any part of the

structure. This change is seen following the publication of CP 4 Ch. V which used different minimum loads for beams and slabs. CP 3, which replaced it in 1952, adopted a high load applied to small areas. A more rational, and more detailed assessment of design loads became possible following an extensive survey of loads in practice which was carried out by BRE in the 1960s (Mitchell & Woodgate, 1971a & b).

The assessment of loads from the action of weather has also became much more sophisticated, to an extent that makes it difficult to display in a simple table. This has been brought about by research that has produced data leading to an improved understanding of the action of wind and snow on buildings and the way in which such natural forces are affected by building shape. The need for this improved understanding has been brought about by the use of lighter construction and demonstrated by occasional failures.

When it was issued in 1952, CP 3 Ch. V included figures for wind loading. In addition to a simple table of average pressures on the roofs of buildings there was a recommendation (Clause 11) that fastenings for wall and roof sheetings within 15 per cent of the span or length from the eaves or verge should designed for higher loads. Diagrams in the explanatory appendices then produced graphs illustrating the results of wind tunnel tests carried out at the NPL. The code was revised as Part 1 in 1967 in metric units but without any figures for wind loading. CP 3 Ch. V: pt. 2 published in 1970 and revised in 1972 provided pressure coefficients for a range of different building shapes.

Snow loads continued to be treated fairly simply in Part 1 of this code but two recent developments should be noted. The structural requirements for agricultural buildings, BS 5502: Section 1.2, which was published in 1980 introduced a level of sophistication in the structural assessment of buildings that we are unlikely to see applied to the majority of structures in the foreseeable future. As the human occupancy of these buildings is low, and the design life may also be limited, the degree of safety may be reduced accordingly. Of course, the vast majority of such buildings are light, single-storey structures where considerable savings in costs may be possible by taking such considerations into account. This code, for the first time, dealt with the variation in snow load brought about by geographical and topographical variations. This allowed much lighter loads to be used in the south and in lowland areas while at the same time the code recognized that high local loads could be caused by drifting snow on roofs of complex shape. The effect of such drifting is of course an equally important factor in the design of light industrial buildings.

A 1.1 Design loads for buildings

Regulation or other source	BS 6399: 1984		CP CH. 5			LCC regulations			Appleby	Dorman Long
Date	1984		1944 general	minimum slabs	beams	1933 slabs		1909&1915 beams	1903	1895
Units	distributed kN/sq. m.	concentrated kN/sq. m.	lbs/sq. ft.	lbs/ft. width	lbs	lbs/sq/ft.		beams	lbs/sq. ft.	lbs/sq. ft.
Room types in more than one building type										
Dining rooms, lounges, billiard rooms	2.0	2.7	80	640	5120					
Assembly areas without fixed seating	5.0	3.6	100	800	6400	100	100	112		
Assembly areas with fixed seating	4.0		80	640	5120	80	70	112		
Boiler rooms etc.	7.5	4.5								
Toilets	2.0									
Bars & vestibules	5.0									
Dense mobile book stack	4.8/m. high 9.6 minimum	7.9								
Stack rooms (books)	2.4/m. high 6.5 minimum	7.0								
Stationery stores	4/m. high	9.0								
Projection rooms	5.0									
Areas for equipment & dressing rooms	2.0	1.8								
Residential occupancy										
Self-contained dwelling units										
All	1.5	1.4				50	40	70	56 to 70	80
Not more than two storeys - one occupation			30	240	1920					
Attics - 1903									34 to 56	
Apartment houses										
More than two floors			40	320	2560					
Communal kitchens, laundries, corridors	3.0	4.5								
Bedrooms, dorms - institutional buildings	1.5	1.8								
Hotels & motels										
Corridors	4.0	4.5							80 to 90	
Kitchens, laundries	3.0	4.5								
Bedrooms	2.0	1.8								
Institutional and educational										
Classrooms	3.0	2.7	60	480	3840	80	70	112		
Chapels	treated as classrooms		80	640	5120					
Bedrooms, dormitories	1.5	1.8				50	40	84		
Drill rooms/drill halls	5.0	9.0				100	100	150		
Laboratories	3.0	4.5								
Reading rooms without or with book storage	2.5 to 4	4.5							70 to 80	
X Ray rooms	2.0	4.5								
Gymnasia/dance halls	5.0	3.6								
Public assembly occupancy										
Public halls/schools										110
Stages	7.5	4.5								
Corridors with foot traffic or trolley loading	4 to 5	4.5								
Museum floors etc.	4.0	4.5								
Offices										
General offices	2.5	2.7	50	400	3200	80	50	100	70 to 80	
Offices at entrance floor (LCC 1933)						80	80			
File rooms (& corridors - BS 6399)	5.0	4.5	100	800	6400					
Offices with fixed computers	3.5	4.5								
Laboratories	3.0	4.5								
Banking halls	3.0									
Retail occupancy										
Shop floors	4.0	3.6	80	640	5120	80	80	112		
Cold storage	5.0/m high 15.0 min	9.0								
Other storage	2.4/m.	7.0								
Industrial occupancy & storage										
Factories, workshops etc	5.0	4.5	100	800	6400			112	125 to 150	
Machinery halls	4.0	4.5	80	640	5120				250 to 500	220 to 420
Workrooms, light, no storage	2.5	1.8							125 to 150	
Foundries	20.0									
Storage not listed separately	2.4/m high		100	800	6400					
Paper storage	4.0/m high	9.0								
Type storage	12.5	9.0								
Warehouses	2.4	7.0	200			200	200	224	150 to 400	120 to 320
Light storage CP 4 Ch. V.			150							
Driveway and vehicle ramps	5	9								
Car parking only	2.5	9	100							
Motor rooms	80			640	5120					

Bibliography

Abbreviations used in this bibliography

AJ   Architect's Journal
BCRA   British Ceramic Research Association
BCSA   British Constructional Steelwork Association
C&CA   Cement and Concrete Association
Concrete   Concrete and Constructional Engineering
CPTB   Clay Products Technical Bureau
DES   Department of Education and Science
DoE   Department of Environment
DSIR   Department of Scientific and Industrial Research
HMSO   His Majesty's Stationery Office
J. Inst. Civ. Engrs. Journal of the Institution of Civil Engineers
J. Inst. Wood Sci.   Journal of the Institute of Wood Science
Proc. Inst. Civ. Engrs. Proceedings of the Institution of Civil Engineers
RIBAJ   Journal of the Royal Institute of British Architects, 3rd Series

ALLEN, JOHN PARNELL (1893), *Practical building construction*, Crosby Lockwood.
ANDREWS, E. S. (1914), 'Slab formulae for reinforced concrete design', *Concrete*, 9, pp. 396-404.
— (1922), 'Steel Frame Buildings, Explanatory Note on the Joint Conference Report' *AJ*, 56, pp. 875-6.
— (1925), 'The strength of filler joist floors', *The Structural Engineer*, 3, pp. 38-41.
APPLEBY, CHARLES JAMES (1897-1903), *Illustrated Handbook of Machinery*, Spon.
ASHDOWN, A.J. (1932), 'The influence of haunches on continuous beams', *Concrete*, 27, pp. 284-95.
— (1948-49), 'Prismatic thin slab structures of long span', *Concrete*, 43, pp. 293-302, pp. 347-52; & 44, pp. 279-85, pp. 317-22.
BAGENAL, HOPE (1924), 'Sound transmission from the architect's point of view - 1, Street noises', *AJ*, 59, pp. 1020 & '2, Noises within doors',.ibid, p. 980.
BAKER, J. F. (1932), 'The Mechanical and Mathematical Stress Analysis of Steel Building Frames' Selected Engineering Paper No. 131 Inst. Civ. Engrs.
— (1935-36), 'The Rational Design of Steel Building Frames', *J. Inst. Civ. Engs*, 3, pp. 127-230.
BARLOW, PETER (1817), *An Essay on the Strength of Timber*, J. Taylor.
BARLOW, S. and FOSTER, G. (1957), 'Universal Beams and their Applications' *The Structural Engineer*, 35, pp. 425-40.
BARNES, A. H. (1941), 'Calculations

without mathematics', *Wood*, 6, pp. 112, 265, 316.
BATES, W. (1984), *Historical Structural Steelwork Handbook*, BCSA.
BENGOUGH, G. D. (1912-26), *Outlines of Industrial Chemistry*, Constable.
BESSEY, G.E. (1934), *Sand lime bricks*, Building Research Board Special Report No. 21, HMSO.
BETHAMS-WILLIAMS, D. (1938), 'The construction of exhibition buildings', *The Structural Engineer*, 16, pp. 448-62.
BILL, MAX (1949), *Robert Maillart*, Zurich: Verlag für Architecture.
BIRKMIRE, WILLIAM H. (1904), *Skeleton Construction in Buildings*, 4th ed., Wiley.
BLACK, W. (1915-16), 'The lines of industrial expansion after the war', *Kahncrete*, 2, p. 145.
BOOTH, L. G. (1971), 'The development of laminated timber arch structures in Bavaria, France and England in the early nineteenth century', *J. Inst. Wood Sci.*, 5, pp. 3-16.
— (1994), 'Henry Fuller's Glued Laminated Timber Roof for Rusholm Road Congregational Sunday School and other early Timber roofs', *Construction History*, 10, pp. 29-46.
BOOTH, L. G. & HEYWOOD, DIANA (1994), 'Josia George Poole and the New School Room, King Edward VI School, Bugle Street, Southampton. An Early Example of Glued Laminated Timber Arches in Buildings in Britain', *J. Inst. Wood Science*, 13, pp. 483-91.
BOULTON, E. H. B. (1938), *Timber buildings for the country*, Country Life.
BOWIE, P. G. (1938), 'Moments in flat slabs', *The Structural Engineer*, 16, pp. 2-13.
BOWLEY, MARION (1960), *Innovations in building materials*, Duckworth
— (1966), *The British Building Industry: Four studies in response and resistance to change*, Cambridge: University Press.
BRADSHAW, R. E. (1963), *An example of reinforced brickwork design*, British Ceramic Research Association Special Publication 38.
BRADY, F. L. (1930), *The corrosion of steel by breeze and clinker concretes*. DSIR Report No. 15, HMSO.
BRAYTON, L. F. (1911), 'Method for the computation of reinforced concrete flat slabs', *Concrete*, 6, pp. 124-31.
BRITISH CONSTRUCTIONAL STEELWORK ASSOCIATION (1964, revised 1965, 1977), *Prefabricated floors for use in steel framed buildings*, BCSA.
BRITISH FIRE PREVENTION COMMITTEE (1904), *The Standards of Fire Resistance of the*

BFPC. Red Book No. 82.
BROOKES, A. (1949), 'Adhesion and the synthetic resins', *Wood*, 14, pp. 305-06.
BROOKES, A. J. (1983, rev. 1990), *Cladding of Building*, Longman.
BULLEN, F. R. (1957), 'Structural features of the new Binns Store in Middlesbrough', *The Structural Engineer* , 35, pp. 408-19
BURRIDGE, L. W. (1936), 'Reinforced Brickwork', *RIBAJ* , 44, pp. 285-95.
BYLANDER, S. (1932-3), 'Welded steelwork in buildings', *The Junior Institution of Engineers, J. & Record of Transactions*, 43, pp. 395-403.
— (1937), 'Steelwork in Buildings - 30 Years of Progress', *The Structural Engineer*, 15, pp. 2-25.
CARTER, JOHN (1774-86), *The Builders Magazine*, Society of Architects.
CASSIE, W. F. (1955), 'Early reinforced concrete in Newcastle upon Tyne', *The Structural Engineer*, 33, pp. 134-7.
— (1953), *Proceedings of the conference on welded structures*, HMSO.
CHANTER, HORACE R. (1946), *London Building Law*, Batsford.
CHAPLIN, C. J. (1936), 'Grading Baltic timbers', *Wood*, 1, p. 238.
— (1937), 'The new LCC timber byelaw', *RIBAJ*, 45, p. 243.
CHILDE, H. (1927), *Manufacture and Use of Concrete Products and Cast Stone*, Concrete Publications.
CLIFTON-TAYLOR, A. & I. A. S. (1983), *English Stone Building*, Gollancz.
COADE, E. (1777), *Etchings of Coade's Artificial Stone Manufacure*, E. Coade.
COCKING, W. C. (1917, 1925), *The Calculations for Steel-frame Structures.*, Scott, Greenwood & Son.
COLE, RAY & COOPER, IAN (1988), 'British Architects: Accommodating Science and Technical Information', *J. of Architectural & Planning Research*, 5, pp. 110-28.
COLEMAN, G. S. (1932), 'The Moment Distribution Method', *Concrete*, 27, pp. 212-17.
CORKHILL, T. (1938), 'Standardised construction', *Wood*, 3, pp. 447-51.
COTTAM, D. (1986), *Sir Owen Williams, 1890-1969*, Architectural Association.
CRABTREE, H. V. (1933), 'Structural steelwork review', *The Structural Engineer*, 11, pp. 158-75.
CREASY, L. R. (1949), 'Steel economy', *The Structural Engineer*, 27, pp. 503-27.
CROSS, H. (1932), 'Analysis of Continuous Frames by Distributing Fixed End Moments', *Trans. Am. Soc. C.E.* 96 , pp. 1-10 (discussion, pp. 11-156).

CURRY, W. (1964), 'The derivation of design stresses for plywood', *Wood*, (May), pp. 45-7.
CURTIN, W. C., SHAW, C., BECK, J. K. & BRAY, W. A. (1982), *Structural masonry designers' manual*, Granada.
CUSACK, PATRICIA (1986), 'Architects and the reinforced concrete specialists in Britain, 1905-08', *Architectural History*, 29, pp. 183-96.
— (1986), 'Apects of Change: Hennebique, Mouchel and ferro-concrete in Britain, 1897-1908', *Construction History*, 3, pp. 61-74.
DAVEY, N. (1933), *Influence of temperature on the strength development of concrete*, BRB Technical Paper No. 14, HMSO.
DAVIS, A.C. (1926), 'Twenty-one years progress in the Portland Cement Industry', *Concrete*, 21, pp. 69-77.
DAWNAY, A. D. (1901), 'Constructional Steelwork applied to building', *The Builder*, 80, pp. 385-90.
DE COLLEVILLE, H. M (n.d.), *Reinforced Concrete Book*, A. William Moss & Sons Ltd.
DE VEKEY, R. C. (1986), 'Towards a UK performance specification for wall ties', in WEST, W. H. W. (ed.), *Proceedings of the First International Masonry Conference*, Stoke on Trent: British Masonry Society, pp. 34-7.
DES (DEPARTMENT OF EDUCATION AND SCIENCE) (1973), *Report on the collapse of the assembly hall of the Camden School for Girls*, HMSO.
DOE (DEPARTMENT OF THE ENVIRONMENT) (1978), *The structural condition of Intergrid buildings of prestressed concrete*, Building Research Establishment Report, HMSO.
DSIR (DEPARTMENT OF SCIENTIFIC AND INDUSTRIAL RESEARCH) (1927), *Fire retardant construction*, Building Research Board Special Report No. 8, HMSO.
— (1931), *First report of the Steel Structures Research Committee*, HMSO.
— (1934), *Mechanical properties of bricks and brickwork masonry*, Building Research Board Special Report No. 22, HMSO.
— (1936), *Final report of the Steel Structures Research Committee*, HMSO.
(1938), *Welding of Steel Structures* - Report of the Welding Panel of the Steel Structures Research Committee, HMSO.
— (1951), *Concrete Block making Machines*, Building Research Board Special Report No.17, HMSO.
DYSON, H. KEMPTON (1908), 'Concrete Block Making in Great Britain', *Concrete*, 3, pp. 224-30.
EDDY, H.T. (1913), *Theory of Flexure and Strength of Rectangular Flat Plates Applied to Reinforced Concrete Floor Slabs*, Minneapolis .

ELLIS, GEORGE (1927), *Modern Practical Carpentry*, Batsford.

ETCHELLS, E. F. (ed.) (1927), *Modern steelwork*, Nash & Alexander.

EVANS, R H. (1935), 'Stresses in the steel reinforcement of concrete structures', The *Structural Engineer*, 13, pp. 354-

— (1936), 'Experiments on stress distribution in reinforced concrete beams', *The Structural Engineer*, 14, pp. 118-130.

FABER, OSCAR (1916), 'Researches on reinforced concrete with new formulae for resistance to shear', *Concrete*, 11, pp. 233-44, 293-305, 358-69, 411-23, 483-91, 532-43, 592-605; (1925), 'Tests on aluminous cement', *Concrete*, 20, pp. 91-101; (1927), 'The structural aspects of the new Horticultural Hall', *A&BN*, 118, pp. 152-6; (1933), 'Recent Developments in Building', *RIBAJ*, 40, pp. 389-406; (1956), 'Savings to be effected by the more rational design of cased stanchions as a result of full size tests', *The Structural Engineer*, 30, pp. 88-109.

FAIRBAIRN, WILLIAM (1854), *On the Application of Cast and Wrought Iron to Building Purposes*, London.

FEWELL, A. R. (1982), 'Machine stress grading of timber in the United Kingdom', *Holz als Roh-und Werkstoff*, 40, pp. 455-9.

FINNIMORE, B. (1985), 'The AIROH house: industrial diversification and state building policy', *Construction History*, 1, pp. 60-71.

FITZMAURICE, R. (1938), *Principles of modern building*, HMSO.

FREITAG, JOSEPH KENDALL (1895), *Architectural Engineering*, N.Y.: Wiley.

— (1912), *Fire prevention and fire protection as applied to building construction*, N.Y.: Wiley.

FRIEDMAN, DONALD (1995), *Historical Building Construction*, N.Y.: WW Norton & Co

GIDEON, SIGFRIED (1962), *Space, Time and Architecture*, 4th ed., Cambridge. MA: MIT.

GLANVILLE, W. H., COLLINS, A.R. & MATHEWS, D.D. (1938), *The grading of aggregates and the workability of concrete*, DSIR, Road Research Board Technical Paper No. 5, HMSO.

GLANVILLE, W. H. & BARNET, P. W. (1934), *Mechanical Properties of Bricks and Brickwork Masonry*, Building Research Station Special Report No. 22, HMSO.

GLOAG, J. E. & BRIDGEWATER, D. L. (1948), *A history of cast iron in architecture*, Allen & Unwin.

GOAD, CHARLES E. (1899), *Conflagrations during the last ten years*, Publications of the British Fire Prevention Committee.

GODFREY, E. (1923), 'Reinforcement for shear in reinforced concrete beams', *Concrete*. 1, pp. 79-

GOLDSTRAW, WILLIAM (1902), *A Manual of the Building Regulations in force in the City of Liverpool*, 2nd. ed., Liverpool: Tiling & Co.

GOODESMITH, WALTER (1933), 'The evolution of design in steel and concrete', *Architectural Review*, 72, pp. 180-92.

GOULD, M. H., JENNINGS, A. & MONTGOMERY, R. (1992), 'The Belfast roof truss', *The Structural Engineer*, 70, pp. 127-9.

GRAY, CHARLES S., KENT, L. E., MITCHELL, W. A. & GODFREY, G. B. (1955), *Steel Designers Manual*, Crosby Lockwood.

GRAY, R. (1950), 'Ridged Steel Arch Roofs', *The Structual Engineer*, 28, pp. 226-36.

GREEN, JOHN SINGLETON (1933), *Concrete Engineering*, Charles Griffin.

GREENHALGH, RICHARD (ed.) (1947), *Modern Building Construction*, 3 vols, New Era Publishing.

GRUNDY, RUPERT FRANCIS BROOKS (1930), *Builders Materials*, Longman.

– (1939), *The essentials of reinforced concrete design*, Chapman & Hall.

HAJNAL-KONYI, K. (1945) 'Structural steelwork' in DREW, J. B. (ed.), *Architects' Year Book*, Vol. 1, Elek, pp. 164-81.

HAMANN, C. W. & BURRIDGE, L. W. (1939), 'Reinforced brickwork', *The Structural Engineer*, 17, pp. 198-250.

HAMILTON, S. B. (1956), *History of reinforced concrete in buildings*, National Building Studies No. 24, HMSO.

— (1958), *A short history of the structural fire protection of buildings*, National Building studies, Special Report No. 27, HMSO.

HAMILTON, S. B., BAGENAL, H. & WHITE, R. B. (1964), *A Qualitative Study of Some Buildings in the London Area*, HMSO.

HASELTINE, B. A. (n.d.), *The design of calculated loadbearing brickwork*, Brick Development Association.

HELSBY, C., HAMMAN, C. W. & SAMUELY, F. (1935a), 'The influence of welding on the design of steel structures', *Welding Symposium*, pp. 133-42.

— (1935b), 'Necessary research for the application of welding', *The Welding Industry*, April, pp. 85-7.

HENDRY, A. W. (1950), 'An investigation of the strength of welded portal frame connections', *The Structural Engineer*, 28, pp. 265-80.

HETHERINGTON, J. NEWBY (1904), *The Royal Insurance Company's Building North John Street and Dale Street, Liverpool*, Batsford.

HILLIER, RICHARD (1981), *Clay that Burns: A History of the Fletton Brick Industry*, The London Brick Co.

HIRSCHTHAL, M. (1933), 'Girderless Flat-slab Bridges for Grade Crossings', *Engineering News Record*, 111, pp. 344-7.

HOOL, GEORGE (1912), *Reinforced Concrete Construction, Volume 1 'Fundamental Principles'*, N.Y.: McGraw Hill

HOLT, H. G. (1913), *Fire protection in buildings*, Crosby Lockwood.

HUNTER, A. (1906), 'Structural Design in Engineering Factories', *The Builder*, 91, pp. 692 & 747-50.

INSTITUTION OF CIVIL ENGINEERS (1910), *Preliminary and Interim Report of the Committee on Reinforced Concrete*, London.

ISLE OF MAN GOVERNMENT (1974), *Report of the Summerland Fire Commission*, Government Office: Isle of Man.

JACKSON, FRANK (1913), 'Modern Steel Building Construction', *RIBAJ*, 20, pp. 413-32.

JAGGARD, W. R. (1913—14), *Architectural and building construction*, Cambridge: Cambridge University Press.

JAGGARD, W. R. & DRURY, FRANCIS E. (1916), *Architectural building construction*, Cambridge: University Press.

JOHNSON, H. C. (1915), 'What is 1:2:4 concrete?', *Concrete*, 10, pp. 85-92.

JOHNSON, P. B. R. (1961), 'Fire protection to steelwork and the structural engineer', *The Structural Engineer*, 39, p. 240.

JONES, R. & BAKER, A. R. (1961), 'High strength bolts - the behaviour of structural connexions using high strength bolts stressed beyond their proof stress', *The Structural Engineer*, 39, pp. 228-34.

JORDAN, R. F. (1936), *The Charm of the Timber House*, Ivor Nicholson & Watson.

KAHN, MORITZ (1917), *The Design and Construction of Industrial Buildings*, Technical Journals.

KIRKALDY, DAVID (1862), *Results of experimental inquiry into the comparative tensile strength and other properties of various kinds of wrought iron and steel*, Glasgow.

KNIGHT & CO. (6th ed. 1899), *Knight's Annotated Model Byelaws of the Local Government Board*, Local Government Publishers.

LANGLEY LONDON LTD (1951), *Savings in Timber and Money in Roofing* . Trade publication.

LAWRENCE, JEANNE CATHERINE (1990), 'Steel Frame Architecture versus the London Building Regulations: Selfridges, the Ritz and American Technology', *Construction History*, 6, pp. 23-46.

LEA, F. M. (1929), *Investigations of breeze and clinker aggregates*, Building Research Board Technical Paper No. 7, HMSO.

— (1936), *Lightweight concrete aggregates*, Building Research Board Special Report No. 15, HMSO.

— (1940), 'Effect of temperature on high-alumina cement', *Transactions of the Society of the Chemical Industry*, 59, pp. 18-21.

— (1971), *Science and Building*, a History of the Building Research Station, HMSO.

LEA, F. M. & BRADY, F. L. (1927), *Slag, coke breeze and clinker aggregates*, Building Research Board Special Report No. 10, HMSO.

LEA, F. M. & DAVEY, N. (1948-9), 'Deterioration of concrete in structures', *J. Inst. Civ. Engrs*, 52, pp. 248-75.

LENCZNER, DAVID (1973), *Movements in Buildings*, Oxford: Pergamon.

LEWIS, E. M. (1957), 'Some notes on the use of high preload bolts in the United Kingdom', *The Structural Engineer*, 35, pp. 167-75. (discussion, 36, pp. 228-42.)

LOADER, R. & SKINNER, J. (1991), 'Management, Construction and architecture: the Development of the Model Factory', *Construction History*, 7, pp. 83-103.

MACINTOSH, R. H. (n.d.), *The No-fines Story*, Edinburgh: Scottish Special Housing Association.

MCKAY, W. B. (1938), *Building Construction*, Longmans.

MAKAY, A. R. (1960), 'Lightweight fire protection and the structural engineer', *The Structural Engineer*, 38, pp. 20-25.

MALINSON, L. G. & DAVIES, I. L. L. (1987), *A historical examination of concrete*, Luxembourg: Commission of the European Communities.

MANNING, G. P. (1929), 'New method of flat slab construction', *Concrete*, 24, pp. 541-4.

— (1934a), 'What is the strength of concrete?', *Concrete*, 29, pp. 421-2.

— (1934b), 'Asbestos cement bar spacers', *Concrete*, 29, pp. 707-08.

MARSH, CHARLES F. (1904, 2nd ed. 1905), *Reinforced Concrete*, Constable.

— (1914), 'Shearing or diagonal reinforcement in beams', *Concrete*, 9, pp. 305-15.

MENZIES, J. B. & GRANGER, G. D. (1976), *Report on the Collapse of the Sports Hall at Rock Ferry Comprehensive School, Birkenhead*, BRE CP 69/76.

MICHAELS, LEONARD (1950), *Contemporary Structure in Architecture*, N.Y.: Reinhold.

MIDDLETON, G. A. T. (1905), *Building materials*, Batsford.

MITCHELL, CHARLES F. (1888), *Building construction and drawing*, London.

MITCHELL, G. R. & WOODGATE, R. W. (1971a), *Floor loadings in office buildings - the results of a survey*, BRE CP 3/71.

— (1971b), *Floor loadings in retail premises - the results of a survey*, BRE CP 24/71.

MITCHELL, G. S. (1903), 'Cheap roofs', *Specification*, 6, p. 43.

MOLE, A. (1949). *Histoire des charpentiers: leurs traveaux*. Paris.

NATIONAL COMMITTEE ON WOOD UTILIZATION (1933), *The Structural Application of Modern Connectors*, Washington, D. C.: US Dept of Commerce.

NEILL, J. A. (1966), *Post-tensioned Brickwork*, CPTB Technical Note, 1, No. 9.

NEVILLE, A. M. (1963), 'A study of the deterioration of concrete made with High-alumina cement, *Proc. Inst. Civ. Engs*, 25, pp.

287-324.

NEWMAN, A. J. (1943), 'Effect of addition of Calcium Chloride to Portland Cements and Concretes', *Concrete*, 38, pp. 159-67.

OZELTON, C. & BAIRD, J. (1976), *Timber Designers' Manual*, Granada.

PALMER, M. F. & FOWLER, R. F. (1958), 'Modern methods of fabricating steelwork', *The Structural Engineer*, 36, pp. 365-76.

PARKER, T.W., NURSE, R.W., & BESSEY, G. E. (1950), *Investigation of building fires: Pt 1 Estimation of maximum temperatures, Pt 2 Colour changes in concrete*, NBS Technical Papers No. 4, HMSO.

PERKINS, W.R. (1917) 'How a four storey model daylight factory was erected in 97 working days', *Kahncrete*, 4, p. 34.

PIDGEON, N. F., BLOCKLEY, D. I. & TURNER, B. A. (1986), 'Design practice and snow loading - lessons from a roof collapse', *The Structural Engineer*, 64A, pp. 67-71.

PITT, P. H. & KNOWLES, C. C. (1972), *The History of Building Regulations in London, 1189-1972, with an account of the District Surveyors' Association*, Architectural Press.

PLOWMAN, J. M. et al. (1966), The testing of reinforced brickwork and concrete slabs forming box beams', *The Structural Engineer*, 45, pp. 379-94.

POST WAR BUILDING STUDIES No. 1 (1944), *House Construction*, HMSO.

— No. 8 (1944), *Reinforced concrete structures*, HMSO.

— No. 15 (1944), *Walls floors and roofs*, HMSO.

POTTER, T(1877, 3rd ed. 1908), *Concrete its use in building and the construction of concrete walls, floors etc.*, Batsford.

POWELL, CHRISTOPHER (1967), 'Structure and materials of low-rise housing systems, a statistical study', *AJ*, 146, pp. 129-30; (1970), *An economic history of the British building industry, 1815-1979*, Architectural Press.

PRICE, D. J. DE SOLLA (1965), 'Is technology historically independent of science? A study in statistical historiography', *Technology and Culture*, 6, pp. 553-68

PUGSLEY, SIR ALFRED (1951), 'Concepts of safety in structural engineering', *J. Inst. Civ. Engs*, 36, pp. 5-31 (discussion, pp. 31-51).

— (1966), *The Safety of Structures*, Edward Arnold.

RAGSDALE, L. A. & RAYNHAM, E. A. (1972), *Building Materials Technology*, 2nd ed., Edward Arnold.

REECE, P. O. (1948), 'Timber connectors', *The Structural Engineer*, 26, pp. 275-31.

— (1951), 'Timber as a structural material', *Wood* , 16, pp. 374-9; (1967), 'Timber engineering - some aspects of research, design and industrialization in relation to Code of practice CP 112', *The Structural Engineer*, 45, pp. 101-10.

REYNOLDS, CHARLES (1932), *Concrete Designer's Handbook*, Concrete Publications.

RITCHIE, THOMAS (1935), 'Apsley House, Finchley Rd.', *A&BN*, 144, pp. 310-13.

ROBERTSON, HOWARD (1928), 'The Modern Movement in Holland - 1, The Horizontal Expression', *A&BN*, 119, pp. 495-8.

ROSTRON, R. MICHAEL (1964), *Light Cladding of Buildings*, Architectural Press.

RUSSELL, PETER (1933), *Competitive design of steel structures*, Chapman and Hall.

RUTHEN, CHARLES (1919) 'British building methods', *Builder*, 117, pp. 413-17.

SAINT, ANDREW (1977), *Richard Norman Shaw*, York: University Press;- (1991), 'Some thoughts about the architectural use of concrete', *AA Files* No. 21, pp. 3-12 & No. 22, pp. 3-16.

SAMUELY, FELIX (1937), 'Sheet steel - the modern structural material. A new factory for Steel Ceilings Ltd', *The Welding Industry*, July, pp. 191-7.

SAMUELY, F. & HAMMAN, C. W. (1939), *Building Design and Construction*, Chapman and Hall.

SCHAFFER, R. J. (1932), *The Weathering of Natural Building Stone*, Building Research Board Special Report No. 18, HMSO.

SCOTT, EARNEST A. (1930), *Arrol's Reinforced Concrete Reference Book*, Spon.

SCOTT, W. BASIL (1925), 'The strength of steel joists embedded in concrete', *The Structural Engineer*, 3, pp. 201-19.

SEARLE, ALFRED BROADHEAD (1912), *An Introduction to British Clays Shales & Sands*, Charles Griffin; (1913), 'Cement, Concrete and Bricks' in BENGOUGH (1912-26) p 412; (1915), *Bricks and artificial stones of non-plastic materials*, J. & A. Churchill.

SILVESTER, F. D. (1948), 'Stress grading, an important experiment in modern timber engineering', *Wood* , 13, pp. 12-18.

SINGLETON-GREEN, J. (1928), 'Practical application of the water/cement ratio theory', *The Structural Engineer*, 6, pp. 265-78.

SJOSTROM, C. (1943), *Prefabrication in timber, a survey of existing methods*, English Joinery Manufacturers' Association.

STRADLING, R. E. & BRADY, F. L. (1927), *Fire resistant construction*, BRB Special Report No. 8, HMSO.

SULLIVAN, L. SYLVESTER (1932), 'City Office Buildings', *RIBAJ* , 39, pp. 601-18.

SUNLEY, J. G. & DAWE, P. S. (1963), 'Strength of finger joints', *Wood*, 28, pp. 387-9.

SUTCLIFFE, G. LISTER (1902), *The Principles and Practice of Modern House-Construction*, Blackie.

SUTHERLAND, JAMES (1969), *High rise concrete blockwork* , Concrete Society Technical Paper PCS 37.

— (1981), 'Brick and block masonry in

engineering', *Proc. Inst. Civ. Engs*, 70, pp. 31-63 (discussion, pp. 811-28).

TAYLOR, FREDERICK WINSLOW & THOMPSON, S. E. (1909, revised 1912 & 1916), *Treatise on Concrete, plain and reinforced*, 2nd ed., N.Y.: Wiley.

THOMAS, K. (1965), *Calculated loadbearing brickwork project at Heathgate, Norwich*, BCRA, Vol. 2, No. 2.

— (1966), *Movement joints in brickwork*, CPTB Technical Note Vol. 1, No. 10, CPTB.

THOMAS, K. & MARSHALL, D. (1966), *Hamilton College, construction of residences in loadbearing brickwork*, CPTB, Vol. 1, No. 11.

THOMAS, W. N. (1929), *The use of Calcium Chloride and Sodium Chloride as admixtures to concrete*, BRB Special Report No. 14, HMSO.

THOMPSON, BENJAMIN (LORD RUMFORD) (1796), *An essay on chimney fireplaces*, Dublin: R. E. Mercier.

THOMPSON, S. E. (1912), The practical design of concrete flat slabs, a supplement to Concrete Plain and reinforced, in TAYLOR, F. W. & THOMPSON, S.E. (1912), *Treatise on Concrete, plain and reinforced*, 2nd ed., N.Y.: Wiley.

-- (1913), 'The practical design of reinforced concrete slabs', *Concrete*, 8, pp 27-33

TIMBER DEVELOPMENT ASSOCIATION (1944, rev. 1947, reprinted 1949) *Prefabricated timber houses*, London.

TREDGOLD, THOMAS (1820), *Elementary Principles of Carpentry*, London.

THE TRUSSED CONCRETE STEEL COMPANY (1908), *Reinforced Concrete and some facts about the Kahn Trussed Bar*, 2nd ed., London.

TURNER, CLAUD ALLEN PORTER (1912), *Examples of the mushroom system of construction and the work of contractors associated and doing business with CAP Turner*, Minneapolis: Heywood Mfg. Co.

TWELVETREES, W. NOBLE (ed.) (1875-89), *Rivington's Notes on Building Construction*, Rivington's; (1900), 'Structural iron and steel', *The Builder*; (1905), *Concrete-Steel*, Whittaker; (1907), *Concrete-Steel Buildings*, Whittaker; (1920), *A treatise on reinforced concrete*, Pitman: London; (1925), *Concrete Making Machinery*, Scott, Greenwood & Son.

VOCE, G. T. (1933), 'An introduction to welded structures', *The Structural Engineer*, 11, pp. 274-89, 320-35.

WALDRAM, PERCY, J. (1924), *Structural Design in Steel Frame Buildings*, Batsford.

WALLACE, W. K. (1941), 'Structural engineering on British railways', *The Structural Engineer*, 19, pp. 193-203.

WALLIS, THOMAS (1933), 'Factories', *RIBAJ*, 40, pp. 301-12.

WALTERS, R. T. (1951), *Design Manual for Timber Connectors*, Mc Andrews & Forbes.

WARLAND, EDMUND GEORGE (1928), 'Steel and Stone Construction', *Building*, 3,

pp. 34-5; (1929, 2nd ed. 1953), *Modern Practical Masonry*, Batsford; (1937), *The Fabric of Modern Buildings*, Pitman; (1947), 'Masonry', in GREENHALGH, R. (ed) (1947), *Modern Building Construction*, New Era Publishing, pp 191-278

WATSON, J. (1926), 'Concrete and Cement', *Building*, 1, p. 163.

WEATHERALL, W. F. (1957), 'Equipment for structural laminating', *Wood*, 22, p. 187.

WEAVER, SIR LAWRENCE (1926), *Cottages: their planning, design and materials*, Country Life.

WEEKS, HUGH (1957), *Truscon, the first 50 years, 1907-1957*, London

WELLER, H. O. (1921), *Sand lime and other concrete bricks*, BRB Special Report No. 1, HMSO.

WHITE, R. B. (1965), *Prefabrication; a history of its development in Great Britain*, HMSO; (1966), *Qualitative studies of buildings*, BRE Special Report No. 39, HMSO.

WILLIAMS, OWEN (1932), 'The portent of concrete', *Concrete*, 27, p. 41.

WILSON, T. R. C. (1939), *The Glued Laminated Wooden Arch*, Washington, D.C.: US Dept. of Agriculture.

WOOD, C. ROLAND (1933), 'Building Regulations', *The Structural Engineer*, 11, pp. 444-9.

WOOD, A. D. & LINN, T. G. (1942, rev. 1950), *Plywoods: Their Development, Manufacture and Application*, W. & A. K. Johnston.

WYNN, A. E. (1921), 'The American 'flat slab' type of building, its advantages and design', *Concrete*, 16, pp. 95-102, 178.

— (1926a), *Modern Methods of Concrete Making*, Concrete Publications - (1926b), 'Controlling the manufacture of concrete to obtain uniform strength', *Concrete* , 21, pp. 413-23, 478-94, 588-96; - (1930), 'Design of concrete mixtures', *Concrete*, 25, pp 90-98, 149-58.

YEOMANS, DAVID (1988a), 'The introduction of the trussed rafter into Britain' *Structural Safety*, 5, pp. 149-53.

— (1989), 'Structural Carpentry in London Building' in HOBHOUSE H. & SAUNDERS, A. (eds), *Good and Proper Materials: The Fabric of London since the Great Fire*, RCHME Conference, RCHME & London Topographical Society; (1992), *The Trussed Roof: its history and development*, Aldershot: Scolar Press.

YEOMANS, D. & COTTAM, D. (1989), 'An Architect Engineer Collaboration; The Tecton Arup Flats', *The Structural Engineer*, 67, No. 10 (May), pp. 183-8.

YORKE, F. R. S. (1937), *The Modern House in England*, Architectural Press.

YORKE, F. R. S. & GIBBERD, F. (1937, 1948), *The Modern Flat*, Architectural Press.

Index